Jaguar Books on Latin America

Series Editors

WILLIAM H. BEEZLEY, Neville G. Penrose Chair of Latin
American Studies, Texas Christian University
COLIN M. MACLACHLAN, Professor, Department of History,
Tulane University

Volumes Published

John E. Kicza, ed., *The Indian in Latin American History: Resistance,
Resilience, and Acculturation* (1993). Cloth ISBN 0-8420-2421-2
Paper ISBN 0-8420-2425-5

Susan E. Place, ed., *Tropical Rainforests: Latin American Nature and
Society in Transition* (1993). Cloth ISBN 0-8420-2423-9
Paper ISBN 0-8420-2427-1

Paul W. Drake, ed., *Money Doctors, Foreign Debts, and Economic
Reforms in Latin America from the 1890s to the Present* (1994).
Cloth ISBN 0-8420-2434-4 Paper ISBN 0-8420-2435-2

John A. Britton, ed., *Molding the Hearts and Minds: Education,
Communications, and Social Change in Latin America* (1994).
Cloth ISBN 0-8420-2489-1 Paper ISBN 0-8420-2490-5

Darién J. Davis, ed., *Slavery and Beyond: The African Impact on Latin
America and the Caribbean* (1995). Cloth ISBN 0-8420-2484-0
Paper ISBN 0-8420-2485-9

David J. Weber and Jane M. Rausch, eds., *Where Cultures Meet: Frontiers
in Latin American History* (1994). Cloth ISBN 0-8420-2477-8
Paper ISBN 0-8420-2478-6

Gertrude M. Yeager, ed., *Confronting Change, Challenging Tradition:
Women in Latin American History* (1994). Cloth ISBN 0-8420-2479-4
Paper ISBN 0-8420-2480-8

Linda Alexander Rodríguez, ed., *Rank and Privilege: The Military and
Society in Latin America* (1994). Cloth ISBN 0-8420-2432-8
Paper ISBN 0-8420-2433-6

Gilbert M. Joseph and Mark D. Szuchman, eds., *I Saw a City Invincible:
Urban Portraits of Latin America* (1996). Cloth ISBN 0-8420-2495-6
Paper ISBN 0-8420-2496-4

Roderic Ai Camp, ed., *Democracy in Latin America: Patterns and Cycles* (1996). Cloth ISBN 0-8420-2512-X   Paper ISBN 0-8420-2513-8

Oscar J. Martínez, ed., *U.S.-Mexico Borderlands: Historical and Contemporary Perspectives* (1996). Cloth ISBN 0-8420-2446-8 Paper ISBN 0-8420-2447-6

William O. Walker III, ed., *Drugs in the Western Hemisphere: An Odyssey of Cultures in Conflict* (1996). Cloth ISBN 0-8420-2422-0 Paper ISBN 0-8420-2426-3

Richard R. Cole, ed., *Communication in Latin America: Journalism, Mass Media, and Society* (1996). Cloth ISBN 0-8420-2558-8 Paper ISBN 0-8420-2559-6

David G. Gutiérrez, ed., *Between Two Worlds: Mexican Immigrants in the United States* (1996). Cloth ISBN 0-8420-2473-5 Paper ISBN 0-8420-2474-3

Lynne Phillips, ed., *The Third Wave of Modernization in Latin America: Cultural Perspectives on Neoliberalism* (1998). Cloth ISBN 0-8420-2606-1   Paper ISBN 0-8420-2608-8

The Third Wave
of Modernization
in Latin America

The Third Wave of Modernization in Latin America

Cultural Perspectives on Neoliberalism

Lynne Phillips
Editor

Jaguar Books on Latin America
Number 16

A Scholarly Resources Inc. Imprint
Wilmington, Delaware

Scholarly Resources Inc.
104 Greenhill Avenue
Wilmington, DE 19805-1897

Library of Congress Cataloging-in-Publication Data

The third wave of modernization in Latin America : cultural
  perspectives on neoliberalism / Lynne Phillips, editor.
      p.   cm. — (Jaguar books on Latin America ; 16)
      Includes bibliographical references.
      ISBN 0-8420-2606-1 (alk. paper : cloth). — ISBN 0-8420-2608-8
(alk. paper : pbk.)
      1. Latin America—Economic policy. 2. Latin America—Economic
conditions—1982–   3. Structural adjustment (Economic policy)—
Social aspects—Latin America. 4. Latin America—Social conditions—
1982–   I. Phillips, Lynne. II. Series.
HC125.T515   1997
338.98—dc21   97-22853
                                                                      CIP

⊗The paper used in this publication meets the minimum requirements of
the American National Standard for permanence of paper for printed
library materials, Z39.48, 1984.

Acknowledgments

The exigencies of doing fieldwork do not usually fit well the demands of an edited volume, and I want first to thank the contributors to this volume for their just-in-time production of high-quality papers and their prompt responses to my endless queries, despite being in various parts of the world during the process. I would also like to thank Bill Beezley for his invitation to consider organizing a book on modernization. His support throughout the project has been much appreciated, and I hope that the product has not steered too far from what he had in mind. Thanks to Nicole Noël for her computer expertise and editorial assistance. For their intellectual sustenance on Latin American issues (anthropological or otherwise), I want to thank Tanya Basok, Denis Baranger, Mario Boleda, Graciela Dinardi, Carlos Larrea, Ignacio Llovet, Blanca Muratorio, Lucia Salamea, Gabriela Schiavoni, Pati Tomic, and Ricardo and Camilo Trumper. For financial aid, thanks go to the Social Sciences and Humanities Research Council of Canada and the Association of Universities and Colleges of Canada. Alan Hall and Rachel Phillips Hall deserve special mention for their support and good-natured acceptance of my many absences. Their patience and humor remind me about the important things in life.

About the Editor

Lynne Phillips teaches in the Department of Sociology and Anthropology at the University of Windsor in Canada and is currently involved in a research project on the impact of free trade on rural households in Argentina and Ecuador. She has published articles with Ricardo Trumper on the cholera epidemic in Latin America in *Alternatives* (1995) and *Race and Class* (1996). She edited *Ethnographic Feminisms: Essays in Anthropology* (1995) with Sally Cole and is currently editing *Transgressing Borders: Critical Perspectives on Gender, Households, and Culture* (1998) with Suzan Ilcan.

Contents

Introduction: Neoliberalism in Latin America

Lynne Phillips

Latin America is undergoing a dramatic transformation commonly re-ferred to as neoliberalism.[1] Although neoliberalism, as an ideology and as a practice, has made significant inroads throughout the Americas, the about-face in Latin America is particularly remarkable given the pre-vious ways of thinking about development, trade, and North-South rela-tions. Neoliberalism involves a shift from "inward-oriented" strategies of development promoting national self-sufficiency to "outward-oriented" free trade aimed at total integration into the world market. This transfor-mation has had far-reaching implications in Latin America not only for how economies are managed but also for politics, the organization of so-ciety, and the dynamics of culture.

The contributions to this volume, all original essays, consider the changes taking place in Latin America today specifically through the lens of anthropology. While there is an increasing amount of literature avail-able to students about neoliberalism in Latin America from "macro" per-spectives (see, for example, Gustafson, 1994), *The Third Wave of Modernization in Latin America* considers the impact of neoliberal poli-cies on the people we do not usually hear from—those most often marginalized or excluded from economic decision making. Focusing on a wide range of issues, the contributors use the current methods and theo-retical frameworks of anthropology to analyze local changes as part of broader international transformations. In this sense, the book also marks the development of the discipline, especially in how anthropologists have come to understand the relationships between the local and the global, the traditional and the modern. Those anthropologists working in Latin America in the postwar years, using modernization frameworks to guide their questions, tended to treat the local as a discrete entity, assuming that modernization would, overall, be a positive development in people's lives. Today, anthropologists understand the local and the global as a more dy-namic, multidirectional relationship—so much so that some speak of the localization of the global (see Chapter 3, this volume).[2] Recent analyses focus not only on how the modern creates the traditional (O'Brien and Roseberry, 1991) but also on how modernity itself is a tradition (see Chapter 1, this volume) and how the traditional may be more modern than modernity (see Chapter 8, this volume). Depending on one's theoretical perspective, there is optimism or skepticism about the benefits of such changes. For the optimists, there exists the possibility of reconfiguring power relations and rethinking social relations and global alternatives. The skeptics or critics express concern about the potential and current costs of globalization for people's abilities to maintain control over their ways of life and modes of thought. Our goal in this volume is not to portray Latin Americans as victims, but to provide the basis for a critique of the global processes that are currently under way and that have implications for all of us. The contributors to this volume clarify that Latin Americans display a remarkable resiliency and creativity in their engagements with neoliberalism and modernity—and North American readers may have something to learn from their struggles.

In *The Third Wave of Modernization in Latin America*, the neoliberal "turn" is not viewed as entirely new for Latin America. As a number of historically oriented essays make clear, the objectives of many aspects of neoliberalism have been around for some time under different guises. Neither is neoliberal thinking complete in Latin America; there are many debates taking place today about the value and appropriateness of neoliberalism for Latin American realities. Neoliberalism is not viewed as a logical outcome of today's global economy nor as the inevitable path along which Latin America must follow. Instead, it is understood as a political project that varies geographically and historically and is subject to transformation.

Modernization

This book was developed around anthropology's historical connection with the concept of modernization. Craig Waggaman, a political scientist, has referred to neoliberalism as "neo-modernization" (1994: 223). A quick review of the post-World War II literature, however, indicates that there is one important difference between the previous explorations of this topic and the current situation—the absence of anthropological analyses. While anthropologists were very much involved in earlier treatments of modernization in Latin America, there has been no systematic attempt to understand the current transformations from an anthropological perspective. With this "gap" noted, the contributors here were asked to assess the current modernization process based on their fieldwork in Latin America.

As the contributions of Pierre Beaucage and Michael Painter make clear, the processes taking place today share some important commonalities with past modernization practices, including the imposition of value systems by the North, the development of the market, and the transfer of resources out of local communities and regions. As this volume took shape, however, significant differences also became evident, particularly the neoliberal assumptions about the role of the state and of society itself. Because the concept of neomodernization overlooks these distinctions, the term neoliberalism has been retained here to describe the current policies being adopted by Latin American governments.

The modernization that took place after World War II insisted that the world was divided into two kinds of societies, the traditional and the modern. While critics later pointed out that this was a false dichotomy which failed to take into account the historical dynamic of colonialism, among other things, it was still a very powerful vision of the world that to some extent persists today. Modernization theory envisioned a process whereby the thinking and practices of traditional peoples would become modern (like "ours") through the expansion of the market. This transformation assumed the dual function of creating modern populations in the "Third World" (a post-World War II term) and rescuing them from poverty. The premise was that people would be provided with employment through the industrialization process, an experience that was to alter cultural values about production and consumption. The promotion of the market, specifically wage labor and mass consumption, acted very much as the "hidden hand" of the modernization project (Rostow, 1960).

Because "internal" factors were of prime importance to why countries remained "undeveloped" in the modernization schema, anthropologists—who had recognized expertise in understanding local level practices—were drawn into the modernization question. Much of their work focused on the "worldviews" of Latin American (primarily rural) communities (Foster, 1963, 1965; Lewis, 1965; Redfield, 1955, 1956; Tax, 1953). Not surprisingly, given the predominance of the modernization paradigm, these worldviews were identified not only as different but as traditional. Moreover, due to the influential work of David McClelland, who was concerned with identifying in traditional societies a psychological orientation (which he called achievement motivation) considered imperative for modernity, it was generally understood that Latin American communities must become modern and that cultural transformations were necessary in order for this to occur.

There were a few other voices in anthropology during this time that, although not explicitly critical of the modernization perspective, provided models for alternative interpretations. Work by anthropologists such as Eric Wolf (1955; 1957), who focused on social relations and structure in Latin America rather than exclusively on culture, not only offered useful tools for dismantling the neutrality of modernization theory but also helped to transform anthropology's approaches to empirical studies in Latin America once criticisms of modernization began to emerge.

Dependency Perspectives

By the late 1960s modernization theory was being seriously questioned, particularly by the "dependency" school.[3] This group of scholars emphasized the dependent relations between Northern and Southern economies and argued, from a variety of theoretical positions, that modernization theory was a thinly veiled rationalization for intervention in the South on the North's terms. Andre Gunder Frank (1969) focused on the historical significance of colonialism, ignored by modernization theorists, to make the argument that the South was underdeveloped rather than undeveloped. Pablo González Casanova (1970) used the term "internal colonialism" to characterize underdevelopment in Mexico, in contrast to the identification of distinct traditional and modern sectors made popular by modernization theorists.

During the 1970s most of the debate from scholars critical of the modernization perspective focused on how to describe global and local economies. Some researchers, arguing that Latin American economies should be characterized as capitalist, understood the dependent relation between the North and the South as created primarily through the market, and they focused on unequal trade relations (Amin, 1976; Emmanuel, 1972) and the historical development of the capitalist market from the sixteenth century (Wallerstein, 1972, 1974). Others argued that the site of production was essential to consider (Laclau, 1971), and because wage labor, especially in agriculture, was not the norm in Latin America, the continent should not be considered capitalist. Several Latin American scholars, offering in-depth analyses of the complexity of capitalist and non-capitalist relations in particular countries, made profound contributions to these debates.[4]

The contributions of anthropology to the dependency perspective were important for specifying the changing character of local and regional production systems in Latin America. The work of Stephen Gudeman (1978), Billie Jean Isbell (1978), June Nash (1979), Carol Smith (1978), and Michael Taussig (1980), among others, marked a shift in the discipline, particularly the insistence on locating local communities and regions more explicitly within the wider context of the nation-state and the global economy.

By the 1980s a number of very significant changes were taking place both in the global economy and in social science thinking. On the one hand, neoliberalism was becoming positioned as Latin America's salvation for the future. Not only had neoliberal policies been successfully "tested" on the Chilean population under the brutal regime of General Augusto Pinochet, but some Asian economies (those of the newly industrialized countries) were being touted as success stories for a neoliberal form of global development. On the other hand, a curious phenomenon called postmodernism had made considerable inroads in the social sciences, a point of view that, in anthropology, began to question the value of both fieldwork and radical "metanarratives," such as Marxism and feminism, which had influenced much of the dependency literature. By rejecting political economy perspectives as a legitimate pursuit, many anthropologists returned to cultural approaches (signaled by the publication in 1986 of Clifford and Marcus's *Writing Culture*) that sidestepped the context of an increasingly neoliberal world. This confluence of ideas was to have a profound impact on Latin America in the 1980s and 1990s.

Debt Crisis and Structural Adjustment

The 1980s have been called the "lost decade" for Latin America, referring to the devastating impact of the debt crisis and the structural adjustment policies proposed by the International Monetary Fund (IMF) and the World Bank to "rescue" debtor countries. The debt crisis reflected the increasingly serious balance of payment problems of Latin American countries. Many nations had been wooed by commercial banks in the North to borrow large amounts of money for economic development purposes. When the world economy fell into recession in 1979, these countries, receiving declining prices for their products, were unable to repay their loans to the commercial banks, and most were forced to default on their loans, beginning with Mexico in 1982.

In response, the IMF proposed conditional financing to Latin American countries, arguing that future loans would be forthcoming if countries steered their economies away from protectionism and toward the needs of the world market (Drake, 1994). This reform took place through structural adjustment plans that emphasized wage freezes, decreases in public expenditures, and support for exports. The devastating impact of structural adjustment policies on the large sectors of Latin American populations, and particularly on women, has been documented (Beneria and

Feldman, 1992; Deere et al., 1990; Moser, 1987), and the unethical nature of this solution, which squeezes the poor in order to ensure the stability of the banking system in the North, has been noted (Corbridge, 1993). Yet, these kinds of policies are still largely intact, a fact that can be explained in part by the power of these external organizations to direct national agendas, and to the apparent inability of critical analyses to influence decision making at the higher levels.

Neoliberalism

Neoliberalism is the process of a growing reliance on the market for organizing social and economic activities. Why this process has taken place in Latin America is a matter of debate. Some researchers view neoliberalism as the cure for the current economic crisis, others view it as a symptom of the crisis, while still others view it as the cause. Many economists point to the wrongheadedness of past practices such as import substitution and state-supported development, blaming them for the current problems of countries that are debt laden, and emphasize neoliberalism as the solution for resolving such problems. Other researchers argue that neoliberalism has been able to gain supporters to the extent that it has because of the dearth of alternative thinking (including increasing concerns about the viability of socialism in the late 1980s) about how social change should take place, what Frans Schuurman (1993) refers to as the "impasse" in development theory. Others identify external agencies such as the IMF and the World Bank as the main instigators of this process. Why neoliberalism has become a dominant way of thinking at this particular point in Latin America's history is most likely attributable to a variety of internal and external pressures, many of which are outlined—with varying degrees of sympathy for neoliberalism—in the analyses of David Hojman (1994), Cristobal Kay (1993), and Ian Roxborough (1992).

Conclusive assessments of the impact of neoliberalism in Latin America are difficult to make because of the ambiguous ways in which neoliberalism has been conceptualized and the different approaches (from empirically grounded studies to highly polemical arguments) that have been undertaken to engage in the neoliberal debate. It is useful to clarify that neoliberalism is neither a theory nor a neutral policy that can simply be applied logically to the world's problems. On the other hand, it is a mistake to view neoliberalism as only an ideology of capitalists, without any resonance for large sectors of the Latin American population.

Hans Overbeek and Kees van der Pijl (1993) define neoliberalism as the current profit-seeking project of transnational capital that derives its moral support from neoconservative values. This is a useful definition for two reasons. First, it grounds the ideology of neoliberalism in the political project of a particular segment of the population while recognizing the hegemonic potential of the project.[5] That is, neoliberalism is understood to be a project that aims to gain consent from the majority of the population by drawing on people's concerns in their daily lives. In this way accusations of the coercive character of neoliberalism are minimized. For example, neoliberal advocates commonly argue that through the development of a free market society, people will have access not only to wealth but to greater freedom and social order. Much of the appeal of neoliberalism is its emphasis on individual autonomy, flexibility, and choice within the general context of protecting law and order, private property, and family life. To treat neoliberalism only as capitalist ideology would discount the extent to which much of the population is concerned about these issues. However, as a number of essays in this volume show, when there remains a gap between the rhetoric about such concerns and the programs in place to do something about them, the hegemonic potential of the project is clearly compromised (see especially Chapter 6).

A second useful aspect of Overbeek and van der Pijl's definition is that it indicates how, as a political project, the face of neoliberalism may vary depending on (among other things) a country's relationship to the global economy and its particular political and socioeconomic formation. Thus, while neoliberalism is a global (transnational) project, we may identify different neoliberalisms. In the case of Latin America, certainly there are some underlying similarities in the ways in which countries are integrating neoliberal policies, but there are also some important differences that are evident in the various contributions to this volume. For example, Linda Green argues that the long history of violence in Guatemala must be considered a central component of the "success" of neoliberalism in the countryside (Chapter 3). This is a "militarized" neoliberalism, with echoes of the Chilean case and, increasingly, Peru, imposed on a people often too fearful to protest (Chapter 4).

On the other hand, the Buechlers note that some nongovernmental organizations (NGOs) are willing to try neoliberal policies because they give some attention to sectors of the population (in this case, small-scale enterprises) previously ignored by macro development models (Chapter 5). This is a kind of "experimental" neoliberalism. In still other cases, in what might be considered "contested" neoliberalism, alternative practices regarding the organization of work and society are still widely available, permitting more room for debate and protest about how neoliberal policies are applied (Chapters 2 and 7). When the ecological consequences of a growth-at-any-cost orientation become part of the everyday problems that people must confront, this too can form part of the contestation over the suitability of a neoliberal approach (Chapters 9 and 10). These are the kinds of processes that can transform the character of neoliberal policies. Indeed, some authors (Florence Babb, Beaucage, and Gustavo Ribeiro and Paul Little) hint at the future possibility of, if not an "inclusive neoliberalism" (which appears to be an oxymoron), at least an "inclusive modernity" in which previous histories of collectivism or autonomy are able to reshape contemporary economic strategies so that they may become more redistributive. In any case, these potential differences in neoliberal approaches speak to the need to integrate specificities into the debates about the changes taking place in Latin America today.

A lack of interest in specificities these days might well be a product of "globalization," a concept that often gives the impression that economic systems and culture have everywhere become the same. But it is important to address the question of what globalization means and to clarify what exactly has been globalized. Certainly, there has been a shift in labor-intensive production involving the fragmentation of production processes and the relocation of parts of the production process to areas of the world where labor is cheaper. This process has engendered an international division of labor that links workers around the world at the same time that it imposes competition among them (Nash and Fernandez-Kelly, 1983; Peck and Tickell, 1994; Rothstein and Blim, 1992). Meanwhile, new ideas about society, culture, and politics have emerged.

Thus, we find both postmodernists and economists discussing the virtues of globalization, although they may mean quite different things by it. What is important for our purposes is that, much like the past mobilization and institutionalization of a particular kind of development in the post-World War II era (as described by Arturo Escobar, 1995), arguments about the market as the key mechanism for the construction of a new society have become widely dispersed. The educational training of intellectuals and political figures in northern schools (Collins and Lear, 1995) and the activities of international organizations, including many NGOs, in which objectives aimed toward the elimination of poverty have been recast as development through trade,[6] are just some of the means by which this dispersal has taken place.

Yet, even when new production sites such as free trade zones transform the working lives of Latin Americans, this accomplishment by no means produces a functional, predictable refitting of people's ideas about how their lives ought to be lived. Despite globalization, everyone does not think the same way. To argue otherwise is to cast doubt upon people's abilities to conceptualize the world creatively and dynamically. The goal of this volume is to offer students the opportunity to see how anthropologists make sense of the massive changes being experienced by Latin Americans today in the name of neoliberalism and to highlight the contours and contradictions of Latin American modernity.

The Third Wave of Modernization is divided into three parts. The first section is titled "Changing Rural Lives," referring both to the external interventions that have produced transformations in Latin America and to how people's lives have been altered by recent events in Mexico, Bolivia, and Guatemala. Pierre Beaucage's opening chapter is a careful consideration of Mexico's historical engagement with modernity. Beaucage understands Salinismo (the neoliberal economic orientation of the country under Carlos Salinas) to be a continuation of a long history of liberalism in Mexico that has had particular implications for its indigenous populations. He discusses the decidedly pragmatic approach to these changes taken by the Nahua of the Sierra Norte de Puebla, a people who "stubbornly want a modernity that brings technology under their control." Next, Michael Painter focuses on how the extensive intervention of the United States in Bolivia since 1952 has fostered a particular development model in the country that both discourages industrialization and makes it extremely difficult for small farmers to survive by growing food crops. He argues that the way in which the misdirected U.S. "war on drugs" policy intersects with the neoliberal policies adopted by the Bolivian government doubly hurts the small farmers who grow coca to survive. Finally, Linda Green explores the connections between economy and culture for the Maya in Guatemala. She demonstrates that a thoughtful analysis of these connections enables us to identify the extensive changes, in particular the eclipsing of spaces that permit alternative survival strategies, that have occurred in the Guatemalan countryside with the entrance of export strategies such as contract farming and *maquilas* (assembly factories).

The essays under the heading "Transforming Urban Enterprises" discuss the changing urban environments in Peru, Bolivia, and Nicaragua and specifically consider their impact on women. Linda Seligmann's contribution looks at the complexity of gender and ethnic relations among market women in Peru and shows how President Alberto Fujimori's neoliberal "medicine" both encourages and limits the possibilities for political practice and survival for these women. The Buechlers' chapter assesses the impact of new lending policies on small-scale vendors and producers in Bolivia. They argue that while the promotion of microenterprises—a neoliberal policy—may be of some economic benefit to this marginalized sector, it may also threaten important kinship ties, encourage longer working days, and, ultimately, fail to empower urban women. Florence Babb then looks at the case of Nicaragua, a country in transition from a socialist orientation that emphasized cooperatives to a neoliberal one that promotes microenterprises. She argues that the transformations undertaken by the previous Sandinista government, combined with the economic crisis that has not been resolved through the neoliberal policies of subsequent governments, has produced "a desire to raise issues that had been overlooked or silenced by established political parties before and after the 1990 elections." This situation, not to mention the initial eagerness of the United States to give economic support to the National Opposition Union (Unión Nacional Opositora, or UNO), made a difference for the kind of neoliberalism that has developed in Nicaragua.

The third section, titled "Restructuring Society and Nature," encompasses a broad set of topics, including education, health, and the environment. Lesley Gill's focus on the 1995 teachers' strike in Bolivia highlights how the literature on social movements, influenced by the postmodern disinterest in class issues, fails to explain the roots and the potential of this conflict. Through her vivid portrayals of the people involved in the events, Gill is able to show us the increasing anxiety and fear in the lives of both teachers and parents, as neoliberal policies to restructure the education system are applied without reference to the realities of the Bolivian case. A theoretical contrast to Gill may be found in Constance Classen and David Howes's essay. They take a postmodern approach to the concepts of health, healing, and the body in northwestern Argentina to argue that globalization offers the potential to mix the concepts of traditional and modern medicine, transforming the boundaries of both in a way that may be beneficial to consumers.

The final two contributions consider the links between neoliberalism and the environment in Mexico and Brazil. Marilyn Gates reviews the Mexican environmental record to reveal that, overall, concrete concern for ecological issues is found only when it is evident that such concerns will not interfere with Mexico's profit-seeking growth model strategies. Her analysis of the differences between Western views of the environment and those of rural peasant farmers clarifies the complex picture that needs to be considered before solutions are proposed. Finally, Gustavo Lins Ribeiro and Paul Little focus on the discourse of environmentalism in Amazonian Brazil. They argue that globalization offers a new "place" for local actors in the global arena, one that holds the potential for their transformation into subjects who can challenge the exclusive policies of neoliberalism.

In the conclusion to this volume, the chapters are put into perspective through a discussion of the contribution of anthropology to the neoliberal debate and an elaboration of some of the problems involved in challenging neoliberalism within the social sciences. It is hoped that the following essays make a timely and valuable contribution to the debates about this "third wave" of modernization and are able thereby to advance the development of alternative ideas about transforming our future.

Notes

1. The term "neoliberalism" is still not familiar to many North American readers, though it is well known in Latin America. Many scholars use the term "neoconservatism" (familiar to North American readers through the policies of the U.S. government in the 1980s) interchangeably with the term "neoliberalism," although the discussion about neoliberalism that follows clarifies that the two terms should not be viewed as synonymous.
2. Robertson (1995) uses the term "glocalization."
3. Most authors now agree that dependency is not a theory as much as a perspective. A useful summary that compares the dependency and modernization approaches can be found in Valenzuela and Valenzuela (1978).
4. See the seminal contributions of Fernando Enrique Cardoso (1972), Cardoso and Enzo Faletto (1979), Agustín Cueva (1977), Theotonio Dos Santos (1970; 1978), Celso Furtado (1970), Raúl Prebisch (1950; 1980), Aníbal Quijano (1971), and Osvaldo Sunkel and Pedro Paz (1970), to name just a few.
5. The work of Antonio Gramsci (1971), especially his notion of hegemony, is a key influence on this perspective.
6. Laura McDonald (1995) cautions that NGO work may not be as progressive for the development of a new civil society in Latin America as it is often assumed (compare with Chapter 10, this volume).

References

Amin, Samir. *Unequal Development: An Essay on the Social Formations of Peripheral Capitalism.* New York: Monthly Review Press, 1976.

Beneria, Lourdes, and Shelley Feldman, eds. *Unequal Burden: Economic Crises, Persistent Poverty, and Women's Work.* Boulder: Westview Press, 1992.

Blomström, Magnus, and Björn Hettne. *Development Theory in Transition.* London: Zed Books, 1984.

Cardoso, Fernando Enrique. "Dependency and Development in Latin America." *New Left Review* 74 (July–August 1972): 83–95.

Cardoso, Fernando Enrique, and Enzo Faletto. *Dependency and Development.* Berkeley: University of California Press, 1979.

Clifford, James, and George E. Marcus. *Writing Culture: The Poetics and Politics of Ethnography.* Berkeley: University of California Press, 1986.

Collins, Joseph, and John Lear. *Chile's Free-Market Miracle: A Second Look.* Oakland, CA: Food First, 1995.

Corbridge, Stuart. "Ethics in Development Studies: The Example of Debt." In *Beyond the Impasse: New Directions in Development Theory*, edited by Frans J. Schuurman, 123–37. London: Zed Books, 1993.

Cueva, Agustín. *El desarrollo del capitalismo en América Latina*. Mexico City: Siglo Veintiuno Editores, 1977.

Deere, C. D., et al. *In the Shadows of the Sun: Caribbean Development Alternatives and U.S. Policy*. Boulder: Westview Press, 1990.

Dos Santos, Theotonio. "The Structure of Dependence." *American Economic Review* 60, no. 2 (May 1970): 231–36.

———. *Imperialismo y dependencia*. Mexico City: Ediciones Era, 1978.

Drake, Paul W., ed. *Money Doctors, Foreign Debts, and Economic Reforms in Latin America*. Wilmington, DE: Scholarly Resources, 1994.

Emmanuel, Arghiri. *Unequal Exchange: A Study of the Imperialism of Trade*. New York: Monthly Review Press, 1972.

Escobar, Arturo. *Encountering Development: The Making and Unmaking of the Third World*. Princeton: Princeton University Press, 1995.

Foster, George. "The Dyadic Contract in Tzintzuntzan, II: Patron-Client Relationship," 1963. In *Contemporary Cultures and Societies of Latin America*, edited by Dwight B. Heath, 271–85. Prospect Heights, IL: Waveland Press, 1988.

———. "Peasant Society and the Image of Limited Good." *American Anthropologist* 67, no. 2 (April 1965): 293–315.

Frank, Andre Gunder. *Latin America: Underdevelopment or Revolution*. New York: Modern Reader, 1969.

Furtado, Celso. *Economic Development of Latin America: Historical Background and Contemporary Problems*. Translated by Suzette Macedo. Cambridge, England: Cambridge University Press, 1970.

González Casanova, Pablo. *Sociología de la explotación*. 2d ed. Mexico City: Siglo Veintiuno Editores, 1970.

Gramsci, Antonio. *Selections from the Prison Notebooks of Antonio Gramsci*. Edited by Q. Hoare and G. N. Smith. New York: International Publishers, 1971.

Gudeman, Stephen. *The Demise of a Rural Economy: From Subsistence to Capitalism in a Latin American Village*. London: Routledge and Kegan Paul, 1978.

Gustafson, Lowell S., ed. *Economic Development under Democratic Regimes: Neoliberalism in Latin America*. Westport, CT: Praeger, 1994.

Hojman, David. "The Political Economy of Recent Conversions to Market Economics." *Journal of Latin American Studies* 26, no. 1 (February 1994): 191–219.

Isbell, Billie Jean. *To Defend Ourselves: Ecology and Ritual in an Andean Village*. Austin: University of Texas Press, 1978.

Kay, Cristobal. "For a Renewal of Development Studies: Latin American Theories and Neoliberalism in the Era of Structural Adjustment." *Third World Quarterly* 14, no. 4 (1993): 691–702.

Laclau, Ernesto. "Feudalism and Capitalism in Latin America." *New Left Review* 67 (May–June 1971): 19–38.

Lewis, Oscar. "The Culture of Poverty," 1965. In *Contemporary Cultures and Societies of Latin America*, edited by Dwight B. Heath, 469–79. Prospect Heights, IL: Waveland Press, 1988.

McDonald, Laura. "A Mixed Blessing: The NGO Boom in Latin America." *NACLA Report on the Americas* 28, no. 5 (March-April 1995): 30–35.

Moser, Caroline. *The Impact of Recession and Structural Adjustment at the Micro-level: Low Income Women and Their Households in Guayaquil, Ecuador*. Bogotá: UNICEF Regional Program for Women in Development of the Americas and Caribbean Regional Office, 1987.

Nash, June. *We Eat the Mines and the Mines Eat Us: Dependency and Exploitation in a Bolivian Tin Mining Community*. New York: Columbia University Press,1979.

Nash, June, and Maria Patricia Fernandez-Kelly, eds. *Women, Men, and the International Division of Labor*. Albany: State University of New York Press, 1983.

O'Brien, Jay, and William Roseberry, eds. *Golden Ages, Dark Ages: Imagining the Past in Anthropology and History*. Berkeley: University of California Press, 1991.

Overbeek, Hans, and Kees van der Pijl. "Restructuring Capital and Restructuring Hegemony: Neoliberalism and the Unmaking of the Postwar Order." In *Hegemony in the Global Political Economy*, edited by H. Overbeek, 1–27. London: Routledge, 1993.

Peck, Jamie, and Adam Tickell. "Jungle Law Breaks Out: Neoliberalism and Global-Local Disorder." *Area* 26, no. 4 (December 1994): 317–26.

Prebisch, Raúl. *The Economic Development of Latin America and Its Principal Problems*. New York: United Nations, 1950.

———. "The Dynamics of Peripheral Capitalism." In *Democracy and Development in Latin America*. No. 1, edited by Louis Lefeber and Liisa L. North, 21–39. Vol. 1, Studies on the Political Economy, Society, and Culture of Latin America and the Caribbean. Toronto: Centre for Research on Latin America and the Caribbean and Latin American Research Unit, 1980.

Quijano, Aníbal. *Nationalism and Capitalism in Peru: A Study of Neo-Imperialism*. New York: Monthly Review Press, 1971.

Redfield, Robert. *The Little Community*. Chicago: University of Chicago Press, 1955.

———. *Peasant Society and Culture*. Chicago: University of Chicago Press, 1956.

Robertson, Roland. "Glocalization: Time-Space and Homogeneity-Heterogeneity." In *Global Modernities*, edited by Mike Featherstone, Scott Lash, and Roland Robertson, 25–44. London: Sage Publications, 1995.

Rostow, W. W. *The Stages of Economic Growth: A Non-Communist Manifesto*. Cambridge, England: Cambridge University Press, 1960.

Rothstein, Frances, and Michael Blim, eds. *Anthropology and the Global Factory: Studies of the New Industrialization in the Late Twentieth Century*. New York: Bergin and Garvey, 1992.

Roxborough, Ian. "Neo-liberalism in Latin America: Limits and Alternatives." *Third World Quarterly* 13, no. 3 (1992): 421–40.

Schuurman, Frans J., ed. *Beyond the Impasse: New Directions in Development Theory*. London: Zed Books, 1993.

Smith, Carol. "Beyond Dependency Theory." *American Ethnologist* 5, no. 3 (August 1978): 574–616.

Sunkel, Osvaldo, and Pedro Paz. *El subdesarrollo latinoamericano y la teoria del desarrollo*. Santiago de Chile: Siglo Veintiuno, 1970.

Taussig, Michael T. *The Devil and Commodity Fetishism in South America*. Chapel Hill: University of North Carolina Press, 1980.

Tax, Sol. *Penny Capitalism: A Guatemalan Indian Economy*. Institute of Social Anthropology Publication 16. Washington, DC: Smithsonian Institution, 1953.

Valenzuela, J. S., and A. Valenzuela. "Modernization and Dependency." *Comparative Politics* 10, no. 4 (July 1978): 535–57.

Waggaman, Craig. " 'The End of History' and Neoliberalism in Latin America: A Concluding Essay." In *Economic Development under Democratic Regimes: Neoliberalism in Latin America*, edited by Lowell S. Gustafson, 223–41. Westport, CT: Praeger Publishers, 1994.

Wallerstein, Immanuel. "Three Paths of National Development in Sixteenth-Century Europe." *Studies in Comparative International Development* 7, no. 2 (Summer 1972): 95–102.

———. *The Modern World-System*. Vol. 1. *Capitalist Agriculture and the Origins of the European World Economy in the Sixteenth Century*. New York: Academic Press, 1974.

Wolf, E. R. "Types of Latin American Peasantries: A Preliminary Discussion." *American Anthropologist* 57, no. 3 (1955): 452–71.

———. "Closed Corporate Peasant Communities in Meso-America and Central Java." *Southwestern Journal of Anthropology* 13, no. 1 (1957): 7–12.

Worsley, Peter. *The Three Worlds: Culture and World Development*. London: Weidenfeld and Nicolson, 1984.

I

Changing Rural Lives

1

The Third Wave of Modernization: Liberalism, Salinismo, and Indigenous Peasants in Mexico

Pierre Beaucage

Ernesto Zedillo became Mexico's president in 1995 and two years later the country was still trying to recover from the political and financial earthquake that marked the end of six years of Salinismo (1988–1994). Few presidents have had a term coined after their name. One of President Carlos Salinas's famous predecessors was Lázaro Cárdenas (1934–1940), whose six-year mandate gave Cardenismo a sense of progressive, nationalistic, and popular policies (for his supporters) and a populist, demagogic, and anti-enterprise doctrine (for his enemies). The two presidents each could stand as the perfect antithesis to the other: Cárdenas advocated national self-sufficiency, while Salinas promoted opening up to international markets. Cárdenas created an all-embracing national party to unify the organized popular sectors and made mass mobilization and state intervention the key to development, while Salinas favored a slimmed-down state, run by high-level technocrats, with parties limiting their concerns to elections. Finally, while Cárdenas associated development with nationalist policies and discourse, Salinas considered the North American Free Trade Agreement (a distinctly antinationalist policy) as the means to ensure future growth and the proof of his administration's good performance. Salinismo had been presented to Mexicans as the gateway to the heaven of the First World, although its aftermath looks more like a descent into hell. In 1995, when Salinas left office, the Zapatista rebellion in Chiapas had not been crushed, inflation had climbed to 52 percent, there were two million more unemployed people, and foreign debt had reached summits higher than the Popocatepetl volcano.

Salinas rejected the neoliberal label and defined his political philosophy as *liberalismo social*, the "social" side supposedly being the aim and "liberalism" the means. Whatever one may think of the compatibility of the two terms, or of their adequacy for defining Salinas's political orientations, when it came to concrete policy they fused into one concept—modernization—including modernization of the state apparatus, education, farming techniques, and social relations in the countryside. Salinas was definitely not the first to set such an objective. In fact, modernization has repeatedly been on the Mexican agenda for two hundred years, and it has usually been closely related to liberalism. Usually, too, modernization was said to imply "some sacrifices," soon to be forgotten when the fruits of modernity would be reaped.

Salinas's successor, Zedillo, although throwing the blame for everything that went wrong upon the departing team, seems to be following the same pattern. In more general terms, it can be argued that, after the Spanish conquest, the most important changes in Mexico have been the many attempts to implant different versions of modernity, and the reactions against such attempts. During this process the Mexican peasantry (a large part of which is indigenous) has been neither a docile object for state policies nor a stubborn opponent to change. What is really at stake in the confrontation between the Mexican government and the Zapatista rebels, for example, and which is reflected in a broader debate within Mexican society, is the meaning and content of modernity.

Since 1983 the country has been working through its third wave of modernization, one in which market forces are meant to become the prime regulator of the economy and, by extension, of society. In this respect, in a very specific way and under a civilian regime, Mexico may be seen as going through a process similar to that experienced in Brazil and Chile, under the military, two decades ago. However, the outcome does not have to be the same, since many basic elements of the social scene are quite different, particularly as a result of the 1910–1917 revolution. In order to evaluate the impact and cost of modernity in the countryside, this chapter will focus on an indigenous region, the Sierra Norte de Puebla, in Central Mexico. A consideration of this lower Sierra region will show that concrete ecological, economic, cultural, and political factors have a strong impact on both the process of modernization and the popular response to it.

Modernity: Category or Process

Modernity used to be a worrisome concept to anthropologists since it seemed to imply the very destruction of their object of study, "traditional" or "primitive" societies and cultures. Jean Baudrillart believes that the notion cannot be given a definition that would be valid for all places and periods. Modernity covers a vast domain, with blurred frontiers, cross-cutting the fields of economics and ideology, esthetics and politics—that is, quite within the scope of modern anthropology. "Fluctuating in its forms, in its contents, in time and space, *it is only stable as a value system, as a myth.* . . . In this, *it resembles Tradition*" (Baudrillart, 1974: 139; author's translation; emphasis added). The basic values of modernity are a secularization of thought and science; the valorization of change and progress following a linear conception of history; an economism that aims at supplying an ever-increasing amount of commodities; and abstract concepts of power and the state, and of time and space. With modernity the individual emerges as the subject of economic and political liberties as well as a subjectivity aspiring to individual happiness. At the same time, modernity tries to shelter the "personal," no longer to be found in public life, in the private realm (Baudrillart, 1974: 140–41).

Absent from Baudrillart's definition (and from many others) is the fact that the transition from tradition to modernity, from the various sociocultural particularisms to a certain form of universalism, necessarily involves a shift in power and a profound reallocation of resources. For this reason, although modernization is in no way a zero-sum game, there is usually a gain for some social actors, and a cost involved for the groups who suffer a loss in their share of control and/or wealth. This shift may occur among those who have fought for the proposed change. The very use of these metaphors of "costs" and "gains" needs an immediate clarification: are these objective phenomena (to be eventually measured through economic and social analysis) or subjective perceptions by the actors themselves? The complexity of these two levels will be evident through an examination of various moments of Mexico's history and the modernization program designed and implemented by the Salinas administration.

The First Wave: Setting Up the Colonial Order

In conformity with Baudrillart's definition that modernity is a process and not a category that can be identified with a given content, it has been recently argued that the global colonization project sponsored by the Spanish state and the Catholic Church might be seen as an attempt at modernizing or "westernizing" the conquered societies while keeping in place some of their basic features (Gruzinski, 1988). This project, best exemplified by the 1542 New Laws (Las Nuevas Leyes de Indias), replaced the earlier, brutal form of domination, called the encomienda, which aimed at quick Christianization combined with rewarding Spanish veterans for their participation in the Conquest.[1] In the New Laws the obligation to convert the "idolatric Indians" was maintained, and the Catholic Church was given all the tools to obliterate thousand-year-old cults and calendrical cycles, and replace them with the worldwide perspective and linear historicity of Christianity (Gruzinski, 1988).

In the areas designed for Indians (*repúblicas de indios*) the same project increasingly marginalized native nobility (caciques) in favor of a uniform system of elected native governors and councillors (the cabildo), under the strict tutelage of the colonial bureaucracy. At the economic level, tribute was maintained and extended outside the frontiers of the Aztec empire, but was progressively monetized. Furthermore, under the repartimiento system the male population was forced to take long journeys to the Spanish-owned mines and farms, and were exposed to foreign ways in administrative cities and market towns. As the main institution responsible for the indigenous population, the Church did not limit itself to spiritual contributions. Monks brought European herbs to cure new and old ailments and introduced fowl and donkeys as well as sheep, whose wool was then used to make garments quite suited to the cold highlands. Thus, Mexico's indigenous peoples were forcibly drawn into the realm of the incipient world system and history, not only technologically but also economically, politically, and ideologically (Gibson, 1964: 136–65).

At the same time, though, the New Laws established a fundamental differentiation and segregation between the natives, locked in the *repúblicas de indios*, and the Spaniards who lived in town and on their estates. No attempt was made to eliminate native languages; it was the priests who learned Amerindian tongues. Indian communities, some of them pre-Columbian, some of them created by the Church (*congregaciones*), obtained the official recognition of their communal lands, on which they could raise crops for their subsistence and for sale in the town markets. Throughout the colonial era, a person's status remained directly linked to his or her caste, a typical ancien régime feature.

The Spanish conquest did bring various elements of a Renaissance modernity. An abstract, linear time replaced the intricate calendars in which the days themselves were gods, and the equally abstract power of the state and courts replaced personal ties with the pre-Columbian lords. Steel tools and domestic animals were spontaneously adopted by Mexican natives; the latter also welcomed the democratic cabildos and often actively contributed to the elimination of caciques. Money was quickly used in the markets, and inside communities as well. At the same time, Indians sheltered large sectors of their former cultures, particularly in the fields of ritual and belief, which the clerics defined as "idolatry" and persistently tried to eradicate. The imposed culture itself was only incipiently modern: the abstract God of Christianity was concealed behind a multiplicity of saints not so different in their attributes and cults from the traditional deities, and colonial society, after the decline of mining at the beginning of the seventeenth century, saw the emergence of a personalized power of landowners (hacendados). There was a definite appearance of individualism, linked with the spread of market relations and the breakdown of many groups, but it was tempered by strong community ties with legally enforced coresponsibility, either for tribute payment or for the cult of the patron saint.

This first contradictory attempt at modernization carried an enormous cost, which was paid for almost exclusively by the indigenous population, in spite of the interventions of some humanists (such as Francisco de Vitoria and Bartolomé de Las Casas) on their behalf.[2] The native population of Central Mexico decreased by over 90 percent between 1530 and 1610 under the double impact of the new diseases and overexploitation in the mines, farms, and cities (Cook and Borah, 1977: 96). Furthermore, they occupied the lowest level in this new caste society. From the perspective of modernization, these events appear as the unavoidable costs to be paid when the natural barriers between two unequally developed cultures are overcome. In the native view, though, the costs far outweighed the gains, as was indicated by the various forms of resistance that developed throughout the colonial period.

It is important to note that the Indians who resisted Spanish and criollo (Mexican-born of Spanish descent) rule, whether they practiced secret cults, proceeded legally against corrupt government officers and greedy landowners, or openly revolted against the state and the Church, did not do so to defend pristine native ways, but to defend the syncretic culture that resulted from the colonial process. Values such as justice, respect and keeping one's word, expressed in the dominant religious discourse, blended quite well with the new village-based, democratic Indian identity. At the same time the dominant order relegated them to a stigmatized social status, *indios,* which denied them these very values.[3]

The Impact of the Bourbon Reforms (1760–1810) and the Porfirio Díaz Era

The latter stages of Spanish colonial rule were inspired by an idea that was becoming dominant in eighteenth-century Europe: liberalism. Liberal ideas first came to the Spanish colonies from outside and above, that is, from the Bourbon reforms (Florescano, 1992: 64). Charles III (1759–1788) implemented drastic changes in the empire, with the aim of increasing the productivity of mining and agriculture, and thus the Crown's revenues.

These state-sponsored, authoritarian, liberal reforms met with hostile reactions from the dominant stratum of colonial society, the criollos, who controlled land and commerce and staffed the middle layers of the state and Church apparatus. The reforms also created resentment among the indigenous population, since they allowed non-Indians to exploit "unused" Indian lands. So the main political impact of the initial introduction of state-inspired liberalism in Mexico was to stimulate efforts against a nationalist movement whose final outlet was the Mexican war of independence (1810–1821).

The criollos retained power during the turbulent twenty-five years that followed Mexico's final independence in 1821. Meanwhile, liberalism was taken up by the mestizo lower-middle class (petty bureaucrats, army officers, underemployed professionals), who used it as a stepping stone for social ascension (Revueltas, 1992: 95). After the Liberal victory of 1856, which also marked the mestizo ascent to power, liberalism became the very ideological basis of the new state. The liberal program, which remained essentially a letter of intent until 1856, may be summarized by the word "progress." Progress meant eliminating the "shackles" left by colonial society. In particular, the land, the country's main resource, had to be taken away from the Church and from the indigenous population, whose "backwardness" was seen to prevent improvements in agriculture.

As a political regime, Mexican liberalism consolidated under Porfirio Díaz (1876–1910). Now that Díaz has become one of the villains of Mexican history there has been a tendency to attribute to him the so-called degeneration of liberalism, but, in fact, Díaz, as a liberal, firmly believed in progress. He spared no effort to establish an efficient administration and to endow the country with a modern infrastructure and economy, including railroads and the telegraph, urban facilities, and large-scale farming centered on sugarcane, coffee, cotton, and cattle. More recent historical research is redefining him as the person who executed, with an iron hand, the plans set by his illustrious predecessor, Benito Juárez, who was an heir to the Bourbon reformers (Guerra, 1985).

Once Díaz came into power, the gap between the liberal discourse and the real forms of state regulation became more and more evident. Liberal discourse was evident in the constitution and in political language, where it still embodied all the elements of the ideology of progress, such as individual freedom, education, elections, and equality in front of the law. However, in practice "national unity" meant centralization of power in Mexico City, "divisions of powers" meant absolute predominance of the executive branch over the legislative and the judicial branches, "public order" meant overt repression of any opposition, and "liberation of the land" meant the expropriation of the land of hundreds of thousands of farmers for the benefit of a few landlords.

This contradictory aspect of Mexican liberalism helps us to understand the diverse reactions it met in such an ethnically and regionally diverse country as Mexico. While the opposition to the land expropriations led to protests and rebellions in many parts of the country, in other areas indigenous peasants adhered to the revolutionary, nationalistic aspects of liberalism and used it to promote their interests. For example, in the Sierra Norte de Puebla the Indians took arms against the French Intervention Army which had allied with the regional landlords and the clergy. Under native leaders such as Juan Francisco Lucas and Dieguillo Palagosti, the Nahua expelled the French and the criollo elite (Thomson, 1991). Given that Lucas later became a regional strongman for Díaz, the Sierra natives were able to keep much of their land, which they converted to private plots, although they did lose important assets to mestizo and foreign planters (Taller de Tradición Oral, 1994).

Privatization involved a deep change in the attitude toward land. Plots could be bought and sold, and could also be mortgaged when cash was needed. A twofold process of land concentration took place: at the regional level, in the hands of the mestizo bourgeoisie from the county towns (*cabeceras*), and at the village level, where some natives, through commerce, usury, and/or political manipulation, obtained control of substantial tracts of land.

In the higher Sierra, where only one crop of corn can be grown per year, landless peasants (the "poor") resorted to sharecropping for the landowners (the "rich") and to seasonal migration to the nearby Veracruz coast. Even today, community organization in the higher Sierra is less developed than in the lower Sierra, and reciprocal ritual ties like compadrazgo (ritual coparenthood) define loose networks between peasant households. In the lower Sierra, privatization stimulated the adoption of cash cropping (first sugarcane, then coffee), which provided agricultural work nearly year-round, and peasant agriculture produced a notable surplus. Today, elaborate community religious structures reinforce local identity, while the main cleavage remains that between Indians and mestizos (Beaucage, 1994). In neither area, however, did privatization mean that land simply became a commodity, to be measured in abstract terms according to surface and money value. To this day, native communities believe that the whole land, cleared and named by "our ancestors" and marked by milestones, belongs to their members, and that outsiders' claims to it result from illegitimate practices (Taller de Tradición Oral, 1994: 130–34).

The spread of coffee orchards in the lower Sierra allowed the indigenous population to increase beyond the level attained when the region was dependent on food crops alone.[4] As in the case of land and labor, however, monetization did not suppress the sacred character of the basic Indian staple, corn. People still take great efforts to grow at least a part of the grain they need, although they know that the market value of the crop is not much over that of the rent (for sharecroppers) and is much under the value of growing coffee (for smallholders) (Beaucage and Montejo, 1984: 14, 18).

As economic transformation was taking place in the country, the political aspects of modernity trickled down to the indigenous peasantry of the Sierra mainly through their participation in national wars. As a Liberal mayor of Cuetzalan, Palagosti, for example, promoted education and public works, and as a native leader he rose in arms with his followers to defend the remaining communal lands against encroachments by mestizo planters (Thomson, 1991). In both types of actions, the leader defended the way of life of the indigenous community, which had been reconstructed after the Spanish conquest and was now considered the basis of indigenous identity. When the Nahua saw their way of life menaced, as was the case during the French invasion (1862–1867), they spontaneously took arms and fought under their leaders, yet, after the war was over, they did everything to avoid forced military recruitment. They extended this pragmatic attitude to other new ideas brought by liberalism. For example, they were enthusiastic supporters of the municipalization of their communities, which they thought could empower them to manage their own affairs (Taller de Tradición Oral, 1994: 126–27). Also, albeit fervent Catholics, they welcomed the abolition of church tithes since they felt that priests abused them. On the other hand, they had mixed feelings regarding the privatization of communal lands and appeared to have accepted it only when it was the only way left to keep their plots. Finally, they tried to avoid the head-tax and forced labor on the new roads and public buildings even when the order came from Palagosti (Beaucage, 1995a: 357).

Their attitude towards modernization would change after the local mestizos, who had education, money, and urban contacts, grabbed economic and political power at the regional level. The reaction of most natives was to withdraw, physically as well as culturally, to the villages, while oral tradition sought to explain how, and by whom, they had been betrayed. However, they did remain closely integrated—for better and for worse—with the modern political, judicial, and economic apparatus they had fought to set up in Palagosti's days.

In Western Europe and North America, liberalism, as a social and political philosophy, had been the product of the slow maturation of a capitalist economy and a bourgeois worldview. In order to be put into practice in nineteenth-century Mexico, liberalism's basic principles—a maximum of economic and political freedom for the citizen and a minimum of state presence—had to be turned into their opposites. Direct and permanent state intervention occurred in all spheres, and repression was oriented not only against the "reactionaries" but against the people themselves, especially when their aspirations (having land to till and maintaining village life) clashed with the liberal view of a nation of anonymous, individual citizens (Florescano, 1992: 64).

Personalized power, demagogy and fraud—once tricks to get into power—became the norm for the Republican government. The reiteration of the liberal principles became mostly an exercise of style for those in power, defining what has been called "*el México imaginario*" (the imaginary Mexico). The modernization program that Porfirio Díaz started, and that has continued throughout this century, has had increasingly high costs including millions of landless peasants, urban misery, and economic and political dependence upon the United States and Europe. But perhaps one of the highest costs would be the creation of an ever-widening gap between the imaginary Mexico and the real culture and practices of the Mexicans, native and non-native, whose main worry is to make ends meet in a world of authoritarianism, deceit, and corruption.

In the early 1900s this cost was resented not only by those who suffered most (peasants, miners, and factory workers) but by large sectors of the petty bourgeoisie, who had no say in the way the state was run and saw their world drift further away from what they had fought for with Juárez and young Díaz. In 1910, Francisco Madero launched his opposition campaign by stressing the gap between the liberal ideals and the Díaz regime. He became president but was not able to mobilize large masses with his legalistic slogan, "Sufragio effectivo, no reelección" (Real vote, no reelection). The aspirations of a majority of peasants, in this mostly rural country, were best expressed by Emiliano Zapata's slogan, "Tierra y libertad" (Land and freedom). It was Venustiano Carranza who finally incorporated the agrarian and labor demands into the new Constitution of 1917 and was able to put an end to the armed struggle.

The Second Wave: Cardenismo (1934–1940) and the Mexican Way to Modernity

Two decades after the revolution the conditions of peasants and workers had hardly changed since Díaz's days in spite of the inscription in the constitution of their respective rights to land (Art. 27) and satisfactory labor conditions, including the right to organize (Art. 123). The gap between the real and the imaginary country was wider than ever as President Plutarco Elías Calles succeeded in twisting the anti-reelection clause and governing from 1924 to 1934 through successors he had well in hand. Many revolutionary leaders allied with the old leading families or turned into caciques. But the participation of large sectors in the revolutionary struggle had made many people more conscious of their rights and of the possibility of changing things by putting pressure on those in power. Anarchist unions were quite effective among factory workers, while agrarian organizations helped workers to occupy the idle fields of the haciendas.

In 1934 the new president, Lázaro Cárdenas, initiated a series of dramatic changes. After tightening his control over the state and the army and sending Calles into exile, he decided to carry out the land reform laws by turning over to the peasants seventeen million hectares of farmland. By so doing, he broke over two centuries of rule by the landowning class and obtained unprecedented peasant support for the regime. To the workers, he gave the right to unionize and ensured a more effective application of the labor code. Then, on the very eve of World War II, he nationalized the foreign oil companies, giving the Mexican state a powerful resource to support its expansion and fund services such as education and public works.

At the same time, Cárdenas incorporated the peasant organizations, workers unions, and independent associations into the Partido de la Revolución Mexicana (transforming the Partido Nacional Revolucionario founded by Calles). Cárdenas justified the transformation by pointing to the danger faced by the Revolution because of its external and internal enemies.[5] Thus, Mexico developed its unique, long-lasting corporatist structure, in which the main social partners, including the labor unions and the associations of peasants and independent producers, would jointly determine who was going to be Mexico's next president. Even those formally excluded from the alliance drew benefits from the new social order. The incipient industrial bourgeoisie could rely on state contracts and high custom duties, and could produce for the internal market the consumption goods that were less available from abroad because of the war. Even the landlords who agreed to cooperate with the regime could convert their reduced assets to intensive production and sell to government agencies or to a thriving post-World War II agrobusiness.

In the rural areas where the agrarian reform never reached (such as the northern cattle-raising ranches, the southeastern coffee-producing zone, and most of the Indian Sierras), economic and political integration was achieved by adapting the traditional system of the cacique. The cacique, usually a large landlord or commercial intermediary, maintained a wide network of clients in mestizo towns and Indian villages. He ensured their political allegiance to the party and in return obtained economic support from the state (for example, farm credit) and a blank check regarding its management of regional affairs. His henchmen ran for positions as mayors and deputies, and he eliminated any competitors.[6] Although marginal to the formal political structure (the cacique seldom held office himself) he had direct connection to the top state and national levels through the party line, the party and the state being one and the same thing.

The economic results of Cardenismo, stimulated by a favorable international conjuncture, have been called, somewhat exaggeratedly, the "Mexican Miracle." From a political point of view it has been labeled "stabilizer development" (*el desarrollo estabilizador*). From 1940 to 1969, Mexico experienced its longest period of uninterrupted economic growth, with Gross Domestic Product increasing at the steady rate of 6 percent per year. By 1960 more people lived in cities than in the countryside and literacy rates had increased steadily while the proportion of landless peasants came to an historic low. The country also experienced a political stability that is unique in Latin America, with the Partido Revolutionario Institucional (PRI) holding power at all levels of government, election after election. Most observers viewed Mexico as a modern society. From high technology to daily life, U.S. influence was to be felt everywhere, yet the country preserved a definite national personality, based on its rich cultural tradition. It was thought that the pockets of poverty and "backwardness" would sooner or later disappear, thanks to economic growth and the expansion of the state's social services.

One explanation of the new, peaceful Mexican scene was that it benefited all major social actors: peasants had land, workers had steady if low-paid jobs, the expanding middle class had one foot in consumer society, and entrepreneurs could rely on protected markets as well as a cheap and docile work force. Social protest existed, such as the strike of the railroad workers in 1959 and the agrarian movement led by Rubén Jaramillo up to the early sixties, but it remained localized and could be put down easily through state intervention.

There is no doubt that a larger number of Mexicans enjoyed a higher level of well-being from this particular form of modernization. In this context, the state developed a specific discourse in which its legitimacy did not come from the individual choice expressed in the ballot box (as in the classical liberal discourse) since everybody knew the winner of the presidential election about one year before the election. The basic references were to "the revolutionary family" and to "the people of Mexico" whose fundamental needs the government claimed to know directly through the rank-and-file of the PRI. The interventionism of the post-revolutionary state broke with some of the basic tenets of liberalism (such as blind submission to the "laws of the market"), yet free enterprise was encouraged, and individual liberties were respected as long as they did not jeopardize the one-party rule.

The PRI's corporatist, hierarchical structure fit traditional conceptions and practices of social relations quite well. Peasants and artisans often sought a protector, merchant or landowner, whom they asked to be their child's godfather. In this ritualized relationship the peasants were expected to remain loyal to their better-off compadre, and the protector was expected to help the peasant during hard times. In postrevolutionary Mexico, a group of peasants asking for land or credit could contact the PRI deputy or secretary and exchange political loyalty for economic and legal support. The system was flexible enough to co-opt the leaders of protest movements, who were often offered jobs in the government, the peasant union or the Party, which they accepted with the justification that they could help their followers better "from the inside." This was not seen as a betrayal as long as some help came, which was usually the case.

The hegemonic discourse and practice of Cardenismo has been labeled both populist and corporatist. These terms fit well with the style of the new leaders (populism) and the typical form of social integration (corporatism). But they do not represent the fact that (contrary to historical Mexican Liberalism, which led to mass expropriation and overt repression) the overall policies of the PRI incorporated many of the basic demands that had been made during the revolution. This is why the term "popular-reformist" seems more adequate, although popular organizations were never in control of the process even in the golden years of Cardenismo.[7] In general, the major cost for the popular movement was the long-term loss of its independence, which almost inevitably came with the benefits of the land or labor reforms.

Over vast, rugged areas such as the Sierra Norte de Puebla, though, there was little land to be redistributed, so the classical cacique system persisted well into the 1970s. Integrated into the national (even international) economic system through the sale of their labor and farm products, masses of indigenous peasants remained unaffiliated within the postrevolutionary corporatist scheme, a situation which was destined to have important political consequences.

Setting Up for the Third Wave: The Wearing Out of the Cárdenas Model (1970–1982)

At the very moment that the model of economic growth and political stability seemed firmly in place, various symptoms appeared to indicate that the model was wearing out. In the summer of 1968 the students of Mexico

City, the nation's future elite, manifested their rejection of a sociopolitical system based on appalling inequalities, media censorship, and a de facto one-party state. The protest was crushed in bloodshed in October. Two years later the farmers could no longer supply all the basic staples the cities needed, for the first time since the Agrarian Reform. Inflation, a long-forgotten phenomenon, came to stay.

Mexican public policy since the 1970s can be summarized as a permanent, relatively incoherent search for a way out of the crisis. President Luis Echeverría (1970–1976) identified one root of the problem as the farming crisis, and he thought the solution was to go back to the Cardenista combination of populism and nationalism. Mexico was then heavily dependent upon its agricultural exports (coffee, citrus fruits, cotton) in order to import the technological package its industry needed. However, his "Third-Worldist" rhetoric could not establish workable alliances with other southern countries—the "coffee cartel" set up in 1974 soon proved to be a failure—nor could the idea of "socialization of the ejido" (in the absence of any large-scale solution for the landless) create a new state-peasant alliance inside the country. If peasants did occupy hundreds of large domains, primarily in the Indian South and in the capitalist mestizo Northwest, it was out of despair, and against government will. When Echeverría left the presidency, the country was in disarray. Large rural areas were in turmoil, and inflation and food dependence were increasing.

His successor José López-Portillo (1976–1982) decided to use the oil wealth to stir up growth at all costs. For him, state capitalism should help the peasants raise their productivity in order to link up with the private sector and produce the food the country needed once again. Through the "Mexican Food System" (Sistema Alimenticio Mexicano), he spent billions of dollars in (often useless) infrastructure and in efforts to "organize the peasant" by distributing credit, machinery, fertilizers, pesticides, and high-yield seeds, which led to excessive bureaucracy in the countryside.

The whole system came to a halt in 1982, when oil prices halved in a matter of months, and Mexico awoke again to the inward spiral of inflation, devaluation, capital flight, and foreign debt payments that were impossible to meet. This time a number of top bureaucrats and businesspeople in Mexico, the U.S. government, and various financial circles realized that the political economy of the popular-reformist alliance was dead and that another formula had to be found.

Under Miguel de la Madrid (1982–1988), the key word was "adjustment" conceived in the monetarist fashion of those days: both government deficit and balance of payments problems had the same cause, that is, expenses bypassed income. The remedy was the same as that applied throughout the Third World—reduce government spending and imports and increase revenues and exports. The peso was devaluated, subsidies to basic food supplies decreased, health and education services were cut, and imports drastically reduced. Hundreds of public enterprises considered unprofitable were either sold to the private sector or, more often, closed down. By the end of the decade, soaring prices and wage control had cut the purchasing power of the minimum wage in half.

The end of the import substitution policy, and with it what Gilly (1988) called the "exhaustion of the Cardenista pact," did not produce the same social and political upheaval in Mexico that marked the end of populism in other Latin American countries such as Brazil or Argentina. Once again, the unique system designed by Cárdenas to mobilize the masses proved to be an excellent tool for controlling both the urban workers and the farmers. Their official federations "voluntarily" agreed to the new Pact of Economic Solidarity of 1987 imposed by the de la Madrid administration. Hence, it became materially impossible for the government to dismantle the heavy, obsolete corporatist system as entrepreneurial groups were requesting (Gilly, 1988: 31). The trouble would come from outside the organized workers, essentially from the dwellers of shantytowns whose movement (Movimiento Urbano Popular) presented the most serious opposition to the new policies. The movement's radicalism increased sharply after the September 1985 earthquake in Mexico City, given the obvious cynicism of the authorities and their lack of care for the tens of thousands of homeless (Monsiváis, 1987: 17–122). The system had stopped giving rewards, however small, to those who were loyal to it. After six years of imposed "sacrifices," Mexico found itself at the end of de la Madrid's term with a paralyzed economy, inflation up to 145 percent per year, and a larger-than-ever debt.

After the 1982 crisis, economic liberalism was definitely on the rise in Mexico. The new liberalism found its first clear expression in a right-wing opposition party, the Partido de Acción Nacional (PAN). Rooted in the industrial North, the PAN brandished the all-time model of Mexican Liberals—the United States. In the middle of the political, economical and ideological disarray which had struck Mexico, U.S. policies appeared to be plain common sense to a majority of norteños (northerners), who always had the impression that they only worked so that Mexico City politicians could spend money and distribute favours to lazy southerners. In comparison with the overall change that the PAN proposed, de la Madrid's belt-tightening measures, imposed by the IMF and U.S. private banks, appeared half-hearted and provisional. While the Right was progressively imposing its new vision of modernization, the left was engaged in a long process of redefinition and reorganization, which would start bearing fruit at the end of the 1980s.

Indigenous Movements during the Transition Period (1972–1986)

In the Sierra Norte de Puebla, two very different peasant movements developed after 1970. In the villages of the Upper Sierra, a successful struggle against an increase of the land tax encouraged the formation of an agrarian movement, the Unión Campesina Independiente (UCI), whose second target became the redistribution of some large domains belonging to the local caciques. Here class identity prevailed over community or ethnic ties, as communities often were divided along class lines. Under a charismatic leader, the organization grew rapidly and developed another base in neighboring Veracruz. In 1976 a UCI demonstration in Veracruz gathered thousands of peasants determined to obtain land and put an end to cacique rule. However, López-Portillo's policy of overt repression, as well as the landlords' death squads, were able to deal serious blows to the movement. In 1979 a split occurred between two leaders that forced remaining members underground, and, by the beginning of the eighties, the group had disappeared (Beaucage et al., 1981).

In the lower Sierra the peasant movement was slower to emerge but was of greater endurance. It finally took the form of a community-based, regional cooperative called Tosepan Titataniske (literally, Together We Shall Win). It reached poor and middle Indian peasants and was strongly defined along ethnic lines. In spite of opposition from the local mestizo intermediaries and their political allies, the Tosepan received some financial support and legal recognition from López Portillo's administration, along with other groups that aimed to increase farm output. Progressive outside advisors of various ideological tendencies, mostly agronomists and educators, provided the technical and administrative know-how to help the newly elected native leaders. At first these leaders came from the middle peasantry. They took their mandate as a service to the communities and did not spare their time and efforts to convince farmers from other villages to join the organization. The Tosepan soon developed into a network of local cooperatives whose main purposes were to sell basic staples at subsidized prices and to market peasant produce (allspice, *sapodilla*, oranges, and some coffee). In the early eighties, the Tosepan Titataniske could claim thousands of members from more than sixty villages (Beaucage et al., 1982; Martínez Borrego, 1991).

From 1976 to 1986, the peasant movement was thriving. The network of local cooperative stores seriously competed with the regional commercial bourgeoisie and put a halt to speculative prices on basic items.

The Tosepan Titataniske attracted a diversity of projects, supported by international and state agencies and volunteers, that promoted important cultural and social changes in education (from kindergartens to high schools), created local stores and warehouses, induced road building and road repair, and supported chicken and pig-breeding businesses. Associations were formed to introduce running water, health clinics and nutrition centers, and literacy classes for adults (in Spanish and Nahuat, later in Totonac). The Taller de Tradición Oral devoted itself to the recollection and diffusion of traditional Nahua culture and folklore. With the regional cooperative as its backbone, never before had there been so many efforts put forward for developing the Sierra. Among the natives, the co-op and the various projects generated enthusiasm and intense participation. In many communities, well-attended weekly meetings were the occasion to discuss all collective matters.

At the same time, the Mexican Coffee Board (Instituto Mexicano del Café, or INMECAFE) also "organized" peasants into the Economic Units of Coffee Producers (Unidades Económicas de Productores de Café, or UEPC) to modernize coffee production with credit, a new technological package, and marketing facilities. The participatory nature of the Tosepan Titataniske was in clear contrast with the UEPCs, where producers were summoned to hear what had been decided for them in INMECAFE's head office.[8] Most peasants opted for a double commitment: they stood with the co-op regarding consumption issues, allspice marketing, community development, and politics, but they followed INMECAFE's advice regarding the production and marketing of their main cash crop, and planted more and more coffee of the new high-yield varieties, while the co-op advocated crop diversification and tried to market various products (often successfully, as in the case of allspice).

At the same time that the movement reinforced Indian identity on a regional basis, paradoxically, it accelerated acculturation processes. The younger generation of men soon abandoned the traditional native dress (white cotton shirts and trousers, broad-rimmed straw hats and rubber-sole sandals) for manufactured clothes and shoes of the style usually worn by rural non-native Mexicans. Urban status symbols such as the digital-dial wristwatch, metal ballpoint pen, and pocket calculator became standard for co-op officials (*comisionados*), teachers, and heads of projects. Nearly every woman now wore plastic sandals instead of walking barefoot, but only a small proportion, among the younger ones, adopted the factory-made dress instead of the traditional large white skirt, wide red belt, and embroidered blouse. This style of dress is still considered elegant and as enhancing a woman's beauty (Beaucage, 1985: 85). At the linguistic level, better schooling in Spanish and access to radio and (in some houses) television meant increased bilingualism. While Nahuat is spoken within the house and for daily intercourse, Spanish invades the co-op meetings since it is the only language understood by the outside counsellors. Also, the adoption of the formal structure and proceedings of a cooperative involves using a large number of Spanish terms that have no Nahuat equivalent (such as *presidente de debates* [speaker] and *orden del día* [agenda]). At regional meetings, participants usually speak directly in Spanish, while at village meetings, they use sentences where a Nahuat structure is filled in with many Nahuatized Spanish terms.

The new institutions in the lower Sierra profoundly changed the spatial-temporal parameters of the community. By setting its main office in Cuetzalan, the mestizo-dominated county head, the Tosepan Titataniske created a properly indigenous physical and social space, something that had disappeared a century ago. After doing their business in town, peasant farmers and families would often come to rest, talk, and take shelter from the rain at the co-op building, conveniently located not far from the marketplace. Similarly, in the villages, most of which previously had no retail stores (with the exception of the liquor stores, where men drink standing under the eaves), the local co-op, together with the electric corn mill, became a new center for social interaction. Women would laughingly comment, "Before, we used to chat at the fountain. Now, with running water in everybody's house, we can't do it anymore. So we go early to the corn mill and we gossip a little."

Social time was also deeply modified. Weekly regional meetings of local representatives, which started on Sunday morning, would usually end after dark, with participants complaining bitterly about having to walk back to the villages in the pouring rain, when the trails were deserted and they could be assaulted. In the villages, the fact that the frequent meetings were held at night (so that people would not lose a workday) contradicted the traditional use of time. In the past, important matters were dealt with at (or even before) dawn, and people went to the fields early and went to bed at dusk (Beaucage, 1995b: 302–3).

Gender relations also underwent a notable change. Since the public sphere was considered essentially a man's business, the change came about gradually. Single women complained about being obliged to assist at evening meetings in order to get corn at the co-op store; when they went, they remained in a corner, breast-feeding, laughing quietly as men quarrelled, or rushing out to remove a screaming child. Eventually some literate young women were hired as store salesgirls and did quite well. As some men commented ironically, "They don't booze, don't cruise customers, and don't meddle with accounts." Finally, some women were elected to positions as co-op executives, on school boards and on other committees. Today, the main problem that women face is how to combine their new public life with their roles as wives and mothers. Although Indian society, albeit patriarchal, is not as machista as mestizo society, problems will still occur when the mother is not there to "give the tortillas" (*tamaka*) to her husband and children.

Modernity as it was exemplified by a decade of change (1976–1986), with substantial material improvements, higher incomes, better health and education services, and meetings where everybody could speak and even criticize, had much appeal for the indigenous farmers. These changes were not perceived as "losing our culture" but, rather, appropriating invaluable outside elements into the culture. There were not many laments about the good old days. On the contrary, the general tone was that of a just Indian revenge, and one could hear statements such as:

"Before, the mestizos considered our grandfathers as stupid (*xoxitos*) because they only knew how to work. They did not have a good instrument (arms). But nowadays, you won't frighten our youngsters."

"The mestizos have exploited us for one hundred years, we won't let them any more."

"They used to keep all the good things for themselves but it is us who do all the work."

While the success of the Tosepan Titataniske put a positive value on a stigmatized Indian identity, people felt the loss of traditional work. Farmers were reducing their cornfields, thus leaving the heavy, but sacred work of producing the basic food for lighter, better-paid coffee planting. And many were leaving farming altogether to become masons, truck drivers, or *comisionados*. As one elderly peasant woman put it, "Here, everything grows. But nobody wants to work anymore" (Beaucage, 1989: 130).

Capitalist Modernity: The Contradictions of the Third Wave

Because the region depended on export products, such as coffee and allspice, which sold well, it did not immediately feel the blow of the financial crisis and the policy changes that had affected the whole country after 1982. However, the poorer peasants, who had to buy corn most of the year, resented Distribuidoras de la Conasupo, Sociedad Anónima (DICONSA), the official food distribution agency, for the continual increases of basic food prices in the co-op stores.

In 1986 the cooperative presented its own candidates for mayor and counselors in Cuetzalan and won against the angered mestizo elite. But the new mayor soon discovered that with no funds coming from Mexico, most community development projects had to be shelved, disappointing his once-enthusiastic followers. With all of the oil money being kept in the United States as payment for a one hundred-billion dollar foreign debt, modernization no longer included the development of public infrastructure throughout the country.

Meanwhile the regional cooperative faced new problems. The red tape of a big organization and modern agrobusiness required trained personnel, and this did not exactly fit the earlier pattern when people were chosen because of their respectability. The new *comisionados* were younger, better schooled, and estimated that they deserved at least a minimum wage salary for their work. They also discovered that, in spite of de la Madrid's commitment to a "clean, business-like" administration, whatever money still came from the government's agencies did so mainly in return for political allegiance. A few young, educated (and more ambitious) Indians managed to hold office at the regional level more or less permanently. Peasants found that some of them spent more time in town and traveling to Mexico City than climbing the hillsides to listen to the people. Moreover, because of the lack of financial assets, the Tosepan had never been able to control coffee marketing, which still belonged to the INMECAFE and the local intermediaries (*coyotes*). As the Tosepan attempted to get into the market through a large loan, the international coffee price plummeted (1988–89) when the Intenational Coffee Organization, under whose auspices importing and exporting countries meet, could not agree on a new floor price for quota exports. In fact, persistent overproduction in the South had led the buyer countries, headed by the United States, to question the very logic of maintaining quotas and floor prices. In the year that followed, coffee lost half its value on the international market. The co-op nearly collapsed and the board of directors increasingly narrowed their political alliance with the PRI in order to be able to maintain a minimum level of funding.

As a result of de la Madrid's cutback policies, mismanagement of the earthquake crisis, and poor economic results, the 1988 presidential election was the first one in sixty years in which the PRI lost. The new president, Carlos Salinas, had been the chief economic advisor to de la Madrid. With confirmed U.S. support (President Bush had decided to avoid the risk of supporting PAN), Salinas confiscated the PAN's orientation, arguing that Mexico's badly needed modernization could not be done by the state and should be left to market forces. Of course, the state is much more than a spectator in the process; it has to create the economic, political, and social conditions that will allow the market forces to "play freely." Salinas's purpose was to reorganize the economy, the state apparatus, society, and culture. While de la Madrid sold unprofitable state concerns, Salinas put the best ones up for sale, including the banks and the public telephone company. A new positive climate was created with the private sector, and foreign capital started to flow in again, stabilizing the peso and lowering inflationary pressures.

With regard to the countryside, his policy was precise and twofold. Since his predecessors' attempts at linking entrepreneurs and smallholders had been met with suspicion and hesitation on both sides, he decided to strike at the heart of the problem and "liberate" the land and the people from the ejido system, which had prevented half the arable land from being bought and sold. Furthermore, the national bank, created to support farmers with easy credit, now had to lend money on the basis of profitability, and INMECAFE, which had run into millions of dollars of debt after the international coffee price fell, was simply liquidated (Paré, 1993).

In order to prevent a social crisis, Salinas created the National Solidarity Program (Programa Nacional de Solidaridad, or PRONASOL), which funneled money to some of those excluded from the new economic plan, such as slum dwellers, laid-off workers, and the peasant Indians of the Sierras. Thousands of small community projects (schools, roads, cooperatives) were funded. For example, after the dismantling of INMECAFE, peasant producers were encouraged to purchase its equipment and plants and start exporting. Most organizations were too heavily indebted to do so, but through political pressures some were able to reschedule their debts, get some fresh money through PRONASOL, and buy coffee from their members. In some areas of Guerrero and Oaxaca, this program seems to be working (Paré, 1993), while in Veracruz and in the Sierra de Puebla failure seems widespread (Hoffmann, 1993). In the Sierra de Puebla, private intermediaries are occupying the scene for the first time since 1970.

After fifteen years of failed efforts and hopes, the peasants from the lower Sierra were quite bitter. They had consciously avoided direct confrontation with the state in order to escape the repression faced by their upper Sierra neighbors. In 1990 they learned that there would be no help for replanting the orchards destroyed by frost. Some peasants left the coffee on the trees, since the harvesters' wages were higher than the value of the beans. Those who had large families to feed cut down part of their coffee orchards ("coffee trees make good firewood") and planted corn instead, since it now took two pounds of coffee to buy one pound of corn. The rest picked whatever they could with free family labor and begged the *coyotes* from nearby towns to purchase it. However, the intermediaries were not eager to buy since the price was low.

The peasants are struggling to adapt in this new economy since they know there is no way back to the old system. After twenty-five years of intense exposure to modernity, nobody wants to return to the old days, where you worked from dawn to dusk and were happy to have enough corn to eat and a few pesos to spend at the fiesta. Young men and women who have had elementary schooling, seeing they cannot make a living in the villages, have left for Mexico City to work as masons' helpers and housemaids.

In 1996, San Miguel Tzinacapan, a large indigenous settlement that played an important role in the founding of the Tosepan Titataniske, still exhibits the symbols of progress people were so proud of a decade ago: a road, electricity, new schools, and many cement houses with terrace roofs. The noise of an occasional car or truck has replaced the whinnying of mules. Yet, it is now more common to hear elderly women in worn-out clothes asking for money and teachers complaining about the growing numbers of undernourished children. Meanwhile, in Mexico's Southeast, faced with the same impossibility of appropriating modernity, the Tzeltal from the Selva Lacandona decided to force the Mexican government to renegotiate its political and economic relationship with indigenous communities. The Nahua of Puebla apparently preferred to try their individual luck in Mexico City.

In August 1995 I went with some Nahua friends to Tecoltepec, a poverty-stricken village in the lower part of the Cuetzalan district, an area barely touched by modernity. The trail was impassable and the frail houses were made of planks and rods. The invitation for breakfast meant that our group of four had to be split in two since no single household could treat four guests with coffee, eggs, and tortillas. Last year a collective effort had brought electricity to the village, but they also badly needed piped water since, during most of the year, women had to haul water uphill along steep, rocky paths. The forty able men of the village were waiting for our arrival. The news we brought was that some money had been found to buy the cement and the pipes. They responded that they would work in turns with the Canadian engineers; men would do the rough work and women could carry sand and light materials. There is no longer the historical distrust of foreigners that had been present in the early 1970s. At the same time the villagers have definite, and quite realistic, expectations. They do not share the idealized vision of their poverty ("harmony with nature") that has been spreading in the North and that would make "development" redundant. The villagers of Tecoltepec stubbornly want a modernity that brings technology under their control: "We don't want a pump," said one of their spokespersons. "In X [another village] they got a pump and one month later it was broken and nobody could ever repair it. So, no matter how far the spring is, we shall all work together until the water flows down by itself to where we need it." In February 1996, after three months of difficulties and effort, water ran from a faucet in the center of the village.

Conclusion

The three waves of modernization in Mexico show some differences with respect to the means of achieving modernity and the social groups who are to be its main beneficiaries. Yet the third wave resembles the first in that "liberating" the means of production from "legal shackles," in a context of acute social inequalities, means that the concentration of wealth rapidly and dramatically increases. In Porfirio Díaz's times, more than 75 percent of arable land came to be held by less than 1 percent of the country's landowners. In a striking parallel, there were twenty-four billionaires in Mexico in 1994, compared with seven a decade earlier when liberal policies were given a new start. In both cases, the large majority found itself marginalized from the benefits of the reforms: in the mid-1990s, approximately 40 million people (out of 90 million) were being excluded. The first wave came to a halt in 1910 with the rebellion of the various classes who had to bear all the costs. From the Mexican Revolution came a different concept of modernization, exemplified by Cardenismo, which took into account some basic needs of peasants and workers. However, Cardenas's lack of effective control over the process, and the all-pervasive liberal notion that economic growth per se can only be positive, without any consideration for demographic or environmental limits, brought this new Mexican model to a halt a generation ago, when it too had excluded millions of people. The rising discontent of the rural and urban poor, in addition to external pressures, forced the Mexican ruling classes reluctantly to admit to the failure of the model in the early 1980s. And so, from 1982 onward, the state proceeded to dismantle the material and institutional bases of the old social contract, but without providing a new one. As in the previous periods, and quite paradoxically in a country that is now mostly urban, it is from the countryside that the greatest challenge to the new liberal policy has come, with the Zapatista uprising of January 1994. In its aftermath, a large coalition of popular forces is now emerging, across party and class lines, to include those trying to reinvent an inclusive form of modernity within which costs and benefits can be more evenly spread.

Notes

1. Under the encomienda regime, natives were "bestowed" on a Spaniard, who had the mission of converting them while he was profiting from their labor. The practice was curtailed by the New Laws (1542), wherein control of people and lands reverted to the Crown when encomenderos and/or their heirs died.
2. Francisco de Vitoria (1486–1546) was a Dominican friar and teacher at Salamanca University. He never came to America but, based on the writings of

Thomas Aquinas, he argued for an Indian right to self-government, thus contesting the legitimacy of the Spanish conquest and the forceful conversion of the natives. In 1539 he was forbidden to write or debate anymore on the topic. Bartolomé de Las Casas (1474–1566), also a Dominican, became a bishop in Chiapas, Mexico. He adopted a more pragmatic position—he accepted the legitimacy of the Conquest and the necessity of converting the Indians, but he claimed that the very way in which the two objectives had been carried out and the abuses of the encomienda regime had led the natives to hate Christianity and would lead to their extinction. In what was called the Great Debate of Valladolid (1550), he successfully confronted Juan Ginés de Sepúlveda (1470–1573), a supporter of Indian slavery.

3. The messianic ideology that inflamed Indian prophets and rebels often was, in fact, a symmetrical reconstruction of the colonial Christian ideology, a reconstruction that placed them instead in the dominant position (García de León, 1985; Gruzinski, 1985).

4. With nine thousand inhabitants, in 1877 the district of Cuetzalan experienced seasonal food shortages (Ramírez et al., 1992: 24–25). One century later, its twenty-five thousand people lived essentially on intensive plantation agriculture and related trades and services.

5. The internal situation was quite critical since the Catholic Church, antagonized by Calles's extreme anticlericalism, had set up a guerilla movement, the Cristeros in Western Mexico. The expropriated landlords and foreign interests could use dissatisfied sectors of the armed forces to set up a coup. By accepting the alliance with the state, peasants facilitated their land claims and secured the grants afterwards; workers could benefit from legalized unions to ensure the application of the labor code. The army and independent small entrepreneurs and professionals were also enticed into this social pact which, in times of turmoil, assured them that their interests would be taken into account.

6. In the Sierra Norte de Puebla, a cacique dynasty based in the large domain of Apulco ruled until the mid-1970s. It controlled the regional rum industry and prevented any agrarian claim on its domains to succeed (Paré, 1973).

7. Populism basically refers to a style of discourse in which symbolic reference is made to "the people," the working class and the peasantry being exalted as the real members of the nation in order to obtain their political support. On the other hand a policy may be genuinely labeled "popular" when it embodies basic demands of large sectors of society such as land for farmers, decent labor conditions for workers, and equal rights for women.

8. For example, in 1982–83, the coffee producers had to revolt against INMECAFE, and thousands of them blocked and occupied the Xalapa offices simply in order to get the arrears that had been held for nearly one year.

References

Baudrillart, Jean. "Modernité." In *Encyclopaedia Universalis*. Vol. 11, 139–41. Paris: Encyclopaedia Universalis France, S.A., 1974.

Beaucage, Pierre. "La jeune fille, les fleurs et l'orphelin: Notes sur la poésie amoureuse nahuatl de la Sierra Norte de Puebla (Mexique)." *Recherches Amerindiennes au Québec* 15, no. 4 (1985): 79–90.

————. "L'Effort et la vie: Ethnosemantique du travail chez les Garifonas du Honduras et les Maseuals (Nahualts) du Mexique." *Labor, Capital and Society* 21, no. 1 (1989): 112–37.

————. "The Opossum and the Coyote: Ethnic Identity and Ethnohistory in the Sierra Norte de Puebla (Mexico)." In *Latin American Identity and the Construction of Difference*, edited by A. Chanady, 149–86. Minneapolis: University of Minnesota Press, 1994.

————. "Ethnies et sociétés: Deux ethnohistoires des Nahuas (Sierra Norte de Puebla, Mexique). In *La construction de l'anthropologie québéçoise: Mélanges offerts à Marc-Adélard Tremblay*, edited by F. Trudel, P. Charest, and Y. Breton, 337–66. Québec: Presses de l'Université Laval, 1995a.

————. "*Yekmaseualkopan.* Y a-t-il une manière moderne d'être nahuat?" In *The Reordering of Culture: Latin America, the Caribbean and Canada in the Hood*, edited by A. Ruprecht and C. Taiana, 291–310. Ottawa: Carleton University Press, 1995b.

Beaucage, Pierre, Mariette Gobeil, María Elisa Montejo, and Françoise Vityé. "Développement rural et idéologie paysanne: Ce qui se passe au village." *Anthropologie et Sociétés* 6, no. 1 (1982): 131–74.

Beaucage, Pierre, and María Elisa Montejo. "Rapports fonciers et rente foncière: Une étude de cas dans la Sierra Norte de Puebla (Mexique)." In *Le café au Mexique et en République Dominicaine: Questions de rente foncière*, edited by P. Beaucage, A. Corten, M. E. Montejo, and M. B. Tahon, 4–30. Montréal: Université de Montréal (Groupe de Recherche sur l'Amérique Latine), 1984.

Cook, Sherburne F., and Woodrow Borah. *Ensayos sobre la historia de la población: México y el Caribe.* Mexico: Siglo XXI, 1977.

Florescano, Enrique. *El nuevo pasado mexicano.* Mexico: Cal y Arena, 1992.

García de León, Antonio. *Resistencia y utopía: Memorial de agravios y crónica de revueltas y profecías acaecidas en la provincia de Chiapas durante dos últimos quinientos años de su historia.* Vol.1. Mexico: Era, 1985.

Gibson, Charles. *The Aztecs under Spanish Rule: A History of the Indians of the Valley of Mexico, 1519–1810.* Stanford: Stanford University Press, 1964.

Gilly, Adolfo. *Nuestra caída en la modernidad.* Mexico: Juan Boldó i Climent, 1988.

Gruzinski, Serge. *Les Hommes-dieux du Mexique: Pouvoir indien et société coloniale. XVIe et XVIIe siècles.* Paris: Editions des Archives Contemporaines, 1985.

————. *La colonisation de l'imaginaire: Sociétés indiennes et occidentalisation dans le Mexique espagnol. XVIe-XVIIIe siècles.* Paris: Gallimard, 1988.

Guerra, François-Xavier. *Le Mexique, de l'Ancien Régime à la Révolution.* Paris: L'Harmattan, 1985.

Hoffmann, Odile. "Il y a dix ans déjà . . . Tentatives et faillites d'une modernisation dans le secteur social; les ARIC caféières du Veracruz." In *Les caféicultures mexicaines: La force de la tradition, les risques de la décomposition*, edited by O. Hoffmann and B. Sallée, no. 39, 43–55. Toulouse: Université de Toulouse-Le Mirail, 1993.

Lerner, Victoria. "Consideraciones sobre la población de la Nueva España (1793–1810), según Humbolt y Navarro y Noriega." *Historia Mexicana* 17 (1968): 327–48, quoted in *Indian Labour in Mainland Colonial Spanish America*, edited by J. A. Villamarín and S. E. Villamarín, 59. Newark: University of Delaware, 1975.

Martínez Borrego, Estela. *Organización de productores y movimiento campesino*. Mexico: Siglo XXI, 1991.

Monsiváis, Carlos. "Los días del terremoto." In *Entrada libre: Crónicas de la sociedad que se organiza*, edited by Carlos Monsiváis, 17–122. Mexico: Era, 1987.

Paré, Luisa. "Caciquisme et structure du pouvoir dans le Mexique rural." *Canadian Review of Sociology and Anthropology* 10, no. 1 (1973): 20–43.

———. "Du paternalisme d'Etat à l'inconnu: Quels modèles après la disparition de l'Institut Mexicain du Café?" In *Les caféicultures mexicaines: La force de la tradition, les risques de la décomposition*, edited by O. Hoffmann and B. Sallée, no. 39: 56–63. Toulouse: Université de Toulouse-Le Mirail, 1993.

Ramírez, Carolina, Gabriel Jaimez, and Pablo Valderrama. *Tejuan titalnamikij . . . Recordamos el pasado*. Puebla: Secretaría de Cultura, 1992.

Revueltas, Andrea. *México: Estado y modernidad*. Mexico: Universidad Autónoma Metropolitana, 1992.

Taller de Tradición Oral del Centro de Promoción Educativa y Cultural. *Tejuan tikintenkakiliayaj in toueytitatajuan/Les oíamos contar a los abuelos*. Mexico: Instituto Nacional de Antropología e Historia, 1994.

Thomson, Guy P. C. "Agrarian Conflict in the Municipality of Cuetzalan (Sierra de Puebla): The Rise and Fall of Pala Agustín Dieguillo, 1861–1894." *Hispanic American Historical Review* 71, no. 2 (1991): 205–58.

2

Economic Development and the Origins of the Bolivian Cocaine Industry*

Michael D. Painter

In the mid- to late 1970s cocaine production emerged in Bolivia's export-driven economy as the dominant industry by generating as much foreign exchange as all other exports combined. While mining, which was Bolivia's dominant export industry from the colonial period, never employed more than 5 percent of the work force, the cocaine industry employed between 7 and 20 percent of the country's work force (depending on the period studied and the method used to make calculations) (Crabtree et al., 1987: 58; OTA, 1993: 5).

*This discussion is based on research supported by the Harry Frank Guggenheim Foundation, the United Nations Development Fund for Women, and the Cooperative Agreement on Systems Approaches to Regional Income and Sustainable Resource Assistance (No. DHR-A-00-9083-00) at Clark University, the Institute for Development Anthropology, and Virginia Polytechnic Institute, funded by the U.S. Agency for International Development, Bureau for Science and Technology, Office of Rural and Institutional Development, Division of Rural and Regional Development. The views expressed are those of the author, and should not be attributed to any of the above-mentioned institutions or individuals acting on their behalf. While solely responsible for any errors of fact or interpretation, the author thanks Sonia Arellano López for commenting on the initial draft.

The institutions participating in the research were the Centro de Estudios de la Realidad Económica y Social (CERES), the Centro de Formación Interdisciplinaria (CEFON) of the Universidad Mayor de San Simón, the Taller de Estudios Sociales (TES), and the Institute for Development Anthropology (IDA), where the author worked until the end of 1994.

Coca leaf and cocaine production had become the livelihood of many families due to an economic crisis triggered by three interrelated circumstances of the 1980s: a drought that effectively eliminated rain-fed agricultural production in most of Cochabamba from 1983 into the early 1990s; a period of hyperinflation during the early 1980s, followed by a radical structural adjustment implemented in August 1985, which marked the adoption of a range of neoliberal economic policies by the Bolivian government; and the collapse of Bolivia's major export industry, tin, during late 1985 and early 1986. This combination of circumstances reduced or removed the ability of many Bolivians to earn a living. At the same time, responding to a booming demand in the United States and other wealthy countries, coca leaf and cocaine production were expanding. Amid the widespread economic devastation, the cocaine industry often appeared to offer the only economic alternative.

While these circumstances were the immediate cause of much participation in coca leaf and cocaine production, reference to them alone is an insufficient explanation of the situation. Several long-term historical factors need to be considered to explain the stagnation of Cochabamba's agricultural economy. This stagnation reinforced conditions, created by the development model adopted by Bolivia following its 1952 national revolution, that had determined the country's subsequent economic growth and development. This model restricted economic opportunities for most people, even as it laid the foundation upon which the cocaine industry would be constructed.

The central features of the post-1952 development model adopted in Bolivia included the creation of an export-oriented agroindustrial elite that depended on state subsidies; the maintenance of a large rural population, able neither to earn a living through farming nor to survive without it; and dependence on economic assistance from the United States to maintain the power relations on which the Bolivian social order rested. This development model has determined who would be the beneficiaries and who would be the victims of the social and economic changes that have occurred since. While this model did not make it inevitable that Bolivia would become a center of cocaine production, it did create the necessary conditions for the cocaine industry to take root and grow. Although the architects of the model could not foresee the rise of the cocaine industry, they were aware of who would benefit and who would bear the costs of the model being implemented. The impact that these benefits and costs had over time, together with the dramatic increase in international demand for cocaine, led to cocaine replacing tin as Bolivia's most important export commodity.

The Pre-1952 Context

As the middle of the twentieth century approached, tin mining was the dominant economic activity in Bolivia. Mining as a whole accounted for 95 percent (tin alone, 74 percent) of Bolivia's exports in 1950 (Crabtree et al., 1987: 57–58). All of Bolivia's tin production was controlled by three corporations belonging to the Patiño, Aramayo, and Hochschild families. The benefits that Bolivia received from its important place as a producer of tin were modest since the country's infrastructural development was tailored to meet the needs of the mining companies. For example, a system of railroads linking the mining centers with coastal ports, from which ore was shipped, and administrative services in Bolivia's major cities was completed by 1917. But there was no road linking the three major cities of La Paz, Cochabamba, and Santa Cruz until the 1950s, after the revolution.

The taxes paid by the tin industry were very small as a share of profit. Nevertheless, they were the major source of revenue for the Bolivian government, which gave the tin barons control over much of the country's political life. While concentrating on the management of their businesses and remaining uninvolved in political administration, they were able to call on the government to pursue economic policies that kept wages low and made it difficult for workers to organize. Troops were always available to repress any unrest (Crabtree et al., 1987: 58; Klein, 1992: 163–69; Malloy, 1970: 43–46).

The inequities of the social order upon which the mining economy rested generated widespread political mobilization during the early decades of the twentieth century, which culminated in 1952 in a successful revolution led by the Nationalist Revolutionary Movement (Movimiento Nacionalista Revolucionario, or MNR). Upon seizing power, the MNR nationalized the tin mines and placed them under the control of a state-owned mining company. The declared intention was that the new state would administer the riches associated with the mining industry for the benefit of all Bolivians.

The Aftermath of the Revolution

Soon after taking power, the MNR government encountered several problems that undermined the promise of redistribution and led to the consolidation of the development model under which Bolivia continues to live. The most important problem was the challenge to MNR control over Bolivia's rural areas posed by uprisings of the native peasantry in the

valleys of Cochabamba. These uprisings were the continuation of an escalating pattern of rural conflict between smallholding peasants and landlords that dated from the late nineteenth century and intensified during
and after the Chaco War (Rivera, 1992: 103–30).

Peasant leaders saw the revolution as an opportunity to press their
struggle against the landlords. The resulting growth of violence and disorder threatened the ability of the new government to control the countryside and contributed to the disruption of food supplies to the cities. In
1953 the government responded by enacting an agrarian reform, which
provided for the expropriation of the large estates and their division among
smallholding peasant families. To ensure that it was not threatened by an
independent rural-based social movement again, the government also established an official peasant union structure. Through this structure, it
distributed patronage to portions of the rural population that it found cooperative and punished those who opposed it (Albó, 1990a, 1990b;
Dunkerley, 1984: 65–74; Klein, 1992: 235–36).

While these steps brought the rural unrest under control, the reorganization of the land tenure system and the disruption of trade and transport linkages between rural areas and the cities contributed to continuing
urban food shortages. The government responded by taking control of the
urban food distribution system and importing massive amounts of food to
satisfy the needs of city dwellers. In addition, the MNR was under enormous pressure to satisfy the expectations of those who had supported the
revolution, including the mineworkers who were seeking pay increases,
urban people who looked to the government to provide jobs, and representatives of various interest groups who were counting on the government to finance development activities that would benefit them. At the
same time, Bolivia was not receiving revenues from the expropriated mines
because of the production disruptions arising from their expropriation
and reorganization. Furthermore, under international pressure, the government decided to compensate the mine owners for the ownership transfers (Klein, 1992: 238).

This combination of circumstances resulted in a profound financial
crisis to which the Bolivian government responded by turning to the United
States for assistance. The United States, for its part, was concerned about
the implications of the 1952 revolution as a model that might be emulated
elsewhere in Latin America. Thus, it sought to use the economic assistance it gave Bolivia to influence the course of political events. Within a
decade of the revolution, Bolivia had received more than $100 million in
U.S. aid. At the time this made it the largest recipient of U.S. aid in Latin
America, and the largest per capita recipient in the world (Eder, 1968:
521–22, 593–94; Klein, 1992: 238–45).

While U.S. economic assistance is widely regarded as having saved the MNR government, the state that was constructed as a result of that assistance bore little resemblance to the one that had been envisioned by many of the revolution's participants. Although nationalist and populist rhetoric remained an important element of Bolivian politics, the country became extremely dependent on continuing U.S. support. During 1955 and 1956, for example, the value of U.S. economic assistance to Bolivia was three times the revenue generated by the Bolivian government in taxes and customs duties. Over the longer term, between 1954 and 1964, Bolivian tax and customs revenues amounted to $287 million, while U.S. aid commitments for the same period totaled $343 million (Eder, 1968: 79, 595–96). No Bolivian government has been able to govern without U.S. economic assistance since 1952.

U.S. Assistance and Agroindustrial Growth

One objective of the economic aid was to promote the development of commercial agriculture in Bolivia's eastern lowlands, particularly in Santa Cruz. Before the 1950s, large rural estates dominated the economy of this region. The boundaries of these estates were recognized by local custom, and their claim to much of the land was not based on a formal title. Within the estates lived peasant families who provided labor and agricultural products to the landowner in return for being allowed to live on the land and use it to produce goods for their own consumption. Lowland native populations also resided within the boundaries claimed by some estates, and paid tribute to the landlords without being formally incorporated into the labor force. The estates produced most of the goods required to satisfy the basic consumption requirements of the people living on them. Since they imported what they did not produce from outside the region, there were no markets for agricultural produce or manufactured goods functioning in the region.

U.S. economic assistance sought to transform these estates into commercial agricultural enterprises, producing initially for Bolivian markets and later for export. To accomplish this change, the United States supported the construction of a paved highway linking the city of Santa Cruz with the upland cities of Cochabamba and La Paz; financed the construction of a distillery to expand the market for sugar cane produced in the area; created a heavy machinery pool to encourage the clearing of expanded areas of forest for cultivation; provided subsidized credit to encourage investment; and provided financial and technical support to formalize titles to land held under customary law. Unlike in the upland and valley regions of the country, little land belonging to large estates was expropriated in the lowlands, although the threat of expropriation was used to encourage landowners to participate in the modernization program (Eder, 1968: 80–83, 648–57; Klein, 1992: 238).

The United States had two major reasons for targeting aid to the large landowners of the eastern lowlands. First, the U.S. and Bolivian governments did not consider it practical to promote agricultural development in the upland areas of the country, due to a range of factors, including biophysical limitations, population density, and political volatility. Second, the United States sought to use agricultural modernization in the eastern lowlands to create a wealthy and politically powerful group of agroindustrial entrepreneurs who defined their interests in ways that were congenial to U.S. interests (Ybarnegaray, 1992: 69–72).

The effort to modernize the agricultural economy of Santa Cruz was largely successful. The region has grown more rapidly than any other area of the country since the 1950s, and it has become an important center of production for a range of agroindustrial crops such as cotton, sugarcane, and soybeans. In addition, Santa Cruz's regional elite has come to play a central role in national politics, with people from the region occupying key positions in every national government since the mid-1960s. However, Santa Cruz's agroindustrial elite became very dependent on continuing economic support from the United States and other international donors, even as it ran up very large commercial bank debts. For its part, the United States, because of its interest in making sure that it remained a strong political force in Bolivia, continued to support this elite, despite Bolivia's inability to wean itself from development assistance and easy credit.

U.S. Assistance and Rural Development

U.S. political interests were also visible in other aspects of the economic assistance it provided to promote rural development in Bolivia. Although it had written off the possibility of promoting agricultural development in upland areas, the United States did provide significant funds that were used by the MNR government to establish and maintain a patronage network to undermine organized opposition by the upland peasantry. Much of the institutional framework that characterized the presence of the Bolivian government in rural upland areas was financed by the United States.[1] The United States also financed a program called Civic Action, under which Bolivian troops were deployed in many areas of the countryside to gain the support of rural residents through the construction of public works. Government institutions interacted with the National Confederation of

Bolivian Peasant Workers, an officially sponsored peasant union, which ostensibly represented the interests of peasant families at the local, departmental, and national levels. Its leaders were salaried employees of the Ministry of Peasant Affairs and Agriculture, and many of them also received regular payments from the military and the Ministry of the Interior (Albó, 1990a: 243–51; Dunkerley, 1984: 88–103; Frederick, 1977: 119–58).

While many of the projects carried out by these institutions constituted important improvements in the lives of the people, their primary purpose was political. Projects were designed to reward government supporters and punish its opponents. Further, these development institutions formed the basis of an intelligence-gathering network throughout the countryside that identified leaders who showed potential for organizing effective opposition to the government. This aspect of U.S. assistance proved useful for neutralizing the growth of potentially hostile social movements. Thus, despite steadily deteriorating living conditions in the countryside, it was not until 1979 that the independent peasant union movement that today represents the majority of Bolivia's rural families was established (Albó, 1990b).

Agroindustrial Elites and Cocaine

While a certain amount of the coca leaf produced in Bolivia has been transformed into cocaine since early in the twentieth century, cocaine manufacture did not become the primary use for coca leaf until the 1970s (Bascopé, 1982: 22; Carter and Mamani, 1986: 92). This change arose from a financial crisis experienced both by the agroindustrial cotton entrepreneurs of the eastern lowlands, whose access to subsidized credit was being threatened, and by upland families still subject to the stagnation of the rural economy.

In the early 1970s many of Santa Cruz's agroindustrial entrepreneurs had responded to incentives provided by the Bolivian government and international donors to invest in cotton production. Between 1967 and 1974, for example, 67 percent of the agricultural loans authorized by the Bank of the State and 48 percent of the agricultural loans authorized by private banks were for cotton production (Ybarnegaray, 1992: 82). Similarly, the Bolivian Agricultural Bank, which had been reorganized with U.S. assistance during the 1950s and was the primary vehicle for U.S.-sponsored agricultural credit during the 1950s and 1960s, allocated 52 percent of its agricultural loans to promote cotton production between 1971 and 1977 (Dunkerley, 1984: 222). As a result of these incentives,

cotton production in Santa Cruz increased from slightly over 8,000 hectares in 1969–70 to about 50,000 hectares in 1974–75 (Pattie et al., 1988:
H–11; Ybarnegaray, 1992: 103).

At the time, credit was available under conditions that encouraged
recipients to treat the funds received more as a grant than a loan (Ybarnegaray, 1992: 76–87). However, when the international price of cotton
dropped precipitously after peaking in 1973–74, many were left in dire
financial circumstances. The Bolivian government took dramatic steps to
bail them out, such as ordering the Bolivian Agricultural Bank to assume
the private debt of the cotton producers and reschedule payments, which
contributed to a mounting public debt in Bolivia that led to a massive
devaluation of the currency. The government absorbed and wrote off the
greatest portion of the cotton producers' debt. As of December 1985, the
government held over $18 million in defaulted agricultural debts, 90 per-
cent of which were owed by farmers in Santa Cruz, and two-thirds had
been granted to support cotton production (Ybarnegaray, 1992: 84).

Despite the bailout, the crisis resulting from the fall of cotton prices
left many commercial farmers shaken and feeling the need to make a quick
profit. Their sense of urgency was in part due to the evaporation of the
easy credit to which they had become accustomed. Access to credit had
declined because of the growing indebtedness of the Bolivian government (to which the bailout of the cotton growers had obviously contributed), declining prices for Bolivia's exports, and increasingly stringent
conditions by international creditors on the granting of credit and the repayment of debts. While the latter change was global in scope and affected governments throughout the continent, Bolivia was hit particularly
hard, suffering the largest decline in absolute and per capita Gross Domestic Product of any country in Latin America (Dunkerley and Morales,
1986: 89, 96; Roddick, 1988: 84). In this context, investment in the transformation of coca leaf into cocaine proved attractive to some members of
the regional elite of eastern Bolivia, including some producers of
agroindustrial export crops, cattle ranchers, and members of the military
(Bascopé, 1982: 53–56, 90–96; Dunkerley, 1984: 222–23, 315–25; Healy,
1986: 104–7).

Smallholding Families and Coca Leaf

Smallholding families in the upland areas of the country were also economically squeezed in the 1970s. While the combination of land redistribution and patronage politics did, for a time, diffuse the explosive social
situation in these areas, it did not address the underlying causes of the
deteriorating living conditions of rural families. The situation in the rural

uplands actually became worse in many respects because of the application of Bolivia's post-1952 development model.

U.S. economic assistance was a contributing factor in this deterioration. As decisive as U.S. assistance was in shaping the course of agroindustrial modernization in Santa Cruz, it accounted for only part of the total foreign assistance package. The largest portion of the aid went to finance Bolivia's imports of surplus agricultural commodities from the United States. Indeed, the United States spent more between 1954 and 1957 to finance the food aid program ($56.6 million) than it did to develop the agricultural sector for the period between 1952 and 1972 ($40 million) (Frederick, 1977: 261–62). In combination with an artificially low exchange rate applied to imported agricultural commodities, the food aid program deepened the problems that domestic producers faced by depressing grain prices to levels that did not even cover production costs. Led by food aid, imports accounted for between 70 and 90 percent of Bolivia's total grain supply for all but two years between 1952 and 1985 (Eder, 1968: 79, 112, 122; Pattie et al., 1988: H–13).

Thus, a combination of factors, including the failure of the government to address the historical causes of stagnation in the agricultural economy, the decision by the Bolivian government and its U.S. sponsors not to invest in upland agriculture, unfavorable exchange rates, and the impact of subsidized grain imports, made it very difficult for rural families to earn a living through agriculture. Many people were compelled to seek ways to earn income off the farm. By 1977, for example, rural families in the upland valley region of southern Bolivia earned an average of U.S.$327 per year, of which 56 percent came from off-farm sources (Deere and Wasserstrom, 1980: 156). Yet smallholding families in upland valleys continued to be very important food producers for Bolivia—they still produced about 70 percent of the food consumed in Bolivia in the late 1970s (Urioste, 1988: 65). Thus, despite increasingly unfavorable conditions, smallholding families continued to farm and, sometimes, to increase production. They had little choice. On the one hand, they could not support themselves solely through farming. On the other, off-farm employment opportunities were so scarce, and so poorly paid, that they could not afford to stop farming, if only to provision themselves. Rural families could continue to produce under such conditions because they worked longer hours at a wider range of productive activities, and relied increasingly on the labor of their children. Nonetheless, there are limits to people's ability to sustain themselves by working harder, especially when so many factors over which they have no control work against them.

The U.S. position, adopted as policy by the Bolivian government, was that the population in upland areas was too dense to permit agricultural

development. Thus, to reduce upland population densities, and the potential for social unrest associated with deteriorating living conditions, the
Bolivian government, with financial support from the United States and
other international donors, began to promote the resettlement of upland
families into the country's lowland areas. Initial efforts took place in Santa
Cruz where five new lowland settlements were established by the end of
1956. A second effort began in 1961, focusing on other lowland areas of
the country, including the Chapare, which has become the major source
of coca leaf destined for cocaine manufacture. The Chapare was desig-
nated a priority settlement area in the National Development Plan for
1962–1971 and in the National Colonization Plan, which was published
in 1963. In 1965, with U.S. support, Bolivia established the National
Colonization Institute to administer settlement activities throughout the
country.

     For the most part, these efforts were considered failures because of
high rates of abandonment and the high costs of resettlement. Nonetheless, the U.S. Agency for International Development and other donors
continued to sponsor colonization projects until the mid 1980s. Many
upland families moved into the tropical and subtropical lowlands using
their own resources and without the support of resettlement programs.
They laid claim to land and began producing a range of crops for their
own consumption and for Bolivia's markets. In the Chapare, for example,
54 settlements, where over 24,000 people resided in 1967, had grown to
247 settlements with a population of over 83,000 by 1981 (Flores and
Blanes, 1984: 82, 88–89). The economic impact of Chapare settlement
was significant. In 1976, settler families in the Chapare were producing
about 39 percent of Bolivia's plantains, 32 percent of its citrus, and
20 percent of its rice on 156,000 hectares of land. Poor roads and inadequate transport were regarded as the major constraint on continuing expansion of agriculture in the Chapare (OAS, 1984: 181).

     Other processes were at work which would have an even greater im-
pact on limiting the expansion of lowland agriculture. Because Bolivia
has a small population—less than seven million people—and because it
is the poorest country in South America, the market for agricultural products is small. Also, while the Bolivian government and international donors promoted settlement, they did not view the settlement areas as places
to invest agricultural development funds. Thus, settlers could not get access to modern agricultural inputs, or the credit with which to acquire
such inputs, to improve the productivity of their labor. The result was
that, as more and more people entered the Chapare and Bolivia's other
settlement areas, they competed with one another for access to the
country's restricted market and drove down the prices for their produce.

Since they had no access to the inputs or credit that would allow this competition to take place on the basis of greater efficiency, it took place on the basis of families' ability to increase production by working harder to produce more. This approach, of course, increased the downward pressure on the price that settler families received for their produce. Eventually they exhausted their ability to respond to declining prices. The only remaining option was to find another crop that had a bigger market and brought a higher price.

Beginning in 1983 and continuing into the early 1990s, much of Bolivia experienced a drought that crippled or eliminated farming in most rainfed areas, forcing many families to abandon their lands in hopes of earning a living elsewhere. The drought exacerbated the impact of a profound economic crisis that manifested itself in two areas that were particularly important in causing families to move to the Chapare. First came a financial crisis that had its roots in the high level of debt that Bolivia and many other Latin American nations were carrying. As a result of trying to deal with a skyrocketing debt rate and sharply falling Gross Domestic Product, Bolivia experienced an annual inflation rate that exceeded 14,000 percent before finally being brought under control by radical structural adjustment measures implemented in August 1985 (Dunkerley and Morales, 1986; Roddick, 1988). For poor people, the cure prescribed for inflation was about as bad as the "disease" had been. The government froze wages for four months (in a year when inflation was running at an annual rate of 14,000 percent) and removed all price controls, resulting in increases of about 1,000 percent in the prices of basic consumer goods. In rural areas this combination meant that prices for agricultural inputs and transport went up dramatically while the price of agricultural produce went down equally dramatically.

A 50 percent decline in international tin prices in October 1985 compounded the effects of the crisis. In March 1986 the London Metal Exchange canceled its contract to trade in tin. The collapse of international tin trading brought ruin to the largest industry in Bolivia's mining sector, the capture of which had been the object of the 1952 revolution. During 1985–86 some 27,000 mine workers lost their jobs; some of them then made their way to the Chapare and other lowland settlement areas. Largely as a result of the mine layoffs, Bolivia's unemployment rate approached 30 percent by the end of 1986 (Crabtree et al., 1987: 5, 20). The large numbers of unemployed further constricted urban food markets, as declining incomes caused people to rely more heavily on imported foodgrains, and to reduce their purchases of food produced in Bolivia.

As these crises unfolded and compounded one another, international demand for cocaine was booming, and some members of Bolivia's dominant social classes responded through investment in the manufacture and sale of cocaine. This investment created an expansion in the market for coca leaf, to which settler families responded quickly. While coca leaf grows well throughout Bolivia's humid tropical and subtropical regions, several characteristics of the Chapare made it particularly attractive for producing coca leaf for cocaine. One is that it is located almost exactly between the upland valleys of Cochabamba, where most of the families who have migrated to the Chapare are from, and the city of Santa Cruz. Sitting astride the major road linking the two areas, the Chapare is easily accessible from both directions. Another is that its broken topography makes the Chapare a good location for concealing and controlling access to the rustic laboratories and processing facilities where the initial steps are taken to extract the cocaine alkaloid from coca leaf. A third characteristic of the area is that the variety of coca leaf grown there, while having a flavor that causes it to be regarded as inferior for traditional forms of consumption, does yield a larger volume of cocaine alkaloid, making it popular among the cocaine producers.

With the rising international demand for cocaine, the various factors affecting Bolivian elites and poor rural dwellers converged to create a boom economy in the Chapare. Bolivian coca leaf production grew from 11,800 metric tons in 1975 to an officially estimated 147,608.3 metric tons in 1988. The Chapare accounted for most of the increased production, nearly all of which was destined for cocaine manufacture. Of the 147,608.3 metric tons produced in Bolivia in 1988, 15,563 metric tons were destined for Bolivia's legal internal market for coca leaf, and 138,234.6 metric tons were produced in the Chapare (DIRECO, 1988: 28–33). The boom was also reflected in the population growth in the Chapare. The 1981 population of slightly over 83,000 had grown to between 196,000 and 234,000 people by 1987 (Durana et al., 1987).

The Economics of Coca Leaf Production

Becoming involved in coca leaf production did not solve the problems of Chapare farm families. Bolivia remains a country whose development policies are hostile to small-scale farm families who want to earn a living through agriculture. As already noted, Bolivia depends heavily on subsidized grain imports, which depresses the price that producers can receive for agricultural produce. Also, credit and other development resources that would permit farmers to invest in capital inputs and compete with one another on the basis of improved labor productivity are monopolized by the agroindustrial elite in the lowlands of Santa Cruz and small pockets of commercial farmers in other areas of the country. Smallholding families therefore compete for access to Bolivia's limited markets based on who can invest the most unpaid labor and still continue to produce in the face of unfavorable conditions. This strategy accelerates the deterioration of agricultural conditions, since more people are offering products at a price that bears no relation to the labor required to produce them, driving prices down even further.

As the population in the Chapare and other lowland settlement areas increased, families intensified the exploitation of their own nonwage labor resources as they vied with one another to sell their produce in Bolivia's urban markets. This competition drove down the prices that producers received for citrus, plantains, and rice (for which the Chapare had been a major supplier in the mid-1970s) and undermined agricultural development based on these crops. Despite strong international demand for cocaine, the same problem affected families engaged in coca leaf production. The well-known profitability of trafficking in cocaine does not extend to the production of coca leaf. If large profits were to be made through coca leaf production, one would expect Chapare farmers to hire large amounts of labor and dedicate their entire farms to that crop. But, while many families do occasionally hire workers, most do not. The mean farm size in the Chapare is 10.4 hectares and the portion of that kept under cultivation is between 1.25 and 4 hectares. Of the land cultivated, the area dedicated to coca leaf ranges from between .6 and 1.6 hectares. In a survey of 194 Chapare farmers, 58 percent said that they hired labor on occasion, 87 percent said that they relied mainly on unremunerated family labor, and 72 percent reported that they supplement the labor of the immediate family by exchanging labor with other families. Farmers stated that the lack of money with which to hire workers, and the limits on the number of family members who would work without wages, were the major limitations on their ability to produce more (Painter and Bedoya, 1991b; Painter, 1995).

As the number of Chapare families relying on nonwage labor to grow coca increased, the mean price of coca leaf declined from about U.S.$80.00 per hundred pounds of dry leaf in 1986 to about U.S.$25.00 in 1990. The competition among a large and growing number of families to sell to a small market compounded the problem generated by the role of nonwage family labor in production by creating a situation in which prices could be manipulated by buyers (Alvarez, 1993: 33–34). Because the Chapare offered advantages over other lowland areas of Bolivia where coca leaf could be cultivated, production remained concentrated in the Chapare rather than being dispersed through much of the tropical lowlands, as had been the case with other crops. As a result, Chapare farm families continued to produce coca leaf, despite deteriorating conditions, not because it was a profitable crop but because it was the only crop families could be sure of selling at any price. Thus, coca leaf proved subject to the same limitations that had afflicted other crops.

Chapare Families and the War on Drugs

The role of Chapare families in coca leaf production made them the object of the so-called War on Drugs, a campaign largely financed with U.S. economic assistance. In Bolivia the war on drugs has two dimensions: to create economic opportunities that generate alternatives to coca leaf production, and to apprehend drug traffickers through law enforcement. Unfortunately, efforts to generate alternatives to coca leaf production as a source of livelihood have been ineffective, and coca-leaf-producing families, rather than drug traffickers, have been the ones most likely to be apprehended in police actions.

Efforts to create alternatives to coca leaf production in the Chapare have proven ineffective primarily because they have focused on the introduction of new crops rather than on addressing the social and economic reasons that families turned to coca leaf production in the first place. Until recently, U.S.-sponsored crop substitution efforts have focused on the introduction of new crops, including coffee, black pepper, and macadamia nuts, among others, and the rejuvenation of crops such as citrus fruits and bananas that had been important sources of family income in the recent past. Agencies responsible for implementing crop substitution concentrated on developing production packages adapted to the physical conditions of the Chapare, which would then be disseminated among farmers through extension. Little attention was given to on-farm constraints such as labor availability or to such marketing issues as where farmers would sell the crops they harvested (Painter, 1990: 20–23; Painter and Bedoya, 1991a: 5–37; OTA, 1993: 84–89).

More attention was paid to the marketing problems associated with substitution crops beginning in the early 1990s. While development efforts to connect crops with markets demonstrated that farmers would respond quickly to opportunities to sell crops other than coca leaf, the lack of investment in upland agricultural development since the 1952 revolution meant that transport facilities, mechanisms to distribute market information, and basic inputs like packing crates for fruit were only available as a result of extraordinary efforts by Bolivian government agencies attempting to promote these alternate crops. Further, the successes of these efforts owed much to external technical, financial, and logistical support, without which they probably would not have been achieved, and certainly would not be sustained.[2] The investment in resources required to achieve these limited successes underscored the fundamental problems that had to be overcome if Chapare farm families were to have a real alternative to coca leaf production (Painter, 1990: 20–23; Painter and Bedoya, 1991a: 5–37; OTA, 1993: 84–89, 105–7).

The impact on Chapare families of the failure to develop alternatives to coca leaf production was compounded by the fact that they, rather than those manufacturing and trafficking in cocaine, bore the brunt of repression meted out in the name of the war on drugs. The level of repression to which Chapare families have been subjected tended to grow through the 1980s, tempered primarily by the fact that by 1987 settlers had formed a strong federation of independent local unions that were linked to Bolivia's national independent peasant confederation. As a result, Chapare families have often been able to respond to large-scale violence with political mobilization that has threatened stability in many areas of the country, a reality that has usually given pause to those who would like to see more force used against them (Painter and Bedoya, 1991a: 70–77; Painter, in press).[3]

A lack of obvious violence does not mean a lack of conflict (Albó and Barrios, 1993: 11–12). For example, in July 1994 the Bolivian government conducted Operation New Dawn, a military operation in the Chapare the stated objective of which was to catch drug traffickers, but the primary impact of which was the repression of settlers. With support from Bolivia's labor movement, the Chapare federations of coca producers organized the March for Life, Coca, and National Sovereignty, which left for La Paz from the Chapare on August 29. The marchers withstood multiple attacks by soldiers and police, who fired tear gas and were supported by helicopters. Despite the attacks, some three thousand marchers (men, women, and children) reached La Paz on September 19, where a substantial portion of the city's population turned out to meet them in a gesture of solidarity. In response to this pressure, the government signed a fifty-four-point agreement with the organizations representing Bolivian labor, the peasant union movement, and the federations of coca farmers, which included provisions to review and modify the country's main antinarcotics law, to establish an interinstitutional commission on human rights, to exercise better control over police and military units in the Chapare, and to abolish conditionalities that made the Chapare eligible for development assistance only if farmers eliminated coca crops at a level stipulated by the government (CEDIB, 1994a, 1994b, 1994c, 1994d).

The ability of Chapare coca farmers to mount this kind of political mobilization successfully has tempered the actions of those inclined to use violence against them, and encouraged the farmers to make their case through collective political action instead of resorting to violence.

Nonetheless, the level of continuing conflict, and the possibility of it escalating, should not be underestimated. The Bolivian government has made and broken agreements with coca farmers in the past. More importantly, the political struggle surrounding coca takes place within the context of broad mobilization against the continuing implementation of neoliberal political policies begun in 1985. Because they contribute to and receive strength from the national peasant and worker movement of which they are a part, Chapare farmers are subject to the ebb and flow of this larger struggle as well as the struggle to defend themselves from being victimized by the war on drugs. Precisely because of their effectiveness in mobilizing large numbers of people and withstanding repression by the police and military, they can become easy targets as the authorities attempt to isolate them from the rest of the peasant and worker movement. Such was the case in 1995, when the government declared a state of siege in response to widespread resistance to its economic policies, and pointed to the mobilization of coca farmers as a justification for its action.

The police subject the Chapare families to a high level of brutality, in the form of beatings, rapes, theft, and destruction of property (Kline, 1987: 25–27; Anonymous, 1988a, 1988b). Much of this is legitimized by the Coca Regulation and Controlled Substances Law, or Law 1008, which was passed by the Bolivian congress in 1988, under pressure from the United States, and provides the legal framework for actions taken by the government in the name of waging a war on drugs. Law 1008 violates provisions of Bolivia's constitution guaranteeing rights of due process to people charged with crimes, which the law's supporters contend is necessary to protect society from the abuses of drug traffickers. However, 60 percent of the people jailed under the law, between its enactment in 1988 and 1991, were from poor rural families. Of these, 99.35 percent were classified as "nearly indigent," and 88 percent relied on public defenders for any legal assistance they received. Furthermore, 95.5 percent of the people jailed under provisions of Law 1008 in La Paz, Cochabamba, and Santa Cruz were there on grounds of suspicion, and only 4.5 percent had been duly tried and sentenced (Blacutt, 1991: 52–53).

The credibility of assertions that violence and repression against rural families constitute a necessary part of an all-out "war on drugs" is undermined by the fact that prominent people who are regarded to be allies of the United States in Bolivia have been permitted to operate freely, without fear of arrest or prosecution (Dunkerley, 1984: 318–19; Kline, 1987: 24–25). Furthermore, Bolivian government officials responsible for waging the war on drugs express the view that the repressive efforts against settler families and rural workers in the Chapare are misdirected. For example, following Operation New Dawn, in which several settlers were killed and many others were beaten and arrested, the undersecretary for social defense, who commands the anti-narcotics units of the national police force, stated that not a single important drug trafficker was arrested ". . . because the big fish are in the cities, and not in the Chapare" (CEDIB, 1994c: 3).

Conclusion

Observers of the cocaine industry have noted that its growth in Bolivia has been linked to widespread corruption, resulting from members of the military, political leadership, and the business sector participating in or turning a blind eye to drug trafficking (Bascopé, 1982; Kline, 1987). While the effects of this problem are widely visible, the seeds of corruption sown by the cocaine industry fell on well-tilled and fertilized soil. The high level of dependence on U.S. economic assistance that was created as part of the post-1952 political order meant that, from the perspective of Bolivian political leaders, internal political and economic agendas were largely subordinated to the requirement that the government continue to receive economic assistance at levels that were a substantial part of total state revenue. From the perspective of U.S. officials responsible for allocating and administering that assistance, the promotion of development, however defined, was consistently less important than promoting narrowly defined geopolitical interests. As a result of these interests, poor people who have organized to oppose the social and political order associated with Bolivia's development model have been the major targets of repression in the name of the war on drugs, while politically powerful people involved in drug trafficking are seldom arrested or convicted.

Bolivian dependence on economic assistance seriously undermined the integrity of state institutions because they would not function, or often, would not exist, if not for U.S. aid. The reality of this dependence has been the point of departure for nearly every Bolivian government since the revolution. Such an arrangement implied an inherent potential for state agencies to be subverted in carrying out functions on behalf of sectors of the national population, when these functions conflicted with the interests of groups or individuals regarded as friendly to the United States.

This potential is realized in the conduct of the war on drugs. Poor rural families were denied access to the opportunities given in abundance to the wealthy. As their economic situation deteriorated, coca leaf production offered a short-term solution to their need to earn a livelihood. They have become objects of repression, not because of their importance in the production of cocaine but because of the inconvenience of waging the war on drugs against those who control the cocaine industry in Bolivia.

Notes

1. These institutions included the National Community Development Service, which carried out public works projects in rural communities; the National Agrarian Reform Institute, which implemented the redistribution of land decreed by the agrarian reform; and the National Colonization Institute, which promoted and administered the resettlement of rural upland families into the lowlands.

2. The Bolivian government agencies responsible for planning and implementing crop substitution efforts (which came to be known as alternative development) were the Subsecretaría Desarrollo Alternativo y Sustitución de Cultivos de Coca (SUBDESAL), the Programa de Desarrollo Alternativa Rural (PDAR), and the Chapare program of the Instituto Boliviano de Tecnología Agropecuaria (IBTA/Chapare). SUBDESAL and PDAR were created with support from the U.S. Agency for International Development (USAID), and received most of their budget for salaries and operating expenses and all of their budget for implementing activities from USAID. IBTA is Bolivia's national agricultural research agency, and IBTA/Chapare formally came under its authority. In fact, it was an autonomous agency wholly funded by USAID, and its budget was kept separate from the rest of IBTA to ensure that funds earmarked for crop substitution activities were not used to pay salaries and operating expenses in other parts of the organization. PDAR and IBTA/Chapare were supported by USAID-funded technical advisors, most of whom were expatriates, including ecologists, agronomists, foresters, hydrologists, animal scientists, extension and marketing specialists, and, from 1988–91, the IDA members of the social science team that conducted this research.

3. The level of violence in the Chapare has been much lower than in South America's other major center of coca leaf production for the cocaine industry, Peru's Upper Huallaga Valley. In the Upper Huallaga, largely unorganized settler families were subjected to all forms of abuse and brutality by drug traffickers, the police, and the military. Because of this lack of organization, many settlers were receptive to the entry of Sendero Luminoso, the only organization openly defending the rights of coca producers. Sendero made the area a major stronghold, and taxed drug traffickers to finance its war against the Peruvian government. The conflict between Sendero and the government brought yet another source of violence to the Upper Huallaga (Painter and Bedoya, 1991a: 70–73).

References

Albó, X. "Del MNR al Pacto Militar-Campesino, a la Confederación Sindical Única." In *La cara india y campesina de nuestra historia*, 3d ed., edited by X. Albó and J. Barnadas, 243–61. La Paz: UNITAS/ CIPCA, 1990a.

———. "Los sindicatos y la nueva forma de lucha campesina." In *La cara india y campesina de nuestra historia*, 3d ed., edited by X. Albó and J. Barnadas, 192–202. La Paz: UNITAS/CIPCA, 1990b.

Albó, X., and R. Barrios. "Presentación." In *Violencias encubiertas en Bolivia*. Vol. 1, *Cultura y política*, edited by S. Rivera Cusicanqui and R. Barrios Morón, 11–24. La Paz: CIPCA and Ediciones Aruwiyiri, 1993.

Alvarez, E. *The Political Economy of Coca Production in Bolivia and Peru: Economic Importance and Political Implications*. Albany: Center for Policy Research, State University of New York, Albany, 1993.

Anonymous (Bolivian exiles). "Represión en Villa Tunari: Cuidado con la guerra de la coca." *Informe R* 8, no. 152, (1988a): 3, 10.

Bascopé Aspiazu, R. *La veta blanca: Coca y cocaína en Bolivia*. La Paz: n.p., 1982.

Blacutt, G. "Comentario sobre la ponencia del Dr. Roger Pando, Subsecretario de Justicia, Ministerio del Interior, Migración, Justicia y Defensa Social." In *Problemas jurídico-legales asociados a la aplicación de la Ley 1008; Procesos, encausamiento y penalidades al narcotráfico*, edited by Sistema Educativo Antidrogadicción y de Movilización Social, 50–54. La Paz: SEAMOS, 1991.

Carter, W. E., and M. Mamani P. *Coca en Bolivia*. La Paz: Editorial Juventud, 1986.

Centro de Documentación e Información Bolivia (CEDIB). *Boletín coca, drogas, narcotráfico y desarrollo*. CEDIB. No. 4, July 31, 1994a.

———. *Boletín coca, drogas, narcotráfico y desarrollo*. CEDIB. No. 5, August 15, 1994b.

———. *Boletín coca, drogas, narcotráfico y desarrollo*. CEDIB. No. 6, August 31, 1994c.

———. *Boletín coca, drogas, narcotráfico y desarrollo*. CEDIB. No. 8, September 1994d.

Crabtree, J., G. Duffy, and J. Pearce. *The Great Tin Crash: Bolivia and the World Tin Market*. London: Latin America Bureau (Research and Action) Limited, 1987.

Deere, C. D., and R. Wasserstrom. "Ingreso familiar y trabajo no agrícola entre los pequeños productores de América Latina y el Caribe." Paper presented to the Seminario Internacional sobre la Producción Agropecuaria y Forestal en Zonas de Ladera en América Latina. Turrialba, Costa Rica, December 1–5, 1980.

DIRECO. "Programa de Reconversión Agrícola." Cochabamba: Ministerio de Asuntos Campesinos y Agropecuarios, SUBDESAL, Dirección Nacional de Reconversión Agrícola, 1988.

Dunkerley, J. *Rebellion in the Veins: Political Struggle in Bolivia, 1952– 1982*. London: Verso Books, 1984.

Dunkerley, J., and R. Morales. "The Crisis in Bolivia." *New Left Review* 155 (1986): 86–106.

———. "Villa Tunari: Dos versiones sobre un mismo hecho." *Informe R*, special section 8, nos. 153/154 (1988b): 1–9.

Durana, J., N. Anderson, and W. Brooner. "A Population Estimate for the Chapare Region, Bolivia." DESFIL Working Paper. Development

Strategies for Fragile Lands Project. Washington, DC: Development Alternatives, Inc., 1987.

Eder, G. J. *Inflation and Development in Latin America: A Case History of Inflation and Stabilization in Bolivia.* Ann Arbor: Bureau of Business Research, Graduate School of Business Administration, University of Michigan, 1968.

Flores, G., and J. Blanes. *¿Dónde va el Chapare?* Cochabamba: CERES, 1984.

Frederick, R. G. "United States Aid to Bolivia, 1953–1972." Ph.D. diss., University of Maryland, 1977.

Healy, K. "The Boom within the Crisis: Some Recent Effects of Foreign Cocaine Markets on Bolivian Rural Society and Economy." In *Coca and Cocaine: Effects on People and Society in Latin America,* edited by D. Pancini and C. Franquemont, 101–43. Cambridge, MA: Cultural Survival, 1986.

Klein, H. S. *Bolivia: The Evolution of a Multi-Ethnic Society.* 2d ed. New York: Oxford University Press, 1992.

Kline, D. "How to Lose the Coke War." *The Atlantic* 259, no. 5 (1987): 22–27.

Malloy, J. M. *Bolivia: The Uncompleted Revolution.* Pittsburgh: University of Pittsburgh Press, 1970.

Office of Technology Assessment (OTA). *Alternative Coca Reduction Strategies in the Andean Region.* Washington, DC: OTA, U.S. Congress, 1993.

Organization of American States (OAS). "The Chapare Region Study, Bolivia." In *Integrated Regional Development Planning: Guidelines and Case Studies from the OAS Experience,* 177–99. Washington, DC: Department of Regional Development, Secretariat for Economic and Social Affairs, OAS, 1984.

Painter, M. "Institutional Analysis of the Chapare Regional Development Project (CRDP)." Working Paper 59. Binghamton, NY: Institute for Development Anthropology, 1990.

———. "Upland-Lowland Production Linkages and Land Degradation in Bolivia." In *The Social Causes of Environmental Destruction in Latin America,* edited by M. Painter and W. H. Durham, 138–66. Ann Arbor: University of Michigan Press, 1995.

———. *The Struggle for Coca: Patterns of Accumulation and Impoverishment in Rural Bolivia.* Tucson: University of Arizona Press, in press.

Painter, M., and E. Bedoya Garland. "Institutional Analysis of the Chapare Regional Development Project (Bolivia) and the Upper Huallaga Special Project (Peru)." Report prepared for the Office of Technology Assessment, U.S. Congress. Binghamton, NY: Institute for Development Anthropology, 1991a.

———. "Socioeconomic Issues in Agricultural Settlement and Production in Bolivia's Chapare Region." Working Paper 70. Binghamton, NY: Institute for Development Anthropology, 1991b.

Pattie, P. S., A. Brown, J. Arledge, I. Asmon, P. Avram, O. Castilla, M. Gertsch, I. Kraljevic, J. Riordan, and J. Smith. "Agricultural Assessment for Bolivia." Paper prepared for Agricultural and Rural Development Office, USAID/Bolivia Mission. Washington, DC: Chemonics International Consulting Division, 1988.

Rivera Pizarro, A. *Los terratenientes de Cochabamba.* Cochabamba: CERES/FACES, 1992.

Roddick, J. *The Dance of the Millions: Latin America and the Debt Crisis.* London: Latin American Bureau (Research and Action), 1988.

Urioste F. de C., M. *Segunda reforma agraria: Campesinos, tierra y educación popular.* La Paz: CEDLA, 1988.

Ybarnegaray de Paz, R. *El espíritu del capitalismo y la agricultura cruceña.* La Paz: CERID, 1992.

3

The Localization of the Global: Contemporary Production Practices in a Mayan Community in Guatemala

Linda Green

Guatemala has been described as a land of "eternal spring and eternal tyranny" (Simon, 1987). To tourists who hurtle along the Pan-American highway en route to the emerald waters of Lake Atitlan or the famous indigenous market town of Chichicastenango, the landscape is stunning. Along the way, travelers glimpse men bent low under the heavy loads suspended on trumplines or women and their children in the brightly colored clothing—for which the Mayas are renowned—laboring over plots of broccoli and snow peas for export, that have sprung up amidst the traditional milpa.[1] These are the Maya, descendants of the civilization that built the famous temples of Tikal, Palenque, and Copan, attractions that bring tens of thousands of tourists each year to Guatemala. For many tourists the Maya represent a picturesque metaphor of a simpler way of life, free from the demands of the modern world.

The reality, however, is very different for the majority of Mayan people who live in the Guatemalan towns and villages of the *altiplano* (western highlands). They exist on the darker side of modernity. Rather than enjoying the benefits of technology, these families experience the degrading underside of capitalist economic relations shored up by a repressive state apparatus. They live in grinding poverty where the average life expectancy for Mayas is forty-five years old and where nine out of ten children under five years old are malnourished.

Recent inscriptions of state power and changes in the penetration of global capital in highland indigenous communities in Guatemala have been profound. The counterinsurgency war, which reached its height between 1978 and 1984, left over one hundred thousand people dead, forty thousand disappeared, one million people displaced within the country, and compelled tens of thousands of men, women, and children to flee across the Mexican border. By the Guatemalan military's own admission over six hundred rural villages in the highlands were destroyed and countless others were partially razed in an effort, they claimed, to sever the guerrillas from their social base of support. It was the most extensive attack on the indigenous highland communities since the time of the Spanish conquest, five hundred years earlier.

One of the notable side effects of the counterinsurgency war has been not only the physical destruction of communities, but the restructuring of community social relations through the militarization of daily life (Green, in press). In the aftermath of war, it is not only that community spatial boundaries have been transgressed, but that many communities now embody the very mechanisms of state terror under the aegis of military control. Army garrisons, civil militias, spies, forced military recruitment of young boys, and rumors of death lists create deep apprehensions and anxiety. People are afraid to speak out about the terror, violence, and dread that permeate their lives. These imposed silences add more fear to the instability. As a result of these new arrangements a sense of trust among community members has been severely undermined.

While political violence has been undoubtedly destructive to community and familial social relations in the highlands, less striking but important economic shifts have also been taking place simultaneously. New forms of capitalist production practices in the *altiplano* are affecting the experiences of everyday life for some rural Mayan households in the Department of Chimaltenango through globalization. Globalization is "the intensification of worldwide social relations which link distant localities in such a way that local happenings are shaped by events occurring many miles away and vice versa. This is a dialectical process because such local happenings may move in an obverse direction from the very distanced relations that shape them" (Giddens, 1990: 63).

Although the restructuring of social relations through capitalist economic arrangements is nothing new to Guatemala's Mayas—highland families have been involved in part-time wage work for almost a century and the wages earned have in part financed their subsistence livelihood— the degree of penetration into community, cultural, and familial practices is qualitatively different. And the direct intrusion into communities, households and families has been possible, in part, as a result of the political violence (de Janvry, 1981; McCreery, 1990; Smith, 1990).

In many communities in the *altiplano* today the economic situation is far worse than it was fifteen years ago. The economic destruction and impoverishment as a result of the political violence has been massive, leading to extensive changes in local patterns of cultivation, trade, and labor movement (Smith, 1990). In the Department of Chimaltenango, for example, there were no corn harvests in some communities between 1981 and 1983 as a result of the counterinsurgency campaign (Krueger and Enge, 1985). During this same period the national economy entered a period of instability, leading to a decline in the production of two of the country's principal agricultural export crops (coffee and cotton) and, as a result, to a decreased demand for the migratory agricultural labor that rural families had provided (AVANCSO, 1994a).

The backbone of this agro-export economy has been a latifundia-minifundia system where peasant farmers from the *altiplano* made the long trek to the south coastal plantations.[2] Initially they were a coerced part-time labor force and later were propelled by the exigencies of capitalist-induced poverty. For the remainder of the year these rural families have subsisted on the small tracts of land that the Uruguayan writer Eduardo Galeano has called "plots of land the size of graves." Here they have eked out a subsistence survival based on milpa production and local part-time wage labor when and if it is available. Plantation work with its slave-like conditions has always been the least desirable for Mayas, and whenever possible many have sought other alternatives to meet their subsistence needs. By the late 1970s, for example, most *municipios* in the Department of Chimaltenango were sending less than 10 percent of the work force to the plantations.[3] Mayas were using their surplus cash from their migratory work to invest in other kinds of local labor ventures rather than becoming fully proletarianized when their land base became too small to be tenable (Smith, 1984). Some were engaged in construction, others in rural development projects such as cooperative schemes and local commerce in addition to milpa production (Smith, 1990). However, a decade later, in the aftermath of war, opportunities for nonagricultural production had diminished significantly as had the demand for migrant labor on coastal plantations. Today, in a reversal of the usual predictions, campesinos have become more rather than less dependent on agriculture for their sustenance. Yet the nature of that production has changed dramatically.

Who Are the Maya?

Although the 21 Mayan indigenous groups in Guatemala are the majority of the population, comprising at least 60 percent of the population, they live under minority rule and their lives remain on the margin; 87 percent live in poverty and 61 percent live in extreme poverty. Most Mayas continue to live in rural towns and villages of the western highlands, although there has been massive internal displacement to urban areas as a result of the civil war (Bastos and Camus, 1994). Despite centuries of disruption and change for Mayan communities, family and community social relations expressed through the weaving of cloth and the growing of the milpa remain central to Mayan material and cultural production practices, not only providing the basis of survival for many, but also the locus of a Mayan epistemology (Green, in press).

Each society has a cultural apparatus through which it transfers and renews cultural values and beliefs. Mayan children receive their education through the milpa and weaving. Young boys learn the importance of corn through their experiences of everyday life. In the milpa they acquire the fundamentals of subsistence agricultural production. It is here where grandfathers, uncles, cousins, and older brothers teach a young boy prayers to the ancestors and spirits at the time of planting. Well before a boy is old enough to wield a hoe on his own he is allowed to drop the corn seeds into the soil alongside his father, who invokes the help of the ancestors and Mother Earth for a successful harvest. Working the soil in this way not only provides Mayas with food to sustain them but reconnects them with the dead and the natural world.

Young girls learn to weave the traditional Maya clothing on a backstrap loom. The production of cloth in this manner has been an important material and cultural expression for Mayan women. Cloth has been used to clothe the body, as a locus of Mayan identity, and has served as supplementary income for women. Weaving has been the site of gender and generational social reproduction where Mayan women produce both art and ideology (Green, in press). As women weave their cloth they are also producing a Mayan epistemology that emphasizes the relationship between human beings—both living and dead—and their universe. In this way a weaver produces, through her labor and her art, a conduit between the past and the future. In this region it is the women who continue to use *traje*, the distinctive clothing of the Maya, to follow the tradition of dressing like their ancestors and to re-create the thread between the past and the present (Carlsen, 1994).

Nontraditional Exports

In the 1980s the U.S. Agency for International Development (USAID) began promoting nontraditional export agriculture as one component of its rural development strategies to ameliorate poverty in the western highlands of Guatemala. In the Department of Chimaltenango, for example, vegetable production for export had become an alternative for many peasant farmers to procure much needed cash. With the demands imposed by the civil patrol system and the decreased labor opportunities of the coffee, cotton, and sugar plantations, the conversion of part of the milpa to contract farming or hiring oneself out as a field laborer were some of the limited options available to local farmers.[4] However, this new global agricultural strategy of small farmers in the "Third World," producing fruits and vegetables for export to the "First World," relies heavily on access to cheap labor (Collins, 1995).

Two types of new agricultural arrangements predominate in this region: contract farming and field labor. Contract farming—that is, small plots of land previously used for milpa production by peasants and now being used for cultivating broccoli, snowpeas, and cauliflower for sale to intermediaries—has proliferated. While some small farmers have profited, recent studies have shown that this is a risky business since many farmers suffer crop failure due to the vagaries of weather (too much or too little rain or frost) or a glut in the market (Rosset, 1991; AVANCSO, 1994b). As a result many farmers have had to default on their loans and have lost their land. Peasants bear the brunt of the failures. Intermediaries provide high-interest loans, seed, and fertilizers which are then deducted from the price of the harvest. Yet, prices are notoriously unstable and it is not uncommon to see vegetables that have been rejected for their poor quality, or for having pesticide residues that are too high, dumped on the side of roadways. Only a few farmers with significant land holdings are able to sustain profits.

Access to land, credit, technical assistance and markets vary considerably according to the size of a farmer's holdings, with the moderately well-off being favored over the poor. Social differentiation, food insecurity, overuse of land, deforestation and an increasing rural proletariat are the realities that characterize economic life in Chimaltenango in the 1990s. One of the structural effects of this shift in land usage is that land that had been utilized previously to produce basic grains for an internal market is now being devoted to export crops (Garst and Barry, 1990). In addition, with an influx of imported basic grains, the local market value of corn and black beans has been undercut, eroding the independence of the peasant farmer.

Contract farming reworks social relations of production. While the peasant farmer continues to own the means of production and to have control over his own labor, it is the contractor who dictates the conditions of that labor and the "pace and rhythm of work" (Watts, 1992: 82). Snow peas in particular are extremely labor intensive and therefore the success of their cultivation involves the use of unpaid family labor. Under these conditions contract farming disguises the exploitation of peasant farmers vis-à-vis their status as independent rural entrepreneurs.

The second agricultural strategy that has been introduced is field labor used in the cultivation of crops such as tomatoes and lettuce for export. On larger land holdings local elites or foreign owners have converted production of domestic crops for local consumption to production of export crops. With the high costs of transport and marketing, low labor costs are crucial for the owners to maintain a competitive edge. The men who work the fields earn U.S.$2.50 for an eight-hour day while young boys earn only U.S.$1.25. The work entails planting, weeding, and fertilizing as well as spraying the plants with pesticides without the benefits of protective safety equipment.

The shift in the commercialization of local agriculture has altered the nature of patron-client relations locally. Although Mayan men often worked for local wealthier ladinos (non-Indians of mixed ancestry) in relations that were undoubtedly exploitative, these relations allowed for negotiations with regard to fulfilling labor obligations. For example, if a family member or neighbor was ill or needed assistance, a worker could petition the owner for flexibility in the work schedule. Under the new conditions of production with the more fragile and labor-intensive export crops, labor demands are more rigid in terms of time. Patron-client relations are being replaced by those of capitalist owner-worker relations that are less responsive to worker needs. While the peasant laborers still may be working the land and even performing activities similar to what they have done in the past, the conditions under which the work takes place have been altered. What is different in these new relations is that the personalistic contract between owner and worker, often from the same region, is replaced by the logic of the market.

Rural Industrialization

Each evening several thousand Maya-Kaqchikel adolescents, both boys and girls—many as young as fourteen years old—leave the dozens of cement-block factories that since 1989 have sprung up along the Pan-American highway in the central highlands of Guatemala. The girls in their colorful *traje* mingle in small groups with adolescent boys as they wait their turn to board recycled American school buses that will carry them home to their villages for the night, a ride that may take them one and one-half hours.

The *maquilas*, or export apparel assembly factories, also have flourished over the past decade in Guatemala. In 1984 there were 6 factories with less than 2,000 workers, and by 1992 there were 275 factories and over 50,000 workers employed. In 1995 the *maquilas* were contracting with more than 80,000 workers. In 1992 garments worth U.S.$350 million were exported to companies such as The Gap, Leslie Fay, and Levi-Strauss. Just two years later those earnings had increased to U.S.$590 million-worth of clothing being exported to the United States. The majority of the investments in the *maquila* factories involve domestic capital, followed by Korean and then North American capital. The young workers, laboring under deplorable conditions, earn on the average U.S.$100 per month (Peterson, 1992; AVANCSO, 1994).

While most of the *maquilas* have been based on the outskirts of Guatemala City, beginning in 1989 *maquilas* were being built increasingly in the newly created free trade zones in the Department of Chimaltenango. One of the largest of these *maquilas* is Sam Lucas, which employs about 1,200 workers. At 6:30 A.M. each morning three school buses leave the central plaza of the town of San Andreas Itzapa filled with Mayan adolescents, and return in the evening between 8:30 and 10:30 P.M., depending on the quota demands of the factory that day. The workers are charged U.S.$.80 per day for transport, a significant portion of the U.S.$4 per day that they earn.

The factory, built from cement blocks with aluminum roofing, is the size of a football field. Inside, long wooden tables divide the workers into lines of about 30 people. Each person repeats the assigned task over and over, whether it is to sew labels on pants, fasten sleeves to a shirt, or cut threads. Production goals are established for each line. For example, one line may have to complete 1,500 shirts each day, while another may be expected to sew on 1,000 labels per day. If the production line reaches its goal, then the workers are paid extra; if not, money is deducted from their wages. Workers complain of harsh working conditions—poor ventilation, the intense heat generated from the ceiling lamps, leg and back pain from standing for long hours—and verbal and physical harassment and abuse by the supervisors and managers for perceived laxity in work habits.

Work discipline and control of time, not unexpectedly, seem to be very important managerial techniques in inculcating these adolescents in capitalist labor practices (Thompson, 1967). Managers continually admonish the workers to not waste time, to finish the work on time, and to arrive on time. If workers arrive late, one half of the day's pay is deducted, and in some instances, they are not permitted to enter the factory. If a worker does miss a day, U.S.$8 is deducted from their salary and if they miss two days they are dismissed. The workers say they often do not receive money for overtime that they are promised. The work hours vary according to the production schedule, so if there is a large order to fill the manager may announce that everyone is obligated to stay until 9:30 P.M. instead of leaving at 6:30 P.M. Before entering and upon leaving the factory, the workers must line up for inspection by the manager and supervisors. This formality requires forty-five minutes and, as a result, buses do not leave to transport the workers home until 7:30 P.M., an hour past paid working hours.

There are no *maquila* unions since people are afraid to organize. Labor union workers who have tried to organize the *maquilas* have met the same fate as the forty trade union leaders who have been murdered or disappeared in Guatemala since the early 1990s. The case of Yovany Gomez is illustrative. Gomez was a twenty-four-year-old organizer who was threatened repeatedly by the Korean manager of a *maquila* she tried to organize in Guatemala City. She was murdered in March 1995. To date, there is not one organized union in the *maquila* industry in a country long noted for its abusive labor practices. Both young workers and their families are well aware of the exploitative conditions under which they are working. Yet the necessity of procuring cash coupled with the lack of a sufficient land base on which to subsist in an economy marked by high inflation has left many families with few options.

However, in some cases adolescents are using their earnings for personal consumption. Girls are using their wages to buy either their traditional woven blouses or the thread to make them, and to purchase the long wrapped skirts worn by the women. Because of financial constraints within the family and the rising prices of textiles, it is difficult for families to provide these girls with their traditional clothing. Through factory work they are able to garner the resources they need to maintain an important symbolic expression of their identity. Adolescent boys may spend their wages on electronic equipment. In some *maquilas* the vendors come right into the factory to sell to the workers. Popular items for purchase include hair dryers, cassette players, radios, and televisions. One father complained that his son left the factory at the end of the month with his paycheck already spent. However, what was more distressing for this father was the fact that his son no longer wished to work in the milpa alongside his father, uncles, and grandfather. Instead, the young man preferred modern factory labor to working the corn fields of his ancestors.

The central preoccupation for many of the families and workers, however, is the way in which factory work affects the perceptions of time and social relations. The effects of these labor practices have the greatest potential for reshaping Mayan cultural practices. Most young workers feel that they have abandoned their families for the long hours of factory work. They have very little time to be at home—rising as early at 4 A.M. and often not returning home until after 9 P.M. in the evening; Sundays are the only days that they have to share time with other family members. The factory production schedule is also at odds with a Mayan sense of mutual aid and obligations to family and neighbors. The young people are unable to participate in any community events and, in effect, their work severs the daily connections between themselves, their family, and their friends. Thus, they are put in the difficult situation of choosing between their individual needs and their commitments to their family and their community. To cope with these pressures many young workers have devised a strategy of intermittent factory work. Several workers quit the *maquila* after a year or two, only to return again after they have stayed home for six months or more to rest and be with their families. Yet, for many, the exigencies of poverty drive them back once again to seek *maquila* work. It is too early to tell whether this will become a cyclical employment pattern and whether this type of strategy will remain acceptable to the *maquila* owners.

Conclusion

What is unique about the present situation for rural Mayan people in the highlands of Chimaltenango is that there has been a substantial weakening of the spaces that they have long utilized to survive. The land surrounding their communities where for centuries they have grown their milpas is being penetrated by new forms of global capitalism. Their communities are militarized in unprecedented ways and daily life is under surveillance. While political repression should not be a necessary factor in disciplining the poor for the introduction of new capitalist work practices, in the case of Guatemala it must certainly be implicated. Today, Mayan communities as refuges from the outside world—whatever their shortcomings, factions, and cleavages—have been reshaped under the weight of violence and repression.

Likewise, the nature of their work practices have also been transformed. It is crucial to locate Mayan culture in work, that is in the milpa and weaving, to understand how culture is produced and what the current changes may signify. As adolescent boys and girls as well as entire families no longer have time and in some cases the desire to do that cultural work, the struggles surrounding culture, power, and social relations at the community and household level take on new meanings locally and globally.

Notes

1. In Guatemala the milpa refers to a plot of land where corn and usually beans and squash are grown together.

2. The latifundia refer to landholding units which range between 45 to over 900 hectares and which usually contain the most fertile agricultural lands in Guatemala. Minifundia refer to the small, fragmented holdings which are less than seven hectares and usually are not sufficient to sustain a family all year (Lovell, 1985). The relationship between latifundia and minifundia can be characterized by the inequality of that relationship, as George Lovell notes: "the fundamental characteristic of landholding in Guatemala in the present day is the concentration of sizable amounts of cultivable land in the hands of the small, wealthy (mostly non-Indian) minority, while an impoverished, but dignified peasant majority, predominantly Indian, ekes out an existence on a tiny percentage of the total national farm land" (Lovell, 1985: 27). Guatemala has one of the most inequitable land distributions in all of Latin America; 2 percent of the population own over 65 percent of the arable lands.

3. A *municipio* is a township usually comprising a principal town and surrounding villages. See Sol Tax for an early discussion of the *municipio* (1937).

4. The civil patrol system was created in 1982 and constituted a rural militia of over a million men by 1985, over half the highland male population over fifteen years of age. The PACS, as they are known in Spanish, function to augment military strength and intelligence in areas of conflict, and more importantly to provide vigilance and control over the local population. Although the Guatemalan constitution states explicitly that the PACs are voluntary, failure to participate or opposition to their formation marks one as a subversive in conflictive zones in the *altiplano* (Americas Watch, 1986).

References

Americas Watch. *Civil Patrols in Guatemala*. New York: Americas Watch, 1986.

Asociación para el Avance de la Ciencias Sociales (AVANCSO). *El significado de la maquila en Guatemala*. Guatemala: AVANCSO, Textos para Debate, 1994a.

———. *Impact ecologico del los cultivos horticolas no-tradicionales en el altiplano de Guatemala*. Guatemala: AVANCSO, Textos para Debate, 1994b.

Bastos, Santiago, and Manuela Camus. *Sombras de un batalla: Los desplazados por la violencia en la ciudad de Guatemala*. Guatemala: Impreso en Fondo de Cultura Editorial, 1994.

Carlsen, Robert. "Discontinuous Warps: Textile Production and Ethnicity in Contemporary Highland Guatemala." In *Crafts in the World Market: The Impact of Global Exchange on Middle American Artisans*, edited by June Nash, 199–224. Albany: SUNY, 1994.

Collins, Jane. "Transnational Labor Process and Gender Relations." *Journal of Latin American Anthropology* 1, no. 1 (1995): 178–99.

de Janvry, Alain. *The Agrarian Question and Reformism in Latin America*. Baltimore: Johns Hopkins University Press, 1981.

Garst, Rachel, and Tom Barry. *Feeding the Crisis*. Lincoln: University of Nebraska Press, 1990.

Giddens, Anthony. *The Consequences of Modernity*. Cambridge, England: Polity Press, 1990.

Green, Linda. *Fear as a Way of Life: Mayan Widows in Rural Guatemala*. New York: Columbia University Press, in press.

Harvey, David. *The Conditions of Postmodernity*. London: Basil Blackwell, 1988.

Krueger, Chris, and Kjell Enge. *Security and Development: Conditions in the Guatemalan Highlands*. Washington, DC: Washington Office on Latin America, 1985.

Lovell, W. George. *Conquest and Survival in Colonial Guatemala*. Kingston, Ontario: Queens University Press, 1985.

McCreery, David. "State Power, Indigenous Communities, and Land in Nineteenth Century Guatemala." In *Guatemala Indians and the State, 1540–1988*, edited by Carol Smith, 96–115. Austin: University of Texas Press, 1990.

Peterson, Kurt. *The Maquiladora Revolution in Guatemala*. New Haven: Center for International Human Rights at Yale Law School, 1992.

Rosset, Peter. "Nontraditional Export Agriculture in Central America: Impact on Peasant Farmers." Working paper no. 20. Santa Cruz: University of California, 1991.

Simon, Jean-Marie. *Guatemala: Eternal Spring, Eternal Tyranny*. New York: W. W. Norton, 1987.

Smith, Carol. "Local History in Global Context: Social and Economic Transitions in Western Guatemala." *Comparative Studies in Society and History* 26, no. 20 (1984): 193–228.

————. "The Militarization of Civil Society in Guatemala: Economic Restructuring as a Continuation of War." *Latin American Perspectives* 67, no. 4 (1990): 8–41.

Stoll, David. *Between Two Armies in the Ixil Towns of Guatemala*. New York: Columbia University Press, 1993.

Tax, Sol. "The *Municipios* of the Midwestern Highlands of Guatemala." *American Anthropologist* 39, no. 3 (1937): 423–44.

Thompson, E. P. "Time, Work-Discipline, and Industrial Capitalist." *Past and Present* 20, no. 38 (1967): 56–97.

Watts, Michael. "Living under Contract: Work Production Politics and the Manufacture of Discontent in a Peasant Society." In *Reworking Modernity*, edited by M. Watts and A. Pred, 65–105. New Brunswick: Rutgers University Press, 1992.

II

Transforming Urban Enterprises

4

Survival Politics and the Movements of Market Women in Peru in the Age of Neoliberalism*

Linda J. Seligmann

The main street to the Cuzco central market is lined with vendors, two or three rows deep on both sides. In the early morning, the rusted-out pickup trucks, taxis, and toiling tricyclists, whose flatbeds are loaded with bulging flour sacks or plastic buckets, potatoes, and reams of cloth, slowly wend their way in serpentine fashion through the streets. The oily air, exhaust, and drone of honking horns make a sharp contrast to the crystalline and frosty peaks that surround the entire city.

The vendors are setting out their wares, inside and outside of the market: razor blades, plastic watches, peppers, shiny red apples, cassette tapes, carrots, onions, cheese, hot plates of food cooking on tiny kerosene-run Primuses, shiny polyester trousers, medicinal herbs, frilly children's Confirmation dresses, used books and newspapers, bloody slabs of meat. Almost anything you might need can be found here if you know where to look for it. Sleepy children are also to be seen, some running errands for their mothers, others bundled up and sandwiched between merchandise in a corner of the stall. The vendors are mostly women, while the men are transporters, hauling the merchandise to its destination or helping their wives, sisters, or daughters to set up their stalls.

*This research took place intermittently between 1988 and 1993 in Cuzco, Peru, once the ancient capital of the Incas. It is a still-growing provincial metropolis with a population of approximately 300,000, the capital of the department of Cuzco and a tourist mecca.

At this hour, the place seems almost orderly, with vendors grouped together according to their merchandise. Come a few hours later, though, and the scene will be one of apparent chaos. The boundaries of groups are barely perceptible; the place is swarming with shoppers and vendors who squat on sidewalks, the floors of the market, anywhere they can find and defend a space. Serious bargaining fills the air as the market women wheedle their wares and their clients cajole them to lower their prices. Nearly invisible to a stranger, wielding power out of proportion to their position and cutting a sinister figure are the municipal agents and wholesalers who amble along from stall to stall, demanding fees and the repayment of debts from the market women.

Down by the railroad tracks not far away, the scene is quite different. There the tracks are lined on one side by huge lorries filled with merchandise being offered by male wholesalers, who are surrounded by women negotiating for their goods. The other side of the tracks is lined by makeshift stalls interspersed with women who sit on the ground by the rails with a few goods spread out before them. Above, the hillsides are strewn with garbage, and dogs scavenge for leftovers.

All of these market women are part of a leading occupational sector of the informal economy. Yet their place within that economy varies according to a number of different factors. Indeed, the informal economy itself has been a lively subject of debate in terms of how to define it and what its relationship is to the formal economy. Most social scientists take one of two positions. One position is that members of the informal economy, because they are evading costly state regulations for establishing and operating formal businesses and because of the lack of fixed capital costs, social welfare protection, and labor laws, can offer the same merchandise at lower costs than can formal businesses, thus encouraging competition between the formal and informal economies. The other position holds that, for the same reasons, formal economies take full advantage of informal sector businesses. Through subcontracting, informal economies nicely complement formal ones, and, in fact, are responsible for much of the value added to products that has often been mistakenly attributed to the formal economy. Thus, rather than existing in opposition to each other, what are known as informal activities are argued to be central to the successful operation of well-established businesses that are categorized as part of the formal economy.[1] The political orientations and activism of people who work within the informal economy are not well understood, in part because of their heterogeneity and mobility, in part because these are questions whose answers must be sought within a changing, historically specific context.

Informal Economies and Women's Identities

Informal economies are hardly homogeneous, and within them different occupational categories, such as that of market women, are also remarkably differentiated. Informal sector enterprises differ in terms of scale and informality. They range from self-employed individuals who sell, trade, or put out products without paying any taxes to small workshops producing goods on a subcontracting basis for formal sector industries.

In either case, structurally speaking, people who work within the informal economy actually share more in common than is often recognized. They are unprotected by health benefits, insurance, or job stability. Also, many informal activities appear to resemble modes of social organization that existed in rural communities. These "traditions" might include credit arrangements with kin and fictive kin, the moral obligations that hedge patron-client relationships, modes of mutual assistance, and information and supply networks grounded in kinship ties.[2]

In highland Peru, market women have inhabited the social landscape for several centuries, but their reasons for becoming market women have varied over time in accordance with gender ideologies, the economic dynamism of rural agriculture, motivations for economic diversification, and aspirations for their offspring. In addition, the income that market women have earned has varied in accordance with the state of the national economy. For women in particular, activities such as market vending or arduous detail work in textile sweatshops offer them jobs they would not otherwise have. Sometimes it gives them much needed flexibility so that they can care for their children and work at the same time, and it gives them considerable autonomy from their husbands, boyfriends, or fathers.[3]

Market women operate at different levels of the economy. Some of them work full-time at marketing and pay rent for their permanent stalls and taxes on their earnings. Others work full-time but operate at a lesser scale, neither paying taxes nor occupying permanent stalls. Still others sell now and then, combining diverse occupations, especially as rural producers and itinerant vendors. This group does not have stalls, pays no taxes, and does not have a license or health card.

Patron-clientelism among market women and their political representatives divides the solidarity among them as much as the economic competition. Patrons provide credit and other valuable kinds of resources and protection; in return, market women and their union leaders will often vote accordingly, sometimes for the patrons themselves.

Multiple images of market women fill the pages of travelogues and monographs. Often, they are depicted as feisty, neither male nor female, neither "Indian" nor "mestizo." These are images that in Peru, at least, are deliberately cultivated by market women themselves and, over time, have come to constitute a repertoire of cultural traditions and practices. However, the literature also includes the admonishments of researchers who decry the way that market women have been romanticized as the vanguard of future revolutions. Both positions are correct, not surprisingly.[4] Many of these women, established or not, will resort to the machinations of the trickster to defend their place and products, fend off the municipal agents, and get a good deal in their negotiations. However, they will also come to the aid of their companions in the marketplace and help out with food, credit, and moral support from time to time.

Class and ethnic self-identification and relationships are complex in Peruvian society. Barriers to upward mobility, traditions of cultural ensembles, such as unique apparel and language, competition among market women whose status differs in the marketplace, patron-clientelism, and questions of occupational change from one generation to the next play critical roles in market women's ethnic and class self-identification, and their ability to form a unified front.[5]

Many market women have already internalized ideal status referents. That is, they believe that better education, Western dress, speaking Spanish, being able to meet their basic needs, owning or renting a house, and educating their children to be professionals will permit them to be accepted as upwardly mobile Peruvian citizens who are mestizas rather than campesinas, *cholas*, or Indians, and who are middle, rather than lower, class.[6] For example, Gregoria Chaca Qoro, an itinerant vendor who lives in the countryside and only occasionally sells her agricultural products in the city, assesses her ethnic and class identification: "I am lower class because I am indigenous, I am poor, and I don't have contact with other kinds of people. I'm a campesina because I live in a village, not the city, and don't have money to spare to buy anything."[7]

In contrast, Elena Quispe and Eulalia Menéndez have permanent stalls. Eulalia's response is that "I am middle class because I live in the city, speak Spanish, and am not doing badly economically. I'm a mestiza because I distinguish myself in my dress as a member of the middle class." Elena considers herself to be a mestiza because she works in Cuzco. Mariana Gonzales Rocca doesn't have her own stall but does pay for a license. She considers herself middle class because she has her own house and "doesn't have problems." She also considers herself as a mestiza because of her dress. Josefina Hancco doesn't have her own stall and doesn't have a license. She considers herself a member of the lower class because she is poor and owns nothing. She also considers herself to be a campesina because she has "never known shoes" and her parents are campesinos.

Market women are quintessential "practitioners of hyphenated ethnicities," yet they struggle with the phenomenon of status inconsistency—that is, the contradiction between their growing expectations of becoming non-Indian and middle class and the persistent negative sanctions they experience from "true" mestizos (Cook and Joo, 1995: 53).[8] At the same time, these very struggles, in the past, have encouraged some market women to abandon their expectations as social climbers and knit together a distinct identity out of being excluded by, yet economically important to, both the mestizo and campesino ranks. However, the devastating impact of neoliberal measures on market women has severely limited their political potential, whether it be through traditional union organizing or identity politics. Even emergent social movements, though they have been more successful avenues of political mobilization, remain weak and subject to a number of constraints.

Neoliberalism in Historical Context

Peru's apparent return to democracy came amidst a civil war between state and paramilitary forces and members of two guerrilla groups, the Shining Path (Sendero Luminoso) and the Tupac Amaru Revolutionary Movement (Movimiento Revolucionario Tupac Amaru, or MRTA). The war had cost over 30,000 lives by 1990. The emergence of democratic principles was symbolized most explicitly by the freely held national presidential elections of 1990. In that election, many market women helped to elect Alberto Fujimori, candidate of the independent party, Cambio 90. They envisioned him to be a "man of the people," the son of Japanese immigrants to Peru who would respond to the plight of the poor and hardworking. In addition, he had been trained as an agronomist and had a pragmatic bent to his character, a welcome change from the wars of rhetoric that had seemed to preoccupy most politicians and the parties with which Peruvians were familiar. In his campaign, Fujimori spoke often of the need to improve the conditions of the many people working part- or full-time in the informal economy as well as those of Quechua peasants in the countryside.

When Fujimori came to office, the economy and national infrastructure were in shambles. By the late 1980s, only 10 percent of Peru's roads were paved. The annual rate of inflation was almost 3,000 percent and people rushed out to spend their money as soon as they received any. Almost all international development agencies had retreated from operation, and after Peru's incumbent President Alan García (1985–1990) had nationalized the banks and refused to pay the foreign debt of over

$23 billion, Peru lost credibility in the eyes of foreign investors and international lending agencies.

The specter of violence hovered over the entire country, much of which remained under emergency law.[9] During the lost decade of the 1980s, Peru had experienced declines in real wages, sinking to less than 40 percent of their 1980 levels by 1990, a figure that only takes fully employed workers into account. Likewise, tax revenues had fallen by more than half during the 1980s. Public sector employees' salaries fell by over 60 percent between 1985 and 1990.[10]

Within two years, Fujimori had succeeded in arresting most of the leaders and many of the followers of Sendero Luminoso and the MRTA. His neoliberal measures, designed to lower hyperinflation and restore economic stability to the country, were enthusiastically endorsed by the International Monetary Fund, the World Bank, and other international lending agencies. These measures aggressively sanctioned privatization, opened the doors to foreign investment, restructured the public sector, imposed austerity measures and taxes on all businesses, and reversed most agrarian reform laws.

On April 5, 1992, Fujimori established an informal pact with the military. He also abolished the judiciary, dissolved the national congress, and suspended the 1979 constitution. Economic growth skyrocketed, not altogether as positive an achievement as it has been portrayed, given how much the economy had shrunk in the intervening decade.[11] Peru was, and still is, touted as a second Chile with one difference: instead of the iron hand of Pinochet, its regime has the semblance of democratic process.

With Peru's formal return to democracy, there was a renewed and intense interest in how to tap into the potential of the informal sector. Hernando de Soto, initially one of Fujimori's advisors, celebrated the ingenuity and resourcefulness of individuals within the informal sector. He argued that if the government reduced state intervention and regulatory procedures altogether and encouraged market mechanisms to flourish, then these individuals would rescue Peru from underdevelopment and become a dynamic middle class. In short, the informal economy would disappear altogether because it would become formalized.[12]

Many analysts have argued that the informal sector is a crucial safety valve, a spill-over mechanism, that prevents unemployment. For a time, that may have been the case for Peru, however, the severity of the neoliberal measures that have been imposed in the country, combined with the violence of civil war that drove people from the countryside to the cities, led to a notable shift in the relationship between the formal and informal sectors of the economy. These measures have increased full-blown unemployment. In other words, the formal sector economy has suffered so greatly both from the downsizing of the economy and the expansion of the urban population that the informal economy can no longer take advantage of its linkages with the formal economy or the buying power of formal sector workers. According to Peru's Labor Ministry, combined under- and unemployment for 1994 was 83.1 percent of the economically active population.[13]

Market Women in the Time of Neoliberalism

By 1993 many market women had become enraged by the kinds of policies Fujimori had implemented and with electoral politics in general. In particular, they opposed the high tax he intended to levy on all members of the informal sector, regardless of scale of operation. They also complained bitterly that the imposition of austerity measures had caused salaries and wages of most of their clients to decline so precipitously that buyers had reduced their purchases of basic necessities. Consequently, not only were market women who sold these kinds of products suffering, but peasant producers were also bearing the brunt of these belt-tightening measures. Vendors, who operated at different levels of the informal economy, complained that no one could afford to buy anything anymore. Several women observed that while these measures were necessary in order to pay the foreign debt, and it was a good thing to reduce the foreign debt, still it was wholly unjust for this "despotic" government to "be killing the poorest and those who suffered most," especially since they had not been responsible for creating the debt in the first place. In one woman's words, "The government, instead of fighting for the people as it promised, was fighting for the most powerful classes and putting us to one side even though we placed a vote of confidence in him [referring to Fujimori]."

The cost of neoliberal measures has had serious repercussions for market women in their ability to survive economically and to organize to fight against these measures politically. Due to economic competition, existing rifts between market women have deepened and fewer market women are able to succeed in making a living from selling their wares. On the other hand, because it is overwhelmingly women who are most burdened with the survival of their families, they sometimes discover common ground in challenging the patriarchal biases of unions and in seeking basic services through alternative modes of political organization.[14]

Family Composition, Generations, and Division of Labor

One cost of neoliberalism that has not been well studied is the effect that
these measures have had on women's occupational strategies and position within their families. Household composition makes an enormous
difference in the capacity of market women to have greater or lesser success in the marketplace. Market women who are most successful are those
who are married, followed by those who can rely on the help of their
extended families and children. As Barbara Geddes has noted, "the costs
and benefits of adjustment are not distributed equally within classes"
(1995: 204). In the case of highland Peru, the economy of most market
women was suffering so extensively prior to restructuring that they were
already relying heavily upon diversifying the labor of their families, and
trying to coordinate the activities of all household members in order to
maximize their opportunities and minimize risk. As Orlandina de Oliveira
and Bryan Roberts note, "the type of job an individual does is a less significant determinant of life chances than other factors such as household
composition and cycle, gender and age" (1994: 68). Because the majority
of market women are single mothers or widows, responsible for both the
economic welfare and caretaking of their children, the labor they can dedicate to work outside the household, in absolute terms, is usually less than
that of men. The stress of surviving economically is extreme in these
cases, especially since, within the informal sector, vending incomes were
already among the lowest, and street vending was already becoming
saturated.

Despite these circumstances, prior to the 1990s many market women
had partially or totally succeeded in fulfilling one of their primary goals
in life—educating their children in order that they would be able to find
better employment than they had been able to find. In the study for this
chapter the occupational data showed that, over the course of three generations, the parents of most market women had been peasants or peons
on haciendas; a few had been vendors. Quite a few of the market women
had begun as domestic servants and then become vendors, going from
itinerant to established positions in the market. Most of their children
were educated; almost all had finished high school and some were in the
university. Those who were older had joined the army or police forces; a
few were helping their mother in the market or working in other occupations within the informal sector; a few had even traveled abroad and were
working in other countries of Latin America or Europe. Many of them
had expected to find work in the public sector since, by 1981, the public
sector employed 66 percent of all nonmanual workers in Peru (de Oliveira
and Roberts, 1994: 54).

De Oliveira and Roberts also observe that as more and more people enter into informal sector employment, the local dimension of labor markets is reinforced. This process makes people unusually dependent on community ties for finding paid work and meeting the needs of their households, which can place considerable strain on relations within households and neighborhoods (de Oliveira and Roberts, 1994). Unemployed grown children are out on the streets, begging, scavenging, hustling, and stealing. Daughters help their mothers with vending or child care, or, in some cases, become prostitutes. In most cases, if the grown children continue to live at home without bringing in much income, they constitute another mouth that must be fed.

If unemployment continues to grow and economic growth does not provide alternative jobs for this large sector of Peru's population, women, who will do whatever they can to ensure the survival of their families, will be disproportionately affected. As one market woman with eight children and an unemployed husband put it, "From the time I wake up until I go to bed, it's the preoccupation a mother has to feed her children, to find food for her children, whether we sell or not, because if we don't sell, there's no food to eat."

Taking to the Streets: The Politics of Gender Interests

Between 1980 and 1994, a few patterns have become more pronounced concerning the political consciousness of market women. Neoliberal measures have heightened tensions and exacerbated competition among the market women. These measures have also delineated, in a far more brutal fashion, the undercurrents of racism that shape most interactions in Peruvian society. Class-based political platforms become far less plausible and credible under these conditions. Imported from the West, the rhetoric of many leftist Marxist-Leninist politicians hardly resonates with these women's subjective understanding of Peru's social landscape. Market women, rather than being united by class interests, find themselves even more factionalized under the conditions of neoliberalism (Hobsbawm, 1990: 152; Escobar, 1992: 62–85).

As the pie gets smaller, the practical aspects of daily survival develop. Market women are less willing to include others who are operating within the same general occupational sector but who are not as well educated, who appear to be more indigenous in dress and language, and are less well off. Almost all of the women interviewed for this chapter mentioned that the major political problems they face are conflicts among the vendors—over space, sale prices, and caretaking of children who accompany their mothers. Interestingly, the more precariously established vendors (*ambulantes*) are far more inclusive than the permanently established ones (*establecidas*), and are far less likely to engage in any kind of political protest or activity. The *ambulantes* would like the government to create permanent stalls for everyone. In contrast, the permanent vendors would like the government to prohibit itinerant vendors from competing with them.

The possibilities for market women to become unified in their political opposition to repressive government measures or oppressive market forces have diminished in the age of neoliberalism. Less-established vendors with fewer resources and recourses primarily take advantage of "everyday" forms of resistance such as information-sharing about the routes of municipal agents and the use of inaccurate scales. They are mostly dejected and desperate, focused on survival, whereas more established vendors experience greater ease in organizing politically and have less to risk. Although the intersection of what Molyneux (1985) calls "practical" gender interests (practical concerns of consumption and survival) and "strategic" gender interests (a shift to more unifying, general concerns of women) are perhaps most apparent in these difficult and stressful conditions, this merging of interests does not mean that market women can act easily on their recognition of these interests.[15]

Almost all "established" market women who rent stalls belong to the Sindicato de Mercados Unidos, a division of the Federación Departamental del Cuzco. A small percentage of nonestablished market women who work on a daily basis in the market belong to the Sindicato de Vendedores Ambulantes. The elected representatives of these unions are primarily men, which has a great impact on the shape and content of political mobilization among market women (Babb, 1989).[16] Both kinds of union organizations emphasize the importance of women as the bulwark of resistance in street demonstrations. In one leader's words, "we use women as tools of mobilization in order to gain respect from the forces of order because one way or another we deserve their respect."

The leadership and members of the Sindicato de Mercados Unidos describe themselves as being members of the working class, and in the past they have been closely allied with the United Leftist Front (Izquierda Unida). The way that they identify their membership contrasts with some of the statements by leaders of the Sindicato de Vendedores Ambulantes, who claim that their union "takes no political actions because the principal members of our union are housewives." Although the latter union maintains that its membership also belongs to a single class, this assertion is more a rhetorical device to encourage solidarity because the *ambulantes* are aware that their political clout, in comparison to that of the *establecidas*, is exceedingly limited.

Because leadership is in the hands of men, certain demands repeatedly made by women—for running water, better hygiene, soup kitchens, and a collective children's nursery—fall on deaf ears. Many of the most intense economic conflicts between established vendors and *ambulantes* are defined by the men simply as the usual domestic squabbles of women. Although men dominate in settling disputes among vendors and leading protest marches, women, by acting in blocs, sometimes prevent men from wholly taking over their organization. More than once, women mentioned that if they feel their leaders are not acting on their demands, they will take to the streets on their own. This kind of statement reveals that a subtle shift may be occurring, from more traditional forms of political organizing to more innovative social movements.

However, a major obstacle to effective political protest for the market women is the splintered nature of their occupational sector. Established market women complain bitterly that their leaders, as well as municipal agents and police, refuse to banish *ambulantes* from the market and instead let them operate with impunity. This statement refers both to the incapacity or unwillingness of political leaders and the forces of law and order to control or repress these "bothersome" women of the market, and also to how women define their concerns within a decidedly patriarchal gender ideology. In addition it pointedly refers to the corruption and patron-clientelism that permeates the way the markets operate.

The Possibilities and Limitations of Social Movements

Market women are far more interested in particular issues that parties or individual politicians address than in loyalty to a particular political party. Social movements often couch their issues in general terms that refer to the common good, and grow out of shared concerns rather than party platforms (Babb, Chapter 6, this volume). These shared concerns, rather than individual representatives, provide the unifying dynamism and incentive to organize. A certain vagueness characterizes the kinds of demands around which social movements often organize. Hence, they are more likely to be inclusive rather than exclusive, somewhat tempering the fierce economic competition and segmentation that the costs of neoliberalism have encouraged.

Recent research into social movements and the role that gender plays in social movements has pointed to the power that "sites" come to have for the purposes of defining how situations become "susceptible to common action" and for the "making of collective identities" (Westwood and Radcliffe, 1993: 20; Escobar, 1992: 78). The concept of "sites," taken from Michel Foucault, refers not only to discursive sites but also to physical-geographic sites, such as neighborhood barrios or the market-place.[17] These sites "invoke both the geography of space and the Foucauldian understanding of discursive space. . . . Sites may also serve to unify individuals who might otherwise be dispersed by the multiplicity of their interests" (Westwood and Radcliffe, 1993: 20–21).

Out of working in the market and residing in the barrios that surround the city of Cuzco, many market women discover common concerns and begin struggling together to reach common goals. "Territorial identities" encourage mutual solidarity embedded in shared memories of the history of the *pueblo jovenes* (squatter settlements) in which most market women live and of the personal and collective struggles in everyday life, including that of the marketplace—caring for children and providing them with food, health services, and education, dealing with absent husbands, obtaining barrio improvements, avoiding the police, facing racism on a daily basis, and organizing transport to and from the market. Such struggles acquire a legitimacy for the women involved in realizing them and simultaneously become a more politicized critique of existing centralized political channels and organizational modes. There are also more opportunities for women to take on leadership roles, often on a temporary basis, within social movements than within unions or political parties.

The daily work of the market women allows for the informality of social movements, often organized spontaneously. As survival becomes more of an issue, an increasing number of market women, established or not, are turning to alternative organizational modes and alliances. These new social movements have the capacity to cut across differentiated occupational sectors. In 1993, after Fujimori announced that all businesses would be required to pay an 18 percent tax to the state, a remarkable demonstration exploded in the streets of Cuzco. The usual tensions between wholesalers and retailers, and between *ambulantes* and *establecidas*, dissolved. The energetic protest of market women from all levels and the truck drivers who supplied their goods not only took the country by surprise but also forced the government to reconsider such a high uniform levy on all businesses. Thus, social movements, because of their spontaneity and issue-oriented nature, have the capacity to oppose reforms and modify policies, even though they have yet to succeed in setting the initial direction of policymaking in Peru.

Movements of the Military

The peculiar relationship between Peru's executive branch and its military is one of the principal reasons why social movements remain fragile as a new motor of political mobilization in Peru. When Fujimori was elected to the presidency, his neoliberal policies were endorsed by a broad spectrum of civil society, all of whom had an interest in stabilizing Peru's economy. Because of the drastic measures that were to be implemented and the conditions of civil war, Fujimori was not averse to allowing the military extraordinary powers. Fujimori's use of military personnel for tasks that had normally been performed by the police and for maintaining social order, especially in the case of strikes and demonstrations, is evidence of the increased militarization of the country (Mauceri, 1995).[18]

Nicolas de Bari Hermoza, Chief of the Joint Command of the Armed Forces, broke with the ostensible neutrality that the armed forces supposedly had maintained since 1980. He announced in his inaugural address that the military "as an institution endorsed each and every one of Fujimori's decrees." This politicization of the military was not embraced by all military officials, but those who opposed it were purged from the ranks.

This new politicization of the military as an institution may allow Fujimori to exert control over the military but it is an unstable control and serves as a substantial threat to democratic process in Peru. It also makes it more likely that any kind of political protest against the regime will be forced to go underground since the deployment of the police and army thwarts most efforts to disrupt or challenge the social order. It is ironic that many Peruvians, including the market women, supported Fujimori for both terms of office because they did not want a return to the violence of Sendero and because Fujimori's policies had brought about foreign investment and some economic growth.[19] Yet, Fujimori's regime, whether it be considered democratic or authoritarian, has brought little in the way of social justice for market women.

Violence and the "Medicine" of Neoliberalism

Lila Paqo Chawa is one of the most wealthy and well-established of market women. She finished high school and her children, unlike those of most other vendors, remain at home with a servant. Her husband, a mechanic, wants her to quit working. Her deceased mother was a vendor without a permanent stall; her father worked in the public sector, in the Ministry of Agriculture. Lila speaks a little Quechua but is more comfortable speaking Spanish. In contrast, her mother spoke only Quechua. When asked how she felt about the current government and what her economic and political concerns were, Lila talked a little about her membership in the union and her participation in demonstrations, even though she said she disliked politics. She whispered a somewhat frantic statement that she had heard that the central market was going to be destroyed and bought by the United States. They were going to build a large hotel and all the vendors would be forcibly moved to San Jerónimo (a town not far from Cuzco). She claimed that this was going to happen because the government thought that the vendors were doing so well, whereas, in her opinion, "the government was drowning them with its policies and those without stable work were the ones who were suffering the most."[20]

The consequences of the rampant deregulation that the Fujimori regime has implemented, supported by most international and national financial agencies, is obliquely referred to in Lila's fantastic statement. There is no question that privatization has had its costs, not the least of which has been the saturation of the informal sector (including that of vending), the high cost of many basic necessities, and the decline in wages and incomes for many Peruvians. While it has also had short-term benefits for the Peruvian economy and its international credibility, such as unprecedented growth in extractive and utilities industries, these benefits have been of limited help to market women. The economic growth of the extractive and utilities industries is not matched by a substantial increase in the numbers employed by such industries. However, the return of tourism may benefit vendors since many market women in Cuzco make handicrafts, and they are relieved that tourism is on the rise again, after having suffered a 70 percent drop during the civil war.[21]

It is unlikely that Fujimori's extreme and repressive deregulation will transform the informal sector into an organized and efficient series of microenterprises. Deregulation and the total withdrawal of the state has worked successfully only in already developed nations such as in Central Italy and Hong Kong. However, rather than rejecting state intervention altogether, a more constructive policy the government should consider, and one with which many market women would agree, is one where the state intervenes in order to provide informal sector workers with greater access to credit to develop transportation facilities, aid in training programs, and incentives for cooperation and linkages among formerly segmented groups for the formation of microenterprises (the Buechlers, Chapter 5, this volume). In the case of vendors, microenterprises could be organized in a variety of ways, all of which would encourage small-scale, dynamic flexibility. As Portes (1994: 129) suggests, such enterprises should be required to provide benefits to workers, offer job tenure, and enforce labor rules. Only then will the reservoir of labor in the informal sector diminish and be less subject to exploitation. In turn, these kinds of measures will enhance social welfare, prevent the flagrant abuse of vulnerable labor, and transform "informal economies of survival into informal economies of growth" (Portes, 1994: 127). The very flexibility of informal sector workers will permit them to handle market uncertainties far better than huge and unwieldy corporations.[22]

Because these proposed policies are long-term goals, they would not provide any short-term fixes. However, they may calm the political instability that Fujimori's medicine portends. Without these policies, it is highly likely that market women, stretched to the limit in terms of time, energy, and patience, and fearful of the power of the military and the memory of Sendero, will limit their participation in future social movements. In turn, their withdrawal may leave the political space open to more violent challenges to Fujimori's regime—in the form of guerrilla movements or military coups.

Notes

1. Moser (1994) and Rakowski (1994) provide a succinct discussion of debates about the informal sector.

2. See Seligmann (in press) for examples of the creative ways in which market women participate in economic, political, and religious activities that build on and transform traditional practices that originate in Quechua communities.

3. See Seligmann (1989, 1993) for a detailed discussion of why, over time, women tend to enter the occupational niche of street vending in Peru. As Sassen (1991: 285–86) points out, while there may be good reasons why women are favored to enter particular niches of the informal economy, structural economic processes linked to the performance of advanced industrialized economies may create the conditions for women to enter the casual labor force in greater numbers and in particular niches.

4. See Seligmann (1989, 1993) for a discussion of these perspectives.

5. As Cook and Joo (1995: 54) point out, ethnic identities tend to be extremely dynamic and complex. Anthropologists' reliance upon essentialist and situationalist approaches to ethnicity are still not entirely satisfactory.

6. See Seligmann (1989) for a discussion of how, in Peruvian society, racism creates obstacles to upward mobility among market women known as *cholas*. *Cholas* may come from indigenous backgrounds but seek the same economic standing and social acceptance as those who consider themselves to be nonindigenous.

7. The names of the market women have been changed to protect them from any possible political repercussions since many of the women are critical of President Fujimori and his policies.

8. See also Zamosc (1994: 56) who speaks of the dynamics and experience of status inconsistency among emerging Indian leaders in Ecuador.

9. Even though emergency law has been lifted in much of the country, in March 1995, 28.5 percent of the Department of Cuzco's population and 22.3 percent of its territory were still living under a state of emergency law (Washington Office on Latin America, 1995).

10. The statistics describing Peru's economy are taken from Mauceri (1995: 11–12) and LASA (1995: 7).

11. According to the National Standard of Living Survey performed in 1994, international reserves have swelled from $150 million in 1990 to $5.3 billion in 1995. The GNP rate rose from 6.4 percent in 1993 to 12.7 percent in 1994. While the poverty rate dropped four points between 1991 and 1994, it is still nearly

seven points over 1985 levels. According to economists Javier Iguíñiz and Jorge González Izquierdo (cited in Howard, 1995), the country is currently living at 1965 levels. Income levels are similar to what they were thirty years ago. Real buying power has decreased by 64 percent over the past decade, and three million Peruvians have joined the ranks of the poor since 1985, with nearly half the population unable to meet basic needs in terms of health, education, and nutrition. Most important of all, the economic growth that has taken place has not generated more employment (Statistics cited from Howard, 1995: 5).

12. Bromley (1994) offers a thoughtful critique of de Soto's prescriptions for the informal sector.

13. Figures taken from *Latin American Press* 27, no. 30, August 24, 1995.

14. Peru's Congress passed a labor reform law in July 1995 that eliminates many of the hard-won rights of women workers, including day care centers in companies that employ more than twenty-five women, a work week of no more than forty-five hours, and an hour break to breastfeed. Protests against the elimination of these rights came from women's groups, not unions.

15. Westwood and Radcliffe (1993: 19–20) offer excellent reasons for why Maxine Molyneux's concepts of practical and strategic gender interests should not be dichotomized, since the distinction does "not take into account the understanding from feminism that the 'personal is political.'" On the contrary, it tends to maintain the distinction between the public and private and between the personal and political. Westwood and Radcliffe argue that political identities are not fixed, and personal concerns about household reproduction and inequalities in the sexual division of labor may indeed translate into strategic gender interests.

16. Despite their rebellious stances, most market women, established or not, offer three reasons for refusing to consider leadership positions in unions: only men know how to lead; one must be literate and educated to be a leader; and they do not have time to take on the burdens of leadership.

17. Discursive sites are defined as "the social and power relations of specific contexts that have both formal recognition and informal negotiations as part of the ways in which they are constructed" (Westwood and Radcliffe, 1993: 20).

18. One example Mauceri offers of the increasing militarization of the state is that "throughout 1991, heavily armed troops were employed to . . . accompany the SUNAT, the National Tax Collecting Agency (Superintendencia Nacional de Administración Tributaria), in closing down street vendors who failed to pay taxes" (1995: 20).

19. In the official count of the results of the 1995 Peruvian elections, Fujimori garnered 64.4 percent of the votes, winning in every department of Peru. In the Congress, Fujimori's party Cambio 90/Nueva Mayoría won a 52.1 percent majority, or 67 of the 120 seats in Congress. Absenteeism was reported at 28 percent (Statistics taken from the Washington Office on Latin America, April 18, 1995, *Report on the 1995 Peruvian Elections*).

20. In "those without stable work" Lila is referring primarily to workers in the informal economy and to those who had lost their jobs in the public sector of the formal economy.

21. Despite the economic possibilities for market women in the tourist industry, there is fierce competition between itinerant vendors and shops that sell tourist goods. Tourism, in fact, constitutes a potential avenue of high returns to vendors if they are able to organize into effective microenterprises. The subject

of the organization of the production and sale of artisan goods to tourists deserves further research.

22. Diverting state and departmental funds for community building, infrastructural development, and the formation of regional markets in the rural provinces of the highlands would lead to similar results. This form of state intervention would encourage the growth of rural agriculture, fortify horizontal linkages, and create ties between rural and urban centers, all processes that would eventually foster far more coherent and dynamic regional economies.

References

Babb, Florence. *Between Field and Cooking Pot: The Political Economy of Marketwomen in Peru.* Austin: University of Texas Press, 1989.

———. "After the Revolution: Neoliberal Policy and Gender in Nicaragua." *Latin American Perspectives* 23, no. 1 (1996): 27–48.

———. "Women, Informal Economies, and the State in Peru and Nicaragua." In *Women and Economic Change: Andean Perspectives*, edited by Ann Miles and Hans Buechler, 89–100. Washington, DC: Society for Latin American Anthropology, 1997.

Bromley, Ray. "Informality, de Soto Style: From Concept to Policy." In *Contrapunto: The Informal Sector Debate in Latin America*, edited by Cathy A. Rakowski, 131–52. Albany: State University of New York Press, 1994.

Cook, Scott, and Jong-Taick Joo. "Ethnicity and Economy in Rural Mexico: A Critique of the Indigenista Approach." *Latin American Research Review* 30, no. 2 (1995): 33–59.

Corcoran-Nantes, Yvonne. "Female Consciousness or Feminist Consciousness? Women's Consciousness Raising in Community-based Struggles in Peru." In *'Viva': Women and Popular Protest in Latin America*, edited by Sarah A. Radcliffe and Sallie Westwood, 136–155. London: Routledge, 1993.

De Oliveira, Orlandina, and Bryan Roberts. "The Many Roles of the Informal Sector in Development: Evidence from Urban Labor Market Research, 1940–1989." In *Contrapunto: The Informal Sector Debate in Latin America*, edited by Cathy A. Rakowski, 51–71. Albany: State University of New York Press, 1994.

De Soto, Hernando. *El otro sendero.* Buenos Aires: Sudamericana, 1987.

Escobar, Arturo. "Culture, Economics, and Politics in Latin American Social Movements Theory and Research." In *The Making of Social Movements in Latin America*, edited by Arturo Escobar and Sonia Alvarez, 62–85. Boulder: Westview Press, 1992.

Geddes, Barbara. "The Politics of Economic Liberalization." *Latin American Research Review* 30, no. 2 (1995): 195–214.

Hobsbawm, Eric. *Nations and Nationalism since 1780: Program, Myth, Reality.* New York: Cambridge University Press, 1990.

Howard, Rebecca. "Daily Life Continues to Be a Daily Struggle." *Peru Solidarity Forum* (1995): 5.

Latin American Studies Association (LASA). "The 1995 Electoral Process in Peru: A Delegation Report of the Latin American Studies Association." Miami: North-South Center, University of Miami, 1995.

Lemarchand, René. "The Political Economy of Informal Economies." Unpublished manuscript, 1992.

Mauceri, Philip. "State Reform, Coalitions, and the Neoliberal *Autogolpe* in Peru." *Latin American Research Review* 30, no. 1 (1995): 7–38.

Molyneux, Maxine. "Mobilization without Emancipation? Women's Interests, State and Revolution in Nicaragua." *Feminist Studies* 11, no. 2 (Summer 1985): 227–54.

Moser, Carol. "The Informal Sector Debate, Part 1: 1970–1983." In *Contrapunto: The Informal Sector Debate in Latin America*, edited by Cathy A. Rakowski, 11–29. Albany: State University of New York Press, 1994.

"Peru: Unions Don't Organize." *Latin American Press* 27, no. 30, August 24, 1995.

Portes, Alejandro. "When More Can Be Less: Labor Standards, Development, and the Informal Economy." In *Contrapunto: The Informal Sector Debate in Latin America*, edited by Cathy A. Rakowski, 113–29. Albany: State University of New York Press, 1994.

Rakowski, Cathy A. "The Informal Sector Debate, Part 2: 1984–1993." In *Contrapunto: The Informal Sector Debate in Latin America*, edited by Cathy A. Rakowski, 31–50. Albany: State University of New York Press, 1994.

Sassen, Saskia. *The Global City: New York, London, Tokyo*. Princeton: Princeton University Press, 1991.

Seligmann, Linda J. "A Woman of Steel: The Life Story of a Peruvian Market Woman." In *Women in the Informal Sector: Case Studies and Theoretical Approaches*, edited by Judith Marti and Tamar Wilson. Albany: State University of New York Press, in press.

———. "Between Worlds of Exchange: Ethnicity among Peruvian Market Women." *Cultural Anthropology* 8, no. 2 (1993): 187–213.

———. "To Be In Between: The *Cholas* as Market Women in Peru." *Comparative Studies in Society and History* 31, no. 4 (1989): 694–721.

Washington Office on Latin America. "Report on the 1995 Peruvian Elections." Memo sent to Peru Peace Network Members, 1995.

Westwood, Sallie, and Sarah A. Radcliffe. "Gender, Racism, and the Politics of Identities in Latin America." In *'Viva': Women and Popular Protest in Latin America*, edited by Sarah A. Radcliffe and Sallie Westwood, 1–29. London: Routledge, 1993.

Zamosc, Leon. "Agrarian Protest and the Indian Movement in the Ecuadorian Highlands." *Latin American Research Review* 29, no. 3 (1994): 37–65.

5

Financing Small-Scale Enterprises in Bolivia

Hans Buechler, Judith-Maria Buechler, Simone Buechler, and Stephanie Buechler*

A s a result of massive rural-urban migration and the economic decline in the 1980s, small-scale activities in urban Bolivia have expanded dramatically.[1] This growth has forced small-scale commodity producers and vendors to search for new ways to finance their activities amidst an influx of competition. Newcomers to this field include former factory workers and miners whose operations have been shut down or reduced as a result of structural adjustment policies that entailed the elimination of subsidies, the cutback of social services, currency devaluations, and wage controls. Competition also comes from people migrating from rural communities where increases in productivity have not kept pace with population growth (see Painter, Chapter 2, this volume).[2] In addition, those engaged in urban production must compete with foreign goods flowing into the country, due to the lowering of import taxes resulting from new trade agreements such as the Andean Pact and as a part of structural adjustment.

Traditional sources of credit to meet the needs of small-scale producers and merchants have become increasingly inadequate. In Bolivia the

*We wish to thank Martha Lanza Meneses, whose initial analysis of the data gathered under the aegis of the International Coalition on Women and Credit and BancoSol in 1994 forms the principal basis for our analysis of the impact of credit on women in La Paz.

This chapter is based on long-term anthropological fieldwork on small-scale marketing and production in La Paz, Bolivia; an impact study of BancoSol conducted for the International Coalition on Women and Credit; and an organizational profile of ACCION International (an NGO concerned with providing credit for small enterprises).

formal financial sector has favored larger borrowers in the nonagricultural formal sector, with a focus on commercial and industrial activities carried out by larger firms. It is estimated that 1 percent of the borrowers in Bolivia receive 45 percent of the loans (Lizano, 1992; Otero, 1993: 23). The very few small-to-medium enterprises that did have access to formal bank loans had increasing difficulties in obtaining such loans due to the structural adjustment policies that forced a reduction of the money in circulation. In an effort to remedy this situation, several nongovernmental organizations (NGOs) have set up credit programs targeted to small enterprises. Some of these organizations have focused their lending on women due to the realization that the elimination of poverty is not possible without the advancement of women. It is now argued that it is only through an increase in women's income that a family's standard of living is enhanced by improvements in health, nutrition, housing, and clothing. Such an improvement is doubly important in the Bolivian context where, in 1991, average incomes adjusted for inflation were only 83 percent of 1987 levels and income distribution has become increasingly unequal as a result of structural adjustment (Arze et al., 1993: 77–78).

Small-Scale Production and Trade in Bolivia

Like many other countries in Latin America, Bolivia's national economy was traditionally dependent on the extraction and export of raw materials, in this case, minerals. Until the agrarian reform of 1953, and even today in the lowlands of Bolivia, the country's elites also owned large farms. Few larger-scale capitalists invested in industry; most manufactured goods were either imported or were produced locally by artisans. Unlike many Latin American countries, Bolivia never went through a period of large-scale import substitution programs. The Bolivian economy has always been characterized by micro- and small-scale production. Although cheap imports and a small number of local factories have made inroads into urban artisan production (making such trades as tinsmithery, which continued to flourish well into the 1980s, all but obsolete), low wages and high transportation costs continue to favor local artisan production of many goods over competing imports. The market for the cheap goods they produce continues to expand with the ever-increasing rural to urban migration.

Small-scale labor-intensive production also proved to be more flexible during the severe economic recession, what has been called the debt crisis, in the early to mid-1980s. The crisis had come about in Bolivia because, like other Third World countries, the country had been encouraged to borrow heavily for large-scale development projects during the

1970s. When these often ill-conceived projects failed to generate promised revenues, the foreign debt, bloated by sharply rising interest rates, became increasingly burdensome. During this period, smaller entrepreneurs could react more flexibly than more highly capitalized ones since their lower indebtedness enabled them to curtail production or even allowed them to make a temporary switch into commerce without going bankrupt.

In addition, small-scale entrepreneurs are able to adapt rapidly to changing economic conditions by engaging in more than one occupation. According to the census of 1992, 13.7 percent of the working individuals in El Alto and 10.4 percent of those working in La Paz had an additional job (Bolivia, 1993a). Examples of microentrepreneurs with multiple occupations include a woman whose main occupation is knitting sweaters for export who also buys and sells cotton goods, a cookie baker who knits sweaters too, and a meat vendor who adds to her income by selling crèche figures during the Christmas fair. In addition, different household members may engage in separate activities but help one another when the need arises. Engaging in more than one occupation also makes it possible "for an individual to temporarily or permanently abandon a trade and switch to another one" (Buechler and Buechler, 1992: 57). For example, in the late 1980s when the government eased import restrictions in connection with structural adjustment, many producers switched to selling imported consumer goods.

Retail trade in many goods, including most foodstuffs (whether locally produced or imported), was also traditionally in the hands of small-scale entrepreneurs whose contribution to commerce further increased after the 1953 agrarian reform, which substantially reduced the role of highland landowners in food distribution. That reform, part of a wide-ranging social revolution that also included the introduction of universal suffrage and the establishment of schools in rural areas, transformed peasants on feudal estates in the highlands into smallholders who often marketed their own produce in the cities. In addition to food, small-scale retailing in street stalls and small shops also includes artisan manufactures, cheaper clothing, and consumer goods. In the late 1980s and into the 1990s, as conditions worsened, the involvement in small-scale activities, particularly commerce, further increased. Mining operations were heavily curtailed in an attempt by the state to rationalize production and reduce massive inflation. During that period the state also reduced public employment and expenditures in health and education, and discouraged industrial investment by maintaining high interest rates (Arze et al., 1993: 47). Desperate for work, large groups of people sought retail sites on the streets, causing many market sites to increase in size.

Even already well-established markets have experienced exponential growth, including the Rodriguez market in La Paz. Once confined mainly to several hundred established market vendors selling in a covered market, in 1967 the Rodriguez market grew to 1,067 vendors on weekdays and 2,332 during the Saturday market, which covered several blocks of vendors selling mainly in the street (J-M. Buechler, 1972: 85). By 1992 the number of vendors selling in the same general area on a Saturday had increased to 3,778 (Rivera Cusicanqui, 1992). The growth in the total number of vendors in La Paz and the newly independent satellite city of El Alto, where many of the more recent migrants from rural areas live and where much of La Paz's industry is moving, is more difficult to establish. In 1967, 12,000 vendors were counted and a total of 15,000 vendors were estimated for the city as a whole, while in 1992, 27,371 vendors were counted in the eight major markets alone (Rivera Cusicanqui, 1992).

The first overall assessment of the importance of small-scale activities in the city of La Paz (which at the time also included El Alto) was obtained with the national census in 1976. At that time, out of a total labor force of 225,654 (in a population of 635,283), 127,415 or 56.5 percent were employed in businesses with five or fewer workers (Bolivia, 1980). The Centro de Estudios para el Desarrollo Laboral y Agrario (CEDLA) estimated that, in 1989, 93,455 persons were employed in commerce alone in La Paz and El Alto (Rivera Cusicanqui, 1992: 18).[3] By 1992 the total population in the two cities had increased to 1,118,870, almost double the population in 1976 (Bolivia, 1993a).

The increase in small-scale activities in La Paz and El Alto mirrors the growth throughout urban Bolivia. In 1992, 55 percent of the economically active urban population were engaged in small-scale activities— 2 percent more than in 1988 and 10 percent more than in 1976 (Arze et al., 1993: 70). In contrast, those engaged in public employment and larger private firms shrank from 44 percent in 1976 to 42 percent in 1988 and 41 percent in 1992.[4]

The Characteristics and Functioning of Small-Scale Enterprises

Social scientists often place small-scale enterprises like those in Bolivia into the category of "informal sector," usually defined as businesses that are not legally constituted or regulated, are not taxed, engage in illegal activities, do not have access to bank credit, and so forth. However, both the automatic association of small scale and low capitalization with characteristics enumerated above and the formal/informal dichotomy itself are misleading (Buechler and Buechler, 1992; H. Buechler, 1992). For example, in Bolivia, marketing in permanent street locations is a highly regulated economic activity. Furthermore, larger "formal" and smaller "informal" firms are often intricately interconnected through a network of dependent relationships, including work being contracted out by larger firms to smaller ones and "wages" of large factories being paid partially in kind to individual workers whose families then resell the goods obtained in this manner. In addition, earnings from factory employment often serve to establish independent firms. Thus, the concept of "informal sector" may hide rather than highlight the centrality of small-scale economic activities to the Bolivian economy.

Opening up a small-scale enterprise can also not be considered as an instant employment solution for the increasing number of rural migrants to the cities. Migrants will work first for others as menial laborers in construction, in domestic service, as stevedores, or for small businesses. They are only in the position to open businesses of their own when they are already well established in the city (Casanovas, 1986).

The manner in which small-scale entrepreneurs in La Paz are initiated into their occupations depends on the nature of these occupations, on gender, and on the rural or urban origin of the entrepreneurs. Entrepreneurs may learn their trades within the household by watching their parents and other family members and gradually increasing their own involvement, or by engaging in more or less formalized apprenticeships in enterprises outside the home. Often, the skills required for a productive enterprise are very general, transmitted to all children of the same sex. Rural to urban migrants are particularly likely to use such skills acquired from their parents. Many of these skills, such as cooking, sewing, floor loom weaving, marketing, and adobe making are general rural skills transmitted to all children of the same sex, who adapt them to the urban context and specific craft or trade they choose (Albó et al., 1982; Buechler and Buechler, 1992). Other skills are specific to a rural community or town that specializes in a particular activity, such as gathering and trading in medicinal herbs or manufacturing musical instruments.

Long-term residents of La Paz have access to a wider range of skills than do recent migrants, and they pass these skills on to their children and to nonrelated apprentices. Indeed, apprenticeship with kin, acquaintances, or strangers is the most common form of acquiring specialized skills. Migrants are more likely than long-term residents to acquire specialized skills from kin. However, perhaps because of their desire for upward mobility, migrant producers are less likely to learn their trade from their parents than are nonmigrants, and fewer first-generation urban dwellers than long-term urbanites in turn pass on the trade to their children. Some producers also learn their trade in factories and, especially in the case of long-term urbanites, from foreigners who have brought skills from their countries of origin. Market vendors, both migrants and nonmigrants, are most likely to learn their skills from their mothers.

From the foregoing discussion of the acquisition of skills, it already becomes apparent that small-scale entrepreneurs are dependent upon a complex network of interpersonal ties to engage in their businesses. Kin are the most important labor resource for all types of small-scale entrepreneurs since, in a situation of job scarcity, a household must maximize labor opportunities for its members. However, even quite distantly related kin are well known to the entrepreneur. Their suitability for a job can be ascertained by making enquiries through other kin, who can also be mobilized to exert pressure on kin workers to conform to expectations. In a 1981 sample of 196 small-scale producers, 70 percent included kin in their work force. Of these, almost three-quarters included members of the owner's nuclear family, and about half involved other kin. Of the total sample, 29.4 percent worked with their spouses and 33 percent with their children (Buechler and Buechler, 1992).

Kin are equally important for vendors, although they rarely employ wage labor except to carry their goods to market. In a 1994 study, only 14.3 percent of the vendors (versus 80.8 percent of the producers) employed wage labor.[5] Instead, they received labor assistance from close kin. There is a clear division of labor between men and women. Vendors' husbands assist with transportation but rarely with selling (except on Sundays), daughters invariably sell and often also act as buyers, and sons help in many ways but they are only half as likely to sell. In half of the cases studied where sons did assist in selling goods, there were no daughters in the family or the daughters were less than seven years old. Sons never help in selling fruit or vegetables, a strictly female domain of the market. Nieces, nephews, and godchildren are mobilized mainly for selling. Kin are almost invariably involved in the decision to enter the market or to sell a specific product, and they are often taught by kin how to sell. For vendors who are migrants, kin are very frequently the source for the produce they sell. Stalls are often purchased from kin or obtained from kin as gifts or through the mediation of kin (J-M. Buechler, 1972; Rivera Cusicanqui, 1992).[6]

Small-scale producers and vendors are dispersed throughout the entire cities of La Paz and El Alto. Small kiosks, newspaper stands, tailor shops, and tiny grocery stores are located even in upper-class neighborhoods. However, most are located in the poorer sections of the city, away from the center and the middle-class suburban areas of Obrajes and Calacoto. Vendors, in particular, must wage a constant battle to avoid being dislodged from the increasingly congested center, which may be why they have a greater propensity to organize market unions and associations. Such organizations provide an interface between the vendors and the municipal government and regulate the allocation of vending sites. In contrast, except for certain prominent artisan groups such as the costume makers and the goldsmiths, artisans, especially those who do not also retail their products themselves, tend not to join formal organizations, and instead remain hidden from public view and, to a degree, outside the control of tax collectors.

Two Case Studies

The lives of Doña Avelina Copana de Garnica, an artisan, and Sofía Velasquez, a meat vendor, give a better sense of the development and functioning of small-scale enterprises in La Paz (Buechler and Buechler, 1996). Doña Avelina is a small entrepreneur who lives in La Paz, the same city where she was born. She speaks both Aymara, one of the two main indigenous languages, and Spanish, and comes from a family with a tradition in costume making. Her entire family, including her husband— a tinsmith—and their six children, are engaged in the family enterprise. Her husband learned the necessary skills to make objects out of sheet metal by being an apprentice in her aunt's workshop for a short period of time. The eight of them live in very small, rented quarters in a district with many other artisans' workshops. Their small workshop is downstairs with a small stove for soldering in the corner. At the back of the room is a tiny cooking area partitioned off by means of a length of fabric. The upstairs consists solely of one bedroom with bunk beds where all of them sleep and where they also perform work for the enterprise. For some of their projects, the Garnicas use the large terrace of Avelina's parents' house across the street from the workshop.

The bulk of their output is destined for ritual use—saints' day celebrations and Alasitas, an annual fair of miniature objects, the purchase of which is supposed to secure the desired objects represented by the miniatures. Production for rituals occupies a large number of La Paz residents. Specifically, Doña Avelina and her family produce masks, noise makers, and whips out of metal, cardboard, and cloth for the Moreno dance, a dance that brings its performers prestige because of the elaborate and expensive nature of the costumes. Avelina is mainly involved in doing the embroidery for the miniatures' costumes and the cutting and pasting of the decorations on the costumes.

Avelina is also very much involved in the managing of the business. She keeps the accounts and supervises the workers. They sell their goods on the basis of orders, and even though she only has a fifth-grade education, Avelina is the one who writes up the contracts and does all of the accounting for the business. Avelina has four hired workers, who were trained by her father and used to work for him. In order to supervise them, she travels every other day to their homes in El Alto, a forty-minute bus ride away, where they work with all the members of their families and occasionally with assistants who are hired by the workers themselves to speed up the job. Since demand fluctuates according to the ritual cycle, only one worker is hired by Avelina and her husband from November until May. From May until August all four are employed because they have numerous orders during these months. September and October are slow months and no employees are hired.

Avelina and her husband occasionally travel to Peru to sell their goods for fiestas. The renown of certain dance types and of particularly talented artisans involved in producing costumes has spilled over the country's borders. However, both she and her husband have been cheated by fiesta sponsors in Peru who, except for a small advance, have refused to pay the Garnicas for the goods they bring. Customs officials also frequently steal one or two items out of each box, knowing that microentrepreneurs are powerless to stop them.

Avelina and her husband have acted as sponsors of the annual fiesta of the patron saint of their neighborhood. Such sponsorships are expensive but bring prestige and important business connections, because people who come to the fiesta then order their artisanry for other fiestas. The artisan production for Alasitas, a fair held during the week following January 24, includes an even larger number of producers, mostly working seasonally. In addition to gypsum effigies of Ekeko, the god of plenty, represented as an old man bedecked with miniature bags of staples, artisans make miniature animals, household items, vehicles, houses, and other desired objects. As a spin-off of fiesta and Alasitas production, artisans like Avelina also produce for the tourist trade, which is becoming increasingly important and which tides the family over slack periods in the annual cycle of rituals. Avelina and her family get contracts from tourist stores in the city. The advantage of selling artisanry to these stores, she says, is that the buyers purchase in large quantities and they pay cash.

Another small-scale entrepreneur, Sofía Velasquez, has been involved in marketing activities since she was a small child. Her mother, a woman who had migrated to La Paz in her teens, would take her to distant valleys to exchange cracklings, the by-product of her tallow candle-making industry. Sofía soon also helped her mother distribute candles to retailers. Later, at the instigation of a friend, she began selling peas and other vegetables in the market on the days when she did not attend school. When her family returned to her mother's community of origin, Sofía took the onions they and other community members produced to the city, sold beer at rural fiestas, and bought eggs at rural fairs for resale to retailers and restaurants in La Paz. Eventually, she made the city her primary residence and traveled from there. Later she switched to trading in mutton and finally to pork.

Like most market vendors, Sofía established long-term economic relationships with both suppliers and clients. Although she must support herself and her teenage daughter, Rocío, with her activities (with little help from the child's father, who also maintains another household), she has been able to give her child a private education and plans to send her to medical school. This is a rare, but not unheard-of, aspiration in Bolivia for someone of her background.[7] Because of her exceptional intelligence, her private school education, albeit only until sixth grade, and her brother's involvement in politics, Sofía has become a leader in the markets where she sells, and heads the market organization that controls the street market in her neighborhood. Such leadership positions also entail sponsoring market feasts, often at considerable personal expense. Women often hold leadership positions at the level of the market unions in which they often comprise the vast majority of the membership. At the level of city-wide federations and regional confederations of unions, men are more likely to occupy top-level positions.[8]

At present, Sofía's daughter cooks food, which Sofía sells in front of her home on the days she is not involved in buying pork in the rural fair closest to her mother's community of origin, or selling pork in La Paz. Sofía considers herself a *chola decente*, a social category that includes well-established urban vendors and artisans such as Doña Avelina. The *cholas* are marked by their attire: wide skirts and a shawl with a tasseled fringe. Depending on whether it is for everyday or for holiday use, the shawl can be made out of wool, embroidered nylon, or even vicuña wool, and the skirt is made from plain cloth or plush velvet. The outfit is not complete without heavy pearl earrings, which, in these days of prolonged recession, are usually made out of gilded silver. Although looked down upon by the elites, the *cholas* pride themselves on their expensive attire, which cost as much as $1,000 for a complete outfit even twenty years ago.

Microcredit and the History of BancoSol

Since the mid-1980s the international development field has increasingly turned to "microenterprise" development programs as an approach to combat the effects of structural adjustment policies. The new focus is on programs that are financially sustainable, without large donor funding, and which provide loans rather than grants to poor people. This approach stems in part from a fear that donor funds can easily be channeled elsewhere by the government or dry up rapidly, as well as from a new business orientation that reflects a conservative trend in economic thinking among many governments and development practitioners. The new focus also stems from the realization that the development field has largely failed to bring about real changes in the lives of most "beneficiaries." Providing micro-entrepreneurs with credit is seen as a way to provide equal economic opportunities to the poor, especially poor women, enabling them to help themselves. The concept of credit fits nicely into the neoliberal argument since it emphasizes equal access to financial resources to support growth of private enterprises and the "free market." The concept emphasizes private initiatives rather than public involvement. The argument is that public services can be further reduced if women's income from private sources increases. The previous handicraft projects for women who did not concern themselves with market realities often did not bring in additional income or empower women politically. Since women's economic empowerment is beginning to be seen as crucial for their overall advancement, access to credit for small enterprises is recognized to be one of the most important steps for achieving this empowerment.

Support by development agencies of microlending institutions is seen as part of this economic solution since the formal financial system has failed to reach microentrepreneurs. Microlending institutions provide small loans for short durations to the self-employed, primarily for productive activities. Different types of microlending institutions exist in Bolivia, including nongovernmental organizations such as ProCredito, the Fundación para la Promoción y el Desarrollo de Microempresas (PRODEM), and programs of nongovernmental organizations such as Catholic Relief Services, credit unions and cooperatives, development banks, and a specialized commercial bank, Banco Solidario S.A. (BancoSol).

In the past decade there has been considerable innovation in the development of different kinds of institutional structures, credit delivery, and financing mechanisms for small entrepreneurs. Concerted efforts on the part of the lenders were necessary in order to overcome the perception of poorer clients that lending institutions were formidable institutions geared towards the wealthy. For example, facilities were made more hospitable to poorer clients. In the case of BancoSol, banks were decorated with photographs of small-scale producers and vendors. The staff was recruited from similar backgrounds to those of the clients and carefully trained. The banks were physically decentralized (both through decentralized branches and the deployment of mobile credit officers), and clients participated within the organizations as members of the board or actually ran the organization, as is the case in credit union and village banks operated by the Foundation for International Community Assistance (FINCA International) in Latin America. Conducive loan policies were introduced, including simple and personal application and repayment procedures that were flexible when necessary (Simone Buechler, 1995: 8–12).

More recently, various types of linkages have been developed between microlending institutions and the formal financial system. Institutions are either becoming part of the formal financial system, as is the case with BancoSol, or remaining outside of the formal financial system, forming linkages instead with commercial and development banks and the money market. Loan guarantee funds have been set up in international commercial banks by international development organizations to be used by local microenterprise programs as collateral to gain access to loans from local banks and in turn lend to microentrepreneurs. National development banks have used NGOs, credit unions, and smaller local banks as intermediaries to reach microentrepreneurs (Simone Buechler, 1995: 13–14).

BancoSol is the first commercial bank in Latin America to focus on serving microentrepreneurs. It grew out of PRODEM, a successful non-profit organization and affiliate of ACCION International in Bolivia.[9] It helped to popularize the solidarity group-lending approach, a credit approach discussed below that has allowed microentrepreneurs to receive small loans without collateral.

In the four years of its operation, PRODEM reached 26,104 clients, and by the end of 1991 was disbursing U.S.$2 million per month (Drake and Otero, 1995: 90–91). However, its potential for growth was ultimately inhibited by a lack of capital. Through ACCION's Bridge Fund letter of credit mechanism, a fund in a U.S. commercial bank that serves as a guarantee to induce local commercial banks to provide greater amounts of lending resources to the ACCION local affiliate and therefore its clients, PRODEM was able to gain access to a small amount of lending capital from local commercial banks. However, it was not able to accept savings deposits because it was a nongovernmental organization and therefore not legally entitled to act as a bank. By 1990, PRODEM was only able to reach less than 3 percent of all the microentrepreneurs in Bolivia (Drake and Otero, 1995: 91–92).

Due to the limitations of PRODEM in reaching more microentrepreneurs and their belief that dependency on donors is ultimately detrimental to development, the idea emerged of creating a formal bank based on the experience of the Grameen Bank in Bangladesh. Initial investors in the bank included Bolivian individuals (U.S.$52,500), Bolivian businesses (U.S.$1 million), the Calmeadow Foundation (U.S.$406,000), ACCION International (U.S.$250,000), ECOS Holding (FUNDES group) (U.S.$250,000), and PRODEM (U.S.$1.4 million) (Drake and Otero, 1995: 92–97).[10]

One of the primary factors contributing to the formation of BancoSol was the leadership of Fernando Romero, one of Bolivia's most powerful businessmen, who became the president of the bank. Romero argued that a new way of thinking about development would occur with the establishment of BancoSol; "the only doubt is how far the transformation will go. We can't continue with the traditional pattern of dependency. We must build institutions that maintain themselves and help the community grow. This is our own sort of perestroika" (Blount, 1992: A17). The political and economic situation in Bolivia was also a determining factor in the creation of BancoSol. Crucial were the government's "no-objection" position, lower inflation, and a projected growth rate in 1992 of 3.5 percent that attracted local and foreign capital (Drake and Otero, 1995: 98).

Some of both the PRODEM and ACCION staff and potential investors were initially critical of starting a commercial bank for the poor (Otero, 1993). Due to their political and social beliefs, some of the PRODEM staff needed convincing that a for-profit bank was a good idea. Investors interested in BancoSol were initially hesitant to establish a bank with such a high interest rate (about 20 percentage points above commercial interest rates), since it was a bank that was supposed to serve the poor (Drake and Otero, 1995: 94). The interest rate of BancoSol is currently 4 percent per month plus various charges, a rate deemed necessary to cover the high costs of lending small amounts, while commercial banks charge only 13 to 15 percent per annum. However, according to one source, the average effective interest rate for loans charged by money lenders in Bolivian cities is from 88 percent to 3,600 percent per year (Otero, 1993: 15).

BancoSol opened its doors in February 1992. The first year, it reached 27,174 clients, made 58,872 loans, and lent U.S.$21,720,000 (Simone Buechler, 1994: 7). In December 1994, BancoSol had twenty-nine branches in four regions. As of December 1995 the bank had 331 employees (up from 73 when it began). In that year, it made 122,477 loans and disbursed over U.S.$72 million to over 61,181 borrowers (out of whom over 16,000 were new borrowers). By December 1995 the bank had lent cumulatively to 417,334 borrowers since 1992. In 1993, 71 percent of the borrowers were women. Although statistics are no longer disaggregated by gender, it is estimated that in 1995 this figure had dropped to 60 to 65 percent (ACCION International, 1995).

BancoSol uses the solidarity group approach to lending. Clients must be part of a five- to seven-member solidarity group to receive a loan. The members are not necessarily related to each other. Each individual in the group receives a separate loan, but all of them are responsible for ensuring the repayment of all the loans. One member of the group is expected to act as the loan payment collector. If one of the members of the group defaults, the others are responsible for repaying that member's loan. The methodology thus relies on peer pressure. It is also considered a less costly way to reach microentrepreneurs who require very small loans.

The solidarity group approach reduces administrative costs by processing one loan for every five to seven members and improves the repayment rate. The minimum and maximum loan amounts for an entrepreneur involved in commerce are U.S.$100 and U.S.$2,700 respectively, and for those in production U.S.$150 and U.S.$3,000. The terms of the loan are eight to forty-eight weeks for an entrepreneur in commerce and twelve to fifty-six weeks for a producer. The groups themselves decide on the terms of the loan. The amount and terms also depend on the number of previous loans received and on the repayment records of the group (Buechler and Meneses, 1994: 2). In order to reduce transaction costs for both the client and the lender, BancoSol has used repayment incentives (higher subsequent loans when repayment occurs on time), solidarity groups, simple loan application procedures, and rapid approval and collection processes. These lower transaction costs enable BancoSol to reach clients at a lower cost and reach microentrepreneurs who do not interest other banks due to their lack of collateral and the need for rapid and small amounts of capital.

BancoSol also collects savings. In December 1995 the total amount of savings was more than U.S.$3 million, which is used for lending capital. There are three different savings plans: an open account in bolivianos and in U.S. dollars in which there is open availability; a capital account in both currencies that permits only two withdrawals per month; and flexible rate-of-interest accounts. This growth in savings has allowed BancoSol to increase the amount of credit available to small enterprises (Otero, 1993: 15–16). However, a large part of these savings corresponds to forced savings required until recently from borrowers, which, in practice, merely increased the cost to the client of the loans.

The growth in the number of borrowers and loans has also had some negative effects on BancoSol's institutional capabilities. With the increase in numbers of clients and branches, arrears have increased. Arrears (late payments more than thirty days overdue) had increased to 5.20 percent from PRODEM's delinquency rate of 0.5 percent (over twenty-one days overdue), but were still below the comparative figure for the Bolivian Banking Industry of 8.3 percent in December 1994 (Otero, 1993: 19; Drake and Otero, 1995: 91). Part of this increase may be due to the lack of training of credit officers as more are required to handle the rapidly increasing numbers of clients. In the beginning, credit officers had been given more extensive training about how to calculate the amount and length of loan that an entrepreneur could handle.

The Effects of the First Two Years of BancoSol

Case Studies

Easier access to credit has affected the lives of small-scale producers and vendors in La Paz, including Avelina and Sofía. Doña Avelina and her husband have both taken out loans from BancoSol. Avelina has been able to hire three more workers (she now has four) since borrowing from this bank. Avelina is one of five people who belong to a "solidarity group." She takes out loans from May until August when, she says, they have the money to pay back the loans on time. She has invested the money she earns on materials that go into the production process, such as sheet metal, solder, paint, glitter, thread, ribbons, and sequins, and also on the salaries of her workers. At the time of the interview she was making payments on a 2,000-boliviano (U.S.$840) loan.

Her husband has savings of about 900 bolivianos (U.S.$378) in BancoSol and she has 400 bolivianos (U.S.$168). The bank requires that borrowers make deposits that represent a percentage of the loan into a savings account at BancoSol. She says they use the money during slow periods to buy food such as noodles, rice, and sugar in large quantities. Avelina says that "since BancoSol lent us money, we are working more and there is more income. We have more contracts.[11] So we also earn a bit more. Last year, 1993, we bought a color television set, in 1992 the Betamax videocassette recorder. I bought it because my children asked me to." However, Avelina had to pawn the videocassette recorder and the color television set early in 1993 to make her payments to BancoSol because of the failure of her Peruvian customers to pay her for goods rendered.

Avelina and her husband were planning to open a store in a market area of El Alto. "[We would] be able to sell more. We would have the use of it, in return for a large, long-term, interest-free loan to the owner. To do this we want to borrow money from Banco El Sol [*sic*]. You see, people from rural areas have easier access to that neighborhood [because it is at the edge of the city]. Most of our clients are from the countryside."

Before Sofía started to borrow from BancoSol in 1992, she financed most of her business from the savings she had made during her earlier business ventures, which began with a small gift from her mother.[12] Sometimes she bought pigs on consignment, paying after she had sold the pork in La Paz. She, in turn, gave credit to those who bought from her and was forced to go through the weekly tedious process of collecting the payments just before making the next trip to the rural fair. When her savings were insufficient, such as the time when a large sum was stolen from her during her travels, she received an interest-free loan from a relative stranger from her community of origin; and when her mother became ill and required medical treatment, she pawned her jewelry. She also borrowed smaller sums at high interest rates from traditional moneylenders.

Sofía had been getting loans for about six years from PRODEM, which she had found out about through her niece who is also a vendor. She explains why she wanted to get credit: "I wanted to obtain a loan because one needs a lot of capital to deal in pork. I used to get loans from other people at a high interest rate. For three days they would charge 5 bolivianos for a 100-boliviano loan. Sometimes, they would not give me a loan at all. At other times, they would ask for pawns. Often, I would pawn my jewelry."

Sofía has had problems with the many solidarity groups she has been part of due mainly to nonpayment on the part of other members. In order to expand her business she took out a loan from BancoSol. In 1994 she was the coordinator of a group and took out 3,000 bolivianos (U.S.$1,260) which she said she uses "to travel for meat. However, sometimes, when sales are bad, I lose part of my capital. When that happens, I have to borrow some money or sell something I own to make the payment. When I have finished paying off the loan, I have to wait for another loan to come through. Then I start traveling again." Sometimes she finds belonging to a group tedious. In one group, she would often have to lend money to one of the members, Nati, who was perpetually late; and when Nati became group coordinator, she would always collect the dues one day late. However, when Sofía was unable to make a payment, the other group members refused to bail her out. Instead, they disclosed her situation, which brought a young credit officer to her door. She was so angry that she retired from the group and formed a new one on her own.

In 1994 she was also taking out loans (albeit illegally, given that BancoSol does not allow simultaneous borrowing from two banks) from PROCREDITO, a nongovernmental organization that gives loans to individuals at a lower interest rate. PROCREDITO does require that the creditor have collateral to back up the loan and encourages creditors to buy consumer goods so that they can get higher loans. In 1995, Sofía ceased to take out loans from PROCREDITO and switched to borrowing from BancoSol exclusively because she refused to buy consumer goods that she could not afford and therefore could not get enough credit from PROCREDITO.

Sofía used to lend money to other microentrepreneurs but now, she says, she is much more careful about her lending because she has to pay her loans back to the bank on time. In the past, she has lost money because her borrowers never paid back the money or paid late. Once a woman died who owed Sofía the equivalent of U.S.$378.95. According to Sofía, "Everything is purchased on credit and with loans. People buy cooking oil, sugar, noodles, shoes on credit. I still owe Bs 20 [20 bolivianos] for the shoes I am wearing, and they are already old. The stores earn double that way. A woman sold me a sweater for Bs 90 with Bs 10 down. When I checked in the Calle Tumusla, they were selling them for 40. So she made Bs 50 on the deal." If many are buying on credit, many are also getting loans. Sofía says of microentrepreneurs, "Everybody from the Alto on down is getting credit from the BancoSol. Even the women who sell drinks from a pail and the unemployed men who sell from their carts take out loans.[13] These days there is a lot of unemployment, so they get loans and work with them."

Even though she has more capital now due to the loans she receives, she says that her earnings have decreased or have remained the same. For the meat she earns only 20 centavos (U.S.$.04) per kilo; and when she has calculated the transportation, she earns only about U.S.$2.00 per trip. She says that of the cooked food sales, fricassee is the most lucrative. Out of a 10-kilo pig her total profits are U.S.$15.79. Her daughter used to sell to the vendors on the street on credit, but many never paid for the food so now they have decided to sell only to passersby. In 1994, Sofía claimed that credit had merely accelerated everybody's business without necessarily improving their living conditions, but during our last conversation with her in November 1995 she credited BancoSol with enabling her to survive during economic conditions that were again becoming increasingly difficult.

Survey Results

In 1994 the effects of credit on producers and market vendors involved in the BancoSol lending were surveyed (Buechler and Meneses, 1994). The study shows that the most likely beneficiaries of the BancoSol program are older, more established vendors and producers. In this respect both Avelina, who is a producer in her early forties with employees, and Sofía, who is in her late forties and an established vendor, are typical. Most of the interviewees were between 31 and 45 years old (55.3 percent) and only 10 percent were under 25. Women with more children were more likely to incur loans (Buechler and Meneses, 1994; and Rivera Cusicanqui, 1992: 25–26). In part, this may be the case because the credit program favors those with more permanent sales sites, who tend to be older, but it may also be because women with larger families have a larger potential work force and therefore sell a more rapid turnover of goods. The greater need to have access to funds may also explain the fact that women who have children and who are in impermanent relationships with men are somewhat more likely to know about PRODEM/BancoSol than married women. A study of 2,480 vendors in La Paz and El Alto found that 60.5 percent of the women in common-law relationships and 58.8 percent of separated and divorced women (versus 55.3 percent of the married women and only 45.8 percent of the single ones) knew about the program (Rivera Cusicanqui, 1992: 19). The clients of BancoSol are not likely to be the poorest entrepreneurs, but they still earned income well below the national average. Both Avelina and Sofía would be situated in the upper half of our sample in terms of their earnings.

In spite of the fact that structural adjustment has led to a sharp decrease in the income of both medium and small-scale producers and vendors between 1987 and 1991, most women engaging in small enterprises have been able to repay the loans they obtained from BancoSol (Arze et al., 1993: 234–35). Avelina's need to borrow from another source to repay the loan appears to be exceptional. The fact that Sofía borrows from another NGO also seems to be unusual. However, like the two women in the case studies, a large percentage of the women surveyed had borrowed at least four times. Indeed, they may have become dependent on such loans to finance their operations. These loans continue to be small, an average of 1,542 bolivianos (U.S.$330), far lower than the maximum (U.S.$2,700 for commerce and U.S.$3,000 for producers) set by BancoSol.

BancoSol clients involved in the study generally have used the loans to buy raw materials. However, the interviewees still needed to sell their previous inventory in order to afford a new supply of raw materials. Only 22 percent indicated that they could now continue producing without having sold their inventory. Nevertheless, access to what constitutes a sizeable sum of money according to Bolivian standards does enable microenterprises to have a higher capital turnover and/or a better assortment of merchandise. Producers have often been able to expand their production substantially by purchasing equipment.

The participants in the survey frequently complained about high interest rates. These high interest rates may be due to high overhead costs, which are reflected in the life-style of top managers and the quality of the banks' buildings that stand out in their surroundings. This impression is partly offset by the fact that the central offices are located in a very shrewdly purchased and renovated colonial building, where the costs appear to have been much lower than the value added. The participants also complained about the processing fees they were forced to pay in addition to the interest, as well as the severity of the punishments for late payment in the form of fines, penalty interest, lower loan amounts, and disbarment from loans for protracted periods of time. As Sofía's case shows, travel, late payment of the microentrepreneurs' customers, and the vicissitudes of life in Bolivia frequently make it difficult for all members of a solidarity group to make their payments on time.

The use of credit has often resulted in a higher workload to pay off the loans. Vendors continue to rely on family labor rather than hired help. While higher workloads may ease slack periods, it also often means that the borrower must make considerable sacrifices to cover interest costs. Indeed, 34.5 percent of the participants were unable to make all their payments on time. The interviewees freely acknowledge the fact that a part of the loan may go to support the husband's economic activities, to purchase real estate, consumer goods, and medical expenses, or even to cover daily subsistence needs. They pride themselves on having purchased land, for example, and in 38 percent of the cases they have made major improvements to their home. There appear to have been few changes in food consumption. While most claim that they have not changed their consumption patterns, those who have are just as likely to have decreased consumption of such foods as meat, fruit, and vegetables as to have increased it.

Informants, including Sofía and Avelina, complain about the increase in competition since they began receiving credit. Seventy percent said that competition had increased, 20 percent said that it had remained the same, and 1.8 percent said that there had been a decrease (8.2 percent did not respond or had no opinion). If this added competition is due to the increase in the urban population, it should be offset by a corresponding increase in the number of consumers. However, real wages decreased dramatically during the crisis of the 1980s, and even though the income of salaried workers has increased in recent years (as did the GNP), in 1991 average family income sank to 81 percent of 1987 levels (Arze et al., 1993: 253).[14] In that year, 70 percent of all economically active persons fell below the poverty line, 10 percent more than in 1987 (Arze et al., 1993: 342). Therefore the increase in demand has not been commensurate with the increase in population.

It is also possible that credit had increased competitive pressures by enabling more individuals to form microenterprises and by permitting established entrepreneurs to offer more goods. In this study, BancoSol clients thought that their competitors were primarily entrepreneurs similar to themselves in the size of their enterprise. Only 15 percent thought of their competitors as larger enterprises such as stores or larger workshops, and even fewer (7 percent) thought of their competition as coming from smaller enterprises such as *ambulantes* (compare Seligmann, Chapter 4, this volume). Mobile vendors comprise only 18 percent of the vendors we interviewed, which reflects BancoSol's policy of allowing only one *ambulante* for every three vendors with permanent sales locations to join a solidarity group. It should be noted, however, that in this case there is no strict division between *ambulantes* and vendors with permanent sites. *Ambulantes* typically include vendors, often men or boys, who sell small amounts of lightweight goods such as brooms and who may never establish themselves in permanent locations. However, the category also includes vendors who are just beginning to gain a hold on sites in established markets or who are pioneers in the colonization of new market locations. Once a new market receives official recognition, the pioneers may eventually become elders, venerated for their struggles to establish the market.

In order to contend with the increasing competition, various strategies have been deployed by producers and vendors, including becoming involved in additional activities and increasing the number of vending sites (Rivera Cusicanqui, 1992: 30). When additional complementary activities were started, they were often spun off to other family members (Rivera Cusicanqui, 1992: 29). In the case of Sofía, her daughter helped with the vertically integrated activity of selling cooked meat at other sites. Enlarging one's vending site by trying to sell more of a product or by having more vendors is often not possible due to the limited number of available consumers in the area and the actual space of the site. Avelina's next step is to open another site in El Alto. In both cases, enlarging one's enterprise seems to indicate that the owner might not necessarily hire more workers in the same vending site or workshop, but coordinate more people's activities in other sites.

While in some other countries, for example, Bangladash, where men have taken over the business once credit was involved and the business was becoming larger, women in La Paz still control their own businesses and finances. Both Doña Avelina, who does the accounting for the family enterprise, and Doña Sofía, who is a single mother, are typical of female entrepreneurs in Bolivia in this respect. A 1992 study of PRODEM shows similar results. In those instances where women shared the credit they received with their husbands, there was no indication of coercion. Instead, the wife typically took the initiative to teach her husband a new skill or induce him to establish his own independent enterprise to deal with a situation of unemployment (Rivera Cusicanqui, 1992: 37). The conclusion that women enjoy considerable latitude in economic decision making in Bolivia is reinforced even in the cases where the repayment of credit has created conflict between husband and wife. The description by one of this study's participants of such a quarrel is typical. When her husband complained, "You should leave this [obtaining credit] alone. Every time I have to give you money to pay the quota," she responded, "Why do I have to plead with you to give me money? You are not giving me money without getting something for it in return."[15]

Microenterprise programs claim to address what the previous chapter has noted as women's "practical" gender needs (those linked to questions of survival such as food, water, and health) and women's "strategic" gender needs (those linked to their political and social emancipation). Whether by design or not, these programs recognize that this distinction is problematic. Economic empowerment is regarded as a step toward other kinds of empowerment. Many of the evaluations of microcredit programs have shown that they empower women economically by enabling them to earn more, which in turn has led to more of a say within the household. In addition—although this is very difficult to measure—some studies claim that, due to their involvement in groups and their interaction with an organization that gives importance to their economic activities, women borrowers have gained a clearer perception of their own interests. These studies have shown that other members of the family and community begin to respect women more. In the case of Bolivia, where women have always been seen as economically important, such changes do not appear to be as salient. What can be established more clearly is that credit programs have enabled women to decrease their dependence on exploitative moneylenders, traders, landowners, and landlords (Simone Buechler, 1994). The study of BancoSol showed that clients were generally no longer relying on other sources of credit. Only 21 percent of those who responded to the question of whether they borrowed money from other sources such as moneylenders, relatives, and rotating credit associations claimed to have done so. Significant is the fact that only 5 percent of those who borrowed did so to pay back a loan to BancoSol.

An ancillary but important role of agencies such as BancoSol has been the creation of lower-level white-collar jobs. The credit officers are mostly women, who often come from the same background as the small-scale entrepreneurs themselves. These individuals may form a systemic link between the small-scale entrepreneurs and the elite-dominated financial system. We were impressed by the knowledge some of these employees had of the concerns of their clients, which contrasted with the frequent condescension of the upper (mostly male) managers.

Nevertheless, as Escobar (1995: 188) and others have argued, "the participation of women in social production is necessary but not sufficient to overcome women's subordination." Many microenterprise programs have failed to adopt an "empowerment approach," developing instead a "productive approach" that does not attempt to transform the way women are linked to productive and reproductive roles. Even so, microenterprise programs have at least shifted away from the perception that women's sphere is coterminous with the domestic sphere, and moved toward recognizing their other activities.

Conclusion

Small-scale enterprises in Bolivia can be regarded as both the continuation of a tradition and as an integral part of a changing, complex national and international economy. From the first perspective, they constitute firms with a repertoire of long-term strategies of adapting to turbulent economic conditions and to the chronic scarcity of capital and raw materials. From the latter vantage point, the flexibility of these firms has long meant that the less flexible state and larger private firms have devolved on them much of the burden of recessions.

The failure of the development model that supported large-scale enterprises may constitute one of the reasons why development agencies decided to support the "informal" sector when it once had considered it backward, outside of the "modernist" project, and "abnormal" (Escobar, 1992). Providing credit for small enterprises constitutes a grudging recognition, on the part of the state and development agencies alike, of the ability of such enterprises to generate employment. This change in the orientation of development is also commensurate with the changes in the economic system toward postfordism,[16] where large-scale and small-scale production coexist side by side and the dichotomy between informal and formal makes even less sense than it did earlier. Thus, the new emphasis in development also entails a recognition of the interlinkages —which have always been present, but which have increased in recent decades—between firms of different sizes.

The change in the global economy, and concomitantly in development models, has brought both new opportunities and new costs for small-scale enterprises. While access to credit has enabled some microentrepreneurs to increase the scale of their operations, the reliance on credit has also increased dependence on the new financial institutions and produced greater exposure to adverse developments in the financial market. Small-scale entrepreneurs have also been forced to change their business practices to reduce risks that might prevent them from paying back their loans on time. Some of these changes were directly dictated by BancoSol's lending policies. The rule that prohibits the inclusion of kin in solidarity groups de-emphasizes ties that are extremely important in other aspects of production and commerce. While distributing the risk for both lenders and clients, and perhaps providing some relief to kin networks that already carry a heavy load, bank policies also place a heavier burden on borrowers because it is difficult for them to establish extra-kin networks of individuals who are sufficiently reliable to meet their obligations to the bank. It remains to be seen whether this increasing dependence will be compensated for by increased family income or whether the effects of structural adjustment, which have been to redistribute income from the poorest segments of the population to salaried employees and the elites, will simply mean that the additional economic productivity resulting from the loans will be offset by increasing competition and the high cost of servicing the loans. Ultimately, the impact of credit programs for small-scale enterprises will depend on national and global economic conditions. Such programs may easily become an excuse for neglecting the more redistributive role of the state associated with the provision of basic services such as health care and education, and thereby reinforce rather than counteract reductions by the state in these areas as an integral part of economic restructuring.

Notes

1. We use the terms "small-scale" flexibly to include what others have called "microenterprises." We have not established a specific upper limit because firms employing dozens of workers are often constituted in a very similar fashion to very small ones in terms of the technology they employ and/or work relationships.

2. Between 1985 and 1990 alone, the percentage of migrants in the urban working age population increased from 6 percent to 10 percent (Arze et al., 1993: 74).

3. This figure is substantially higher than that reported in the preliminary analysis of the official census of economic units undertaken in 1992 that counted only 80,928 individuals employed in 58,236 commercial establishments (Bolivia, 1993b).

4. The balance of the gain in the share of the labor force experienced by small-scale enterprises resulted from a decline in the percentage of the work force employed in domestic service.

5. In our study, the 64 vendors and storekeepers (excluding food vendors who could also be regarded as producers) received some form of labor assistance

in 73.4 percent of the cases, 31.3 percent from husbands, 23.4 percent from sons, 32.8 percent from daughters, 1.6 percent from parents and 7.8 percent from a niece, nephew or godchild. Only 7.8 percent claimed to have hired help.

6. It is also noteworthy that an important part of the support network of both producers and vendors with rural origins are members of their communities of origin, whether they are related or not. Those from the same community who have previously established themselves in the city provide places to stay and become sources of jobs and apprenticeships for new migrants. Those who remain behind become sources for produce or raw materials.

7. Sofía's mother had been upwardly mobile as a result of her successful candle enterprise (an echo of her great-grandmother's urban middle-class status).

8. It should be noted, however, that in the late 1980s the liaison person for the Museum of Modern Art in charge of organizing special exhibits of artisan goods was a *chola*.

9. ACCION International is a private, nonprofit organization that has a network of forty relatively autonomous affiliate organizations in fourteen countries in Latin America, the Caribbean, and the United States. Its headquarters are in Cambridge, Massachusetts, and its relatively new regional training and research center, Centro Acción, founded in 1992, is in Bogotá, Colombia. ACCION was founded in 1961, but since 1973 it has concentrated on creating jobs and generating income for the poorest of the economically active population, recognizing that an increasing number of rural migrants to the cities were turning to self-employment as the only way to survive. ACCION International's funding for program services primarily comes from private contributions, U.S. government grants, international and foreign government grants, interest, and fees. ACCION International helps fund most affiliates by using a guarantee financing mechanism. In 1984, ACCION created the Bridge Fund, a reserve placed in a U.S. commercial bank, which can be used by the affiliates as a guarantee to a local bank. An affiliate can go to a local bank for a loan, and the local bank is assured approximately 55 percent of the loan from the reserve if the affiliate cannot pay back the loan, thereby reducing the risk it incurs. The Bridge Fund is capitalized with loans and donations from foundations such as the Ford Foundation and the MacArthur Foundation, governments, including the U.S. Agency for International Development, individuals, and churches.

10. The Calmeadow Foundation, which has recently changed its name to Calmeadow, is a Canadian organization which has worked closely with PRODEM and with aboriginal groups in Canada on the issue of microenterprise development. In addition to being a funding agency, they are involved in technical assistance and have produced a guide to the planning and implementation of microenterprise programs. The FUNDES group is a Swiss foundation that promotes microbusinesses and has set up a guarantee fund for microbusiness loans.

11. This is presumably because the loans provide the family with the financial means to fulfill them.

12. For a fuller description see Buechler and Buechler, 1996: 106–14.

13 This is probably an exaggeration.

14. For example, Estes (1988: 151) found that average factory wages in 1986 were only one third (U.S.$35 a month) of what they had been in 1980. During the same period the price of rice had gone up 20 percent and the cost of a bus ride had doubled.

15. The pattern of gender equality in economic decision making may be a carryover from the division of labor in rural communities. While women and men undertake different tasks in agriculture, there is little gender discrimination except in inheritance patterns (see Buechler and Buechler, 1971; Carter and Mamani, 1982).

16. Postfordism refers to an economy based on flexible production patterns characterized by outsourcing to smaller firms, wherever labor is cheap, which enables larger companies to increase and contract production rapidly. At the same time, however, the power of labor unions is undercut and benefits to workers are weakened or eliminated. Postfordism also forces the firms to which the work is outsourced to bear the brunt of downturns in the economy.

References

ACCION Internacional. Unpublished statistics. 1995.

Albó, Xavier, Tomás Greaves, and Godofredo Sandoval. *Chukiyawu: La cara Aymara de La Paz. II. Una odisea: Buscar "Pega."* La Paz: Cuadernos de Investigaciónes CIPCA, no. 22, 1982.

Arze, Carlos, Hugo Dorado, Huáscar Eguino, and Silvia Escóbar de Pabón. *Empleo y salarios: El circulo de la pobreza.* La Paz: CEDLA, Programa de Ajuste Estructural, Serie Estudios e Investigaciones, 1993.

Blount, Jeb. "Profit's Not a Dirty Word: Bolivia's Bank for the Poor." *Wall Street Journal,* April 10, 1992.

Bolivia. *Empleo en el sector informal de la ciudad de La Paz.* La Paz: Ministerio de Trabajo y Desarrollo Laboral, Dirección General de Empleo, 1980.

———. *Censo 1992: Resultados finales,* Vol. 2. *La Paz.* La Paz: Ministerio de Planeamiento y Coordinación, Instituto Nacional de Estadística. 1993a.

———. *II censo establecimientos economicos 92: Resultados prelimi-nares.* La Paz: Instituto Nacional de Estadística, 1993b.

Buechler, Hans. *The Masked Media: Fiestas and Social Interaction in the Bolivian Highlands.* The Hague: Mouton, 1980.

———. "Aymara Curing Practices in the Context of a Family History." In *Health in the Andes,* edited by J. Bastien and J. Donahue, Washington, DC: 38–49. American Anthropological Association, No. 12, 1981.

———. "The 'Informal Sector' Revisited: Thoughts on a Misleading Dichotomy." *Anthropology Newsletter* 33, no. 9 (December 1992): 12–13.

Buechler, Hans and Judith-Maria. *The Bolivian Aymara.* New York: Holt, Rinehart and Winston, 1971.

———. "El Aymara boliviano y el cambio social: Reevaluación del concepto de 'intermediario cultural.' " *Estudios Andinos* 2, no. 3 (1971–72): 137–49.

———. *Manufacturing Against the Odds: Small-Scale Producers in an Andean City.* Boulder: Westview Press, 1992.

————. *The World of Sofía Velasquez: The Autobiography of a Bolivian Market Vendor*. New York: Columbia University Press, 1996.

Buechler, Judith-Maria. "Peasant Marketing and Social Revolution in the Province of La Paz, Bolivia." Ph.D. diss., McGill University, 1972.

————. "Something Funny Happened on the Way to the Agora: A Comparison of Bolivian and Spanish Galician Migrants." In *Women and Migration,* edited by Judith-Maria Hess Buechler, (Special Issue), *Anthropological Quarterly* 49, no. 1 (January 1976): 62–69.

————. "The Dynamics of the Market in La Paz, Bolivia." *Urban Anthropology* 7, no. 4 (Winter 1978): 343–59.

————. "The Visible and Vocal Politics of Female Traders and Small Scale Producers in La Paz, Bolivia." In *Women and Economic Change: Andean Perspectives,* edited by A. Miles and H. Buechler, 75–88. Washington, DC: Society for Latin American Anthropology Publication Series, 1997.

Buechler, Simone. "The Key to Lending to Women Microentrepreneurs." *Small Enterprise Development: An International Journal* 6 (June 1995): 4–15.

————. "Women, Microenterprise, and Finance: Keys to Poverty Reduction, Employment, and Integration of Marginalized Groups." Paper prepared for the Second Preparatory Committee for the United Nations World Summit on Social Development, New York, January 1994.

————. "ACCION International and Its Affiliate, BancoSol." A case study prepared for the Expert Group Meeting on Women and Finance for the United Nations Fourth World Conference on Women held by Women's World Banking, New York, January 24–28, 1994.

————. "Credit Approaches and Women Microentrepreneurs." Unpublished report, United Nations Development Fund for Women, New York, 1993.

Buechler, Stephanie, and Martha Lanza Meneses. "Primero, con la cabeza hay que hablar: Impacto del crédito en las mujeres." Paper prepared for the International Coalition on Women and Credit, La Paz, Bolivia, 1994.

Carter, W., and M. Mamani. *Irpa Chico: Individuo y comunidad en la cultura aymara*. La Paz: Editorial "Juventud," 1982.

Casanovas, Roberto. "El sector informal urbano: Apuntes para un diagnóstico." In *El sector informal urbano en Bolivia,* 141–72. La Paz: CEDLA, FLACSO, 1986.

Drake, Deborah, and Maria Otero. *Alchemists for the Poor: NGOs as Financial Institutions*. Cambridge, MA: ACCION International, Monograph Series, 1995.

Escobar, Arturo. "Culture, Economics, and Politics in Latin American Social Movements Theory and Research." In *The Making of Social Movements in Latin America: Identity, Strategy and Democracy,* edited by Arturo Escobar and Sonia E. Alvarez, 62–85. Boulder: Westview Press, 1992.

———. *Encountering Development: The Making and Unmaking of the Third World.* Princeton: Princeton University Press, 1995.

Estes, Valerie. "These Days, to Be Bolivian Is to Die Slowly: Women Factory Workers in La Paz." In *Lucha: The Struggles of Latin American Women,* edited by Connie Weil, 141–60. Minnesota Latin American Series, Minneapolis: Prisma Institute, 1988.

Lizano, E. *Access of Small Enterprises to Conventional Sources of Financing: The Cases of Bolivia, Chile, and Colombia.* Washington, DC: World Bank and FUNDES, 1992.

Otero, Francisco. "BancoSol-Bolivia." An Issue Paper prepared for UNIFEM for the United Nations World Summit on Social Development, Copenhagen, March 6–12, 1993.

Rivera Cusicanqui, Silvia. "Informe preliminar de investigación, proyecto: 'Crédito, potenciamiento de la mujer y bienestar familiar en Bolivia.' " Unpublished report, La Paz, Bolivia, 1992.

6

From Cooperatives to Microenterprises: The Neoliberal Turn in Postrevolutionary Nicaragua

Florence E. Babb*

The rapid dismantling of socialist economies over the last decade, when the Soviet Union and Eastern Europe underwent dramatic transformations, has led to intense debates over the perceived failures of socialism and, for some, the inevitability of capitalism. In such discussions, comparisons with China are sometimes drawn, but little mention is made of Latin American experiments with socialism. When attention does turn to this part of the world, it is most often to Cuba that analysts direct their gaze (Weisskopf, 1992). Predictions of the imminent failure of that thirty-five-year experiment in socialist development have been more frequent since the collapse of the Soviet Union.

From 1979 until 1990, however, international attention was focused on Nicaragua, a small Central American nation that had successfully overthrown a forty-three-year dictatorship, begun a process of social transformation, and charted a new path of development. The U.S. government took a keen interest in the revolution that was under way, and so did a number of Third World countries intent upon overcoming histories of underdevelopment and gaining greater independence in the international

*I gratefully acknowledge the Nicaraguan women and men who gave their time and their friendship and made this work possible. Research in Nicaragua was funded in 1991 by a Fulbright Senior Research Award, and in 1992 by a Wenner-Gren Foundation for Anthropological Research Regular Grant and a Faculty Scholar Award from the University of Iowa. The research continued through 1993, and I returned in 1996, with the support of the Faculty Scholar Award and an International Travel Grant from the University of Iowa. An earlier version of this work was published in *Anthropology of Work Review* 16, nos. 3–4 (Fall–Winter 1995): 2–8.

arena (Enríquez, 1991: 1). A landmark collection of essays on problems of Third World socialism written by leftist academics took its inspiration from the Nicaraguan experience (Fagen et al., 1986). Yet, a more recent collection of essays, *Free Trade and Economic Restructuring in Latin America* (Rosen and McFadyen, 1995), barely mentions Nicaragua. In the book's foreword, Salvadoran political scientist and former presidential candidate Rubén Zamora points to the fall of existing socialism and the rise of neoliberalism—signaling a return to free market economics—as the global processes that frame current struggles in Latin America (Zamora, 1995). He goes on to make the salient remark that popular movements in the region present the left with alternatives to the old party structures and organizations linked to them. He could be describing postrevolutionary Nicaragua, but the country is only referred to in passing (Zamora, 1995: 7–9).

Unlike Cuba and other examples of Communist-Party-directed socialism (or "actually existing socialist systems"), many of which have recently seen their demise, Nicaragua's socialist-oriented Sandinista government was less orthodox in its plan of social reconstruction following a successful revolutionary insurrection. The Sandinista National Liberation Front (Frente Sandinista de Liberación Nacional, or FSLN) allowed for a mixed economy, private enterprise alongside an expanded state sector. For this reason, it is looked to less often as an example from which to draw lessons about the future of socialism. But the Nicaraguan revolution brought about a program of social transformation that went far enough to attract both international acclaim and a rather predictable reaction from the United States—which, through its economic embargo and its funding of the counterrevolutionary (Contra) war, contributed significantly to the problems that brought down the Sandinistas after only a decade in power.

Nicaragua went through two transitions in a fairly short period of time: from a market economy dominated by the elite Somoza family that was transformed by the Sandinistas in 1979 into a state-regulated economy, back to a market-driven program under the government of the National Opposition Union (Unión Nacional Opositora, or UNO), mandated by the International Monetary Fund (IMF) and set in place by the U.S. Agency for International Development (USAID) after the 1990 elections (Spoor, 1994: 517). These were not simple shifts back and forth between capitalist and socialist models, but rather negotiated processes that often allowed for unexpected economic juxtapositions. The UNO government continued to bend somewhat to the interests of the Sandinistas, who until their recent split into two tendencies, one more orthodox and one declaring itself "renovationist," represented the most powerful political party in the country (*Barricada Internacional*, 1995). The result is that while state intervention in the market characterized the last decade, the current period is marked by a significant degree of economic regulation by the government. At the same time, it may be noted that the market liberalization and structural adjustment that are generally associated with the UNO regime actually began under the Sandinistas in 1988. Thus, the Nicaraguan economy presents a far more complicated situation than the apparent "state versus market" dichotomy would suggest (Spoor, 1994).

"The neoliberal turn" referred to in the title of this essay might suggest a simple reversal of political direction and of economic policy after the 1990 elections. Indeed, there is evidence supporting the argument that there has been a rather systematic undoing of economic reforms introduced by the Sandinistas. Where the FSLN promoted the distribution of available resources among the broad population, the UNO government adopted a neoliberal plan that supported the privatization of industry, health, and education, and cut back on state-provided services, subsidies, and basic food packages. In the competitive context of the 1990s, former landowners reclaim their holdings and large industries drive out smaller ones that are no longer protected by the state. Low-income women are disproportionately affected in the process.

Nevertheless, the revolution left its legacy and Nicaraguans have not passively allowed their hard-won rights to be taken away. It was widely expected that the UNO government would "undo the revolution," but the transition has been more complex. If the revolution truly transformed Nicaraguan society, it should "build strong buffers against the neoliberal tide" (Spalding, 1994: 156–57).

Economic Restructuring under the Sandinista Government

The Nicaraguan revolution sought to break with the agroexport economy of the Somoza period and to establish a redistributive economy that would benefit a population that had long suffered from international dependency. Heavy reliance on coffee and cotton production made the country vulnerable to price fluctuations, and the Somoza family had done little to promote economic development. The Sandinistas introduced a broad program of agrarian reform and a policy of self-determination and redistribution. To that end, they nationalized production in key sectors of the economy and set up import and exchange controls. However, their economic planning allowed for continued support of the private sector to a significant degree, and generous loans were made available to capitalists willing to reactivate their enterprises (Walker, 1986: 68). Whether the model would have succeeded is uncertain, as structural problems inherited from the

Somoza period and the assault of the Contra war undermined the nation's development (Spalding, 1987: 4).

Even so, the early years of the revolutionary government saw notable structural change. Some outstanding initiatives were in the areas of health care and education, which were made available to all. Resources more closely linked to the economy were redistributed as well. While rural land reform stood out as a critical element in economic restructuring, change was also brought about in the urban area. New policies awarding land to squatters and efforts to bring water and electricity to their settlements attracted labor to the cities, especially Managua, whose population rose to almost a million, or about a quarter of the country's total size. When low-paid urban workers turned to employment in the informal sector, where earnings were sometimes higher, the government countered by raising wage levels in formal sector jobs. Provision of basic food items and subsidies of imported goods continued until the government could no longer afford to underwrite the basic consumption of the entire country, and turned to offering incentives to the most productive sectors of the formal economy (Gibson, 1987: 40).

The Sandinista government encouraged formal sector employment primarily in the state sector and in services, rather than in industry, and tried to attract those informal traders who swelled the markets to new work sites. Nevertheless, an abundance of workers continued to produce and sell needed goods in small, independent associations of fewer than a dozen individuals. These workers were encouraged to organize collectively within the National Association of Small and Medium Industries (Camara Nacional de Mediana y Pequeña Industria, or CONAPI), and were offered state-supported training and lower prices for primary goods needed in their cooperatives. Programs to provide training for women in nontraditional employment were among those introduced. In many cases, the state bought and sold the items produced by the cooperatives, further enabling small producers to remain in business.

By the mid-1980s, efforts toward social and economic development had been seriously undercut both by the U.S. trade embargo imposed under the Reagan administration and by the need to defend the country in the face of the U.S.-supported Contra war. Nicaraguan economic policy moved from a revolutionary planning process to a program aimed at stabilization. In 1988–89 the Sandinistas responded to hyperinflation and declining economic growth by cutting back on employment in the public sector and on state spending in general. Nominal wage increases, intended to soften the blow, were inadequate to protect the poorest Nicaraguans from the harsh effects of the adjustment measures (Ricciardi, 1991).

Reorganization of Work under the UNO Government

If the Sandinistas' stabilization and adjustment program was hard on many Nicaraguans, the IMF-directed neoliberal agenda of the UNO government was far more crushing (Babb, 1996). New structural adjustment measures were introduced quickly after the 1990 elections in a country whose former revolutionary government had provided a safety net of support. Privatization, the withdrawal of protective tariffs, and cuts in social services were some elements that clashed loudly with the policies of the Sandinistas. Yet, the measures promoted by the UNO government met resistance from some business elites as well as from the popular sectors, with both groups fearing they would lose from the withdrawal of economic support (Spalding, 1994: 158). Thus, the neoliberalism endorsed by the U.S. government and some privileged Nicaraguan sectors was modified as a result of mobilized opposition by diverse segments of the population—a convergence of cross-class interests that has been seen in the country's recent history.

A major devaluation of the currency in March 1991 was preceded by an extensive televised explanation by President Violeta Chamorro's son-in-law and minister of the presidency, Antonio Lacayo, who managed to avert strong opposition to the plan. Soon afterward, twenty-eight thousand state workers who agreed to leave their jobs were granted generous severance pay funded by the USAID under the Occupational Conversion program (Spalding, 1994: 169). These and other efforts to win public acceptance paid off as many former state employees were mollified long enough to set up small independent businesses—a large number of which were failing by 1992, the so-called Year of Reactivation. Other concessions to neoliberalism's opponents included the provision that workers in former state farms and industries would be allowed to control a quarter to a third of the newly privatized businesses. These concessions did not necessarily lead to significant worker participation or empowerment, but received approval from enough Sandinistas to lessen dissatisfaction over the economic model.

Yet, the deepening economic crisis during the 1990s took a great toll on small producers in the country. The majority of small producers and businesses experienced increasing competition as larger industries—both national and international—received UNO government support. No longer having the benefit of favorable terms of credit or protective tariffs on imported goods, cooperatives and other small businesses failed at higher rates. Meanwhile, foreign interests were welcomed to Managua's Free Trade Zone, where they could employ workers at relatively low wages.

Many low-income women and men in Managua came to have less and less confidence in the government bringing about better conditions in their lives. The currency was stabilized in the 1990s, but unemployment and underemployment approached 60 percent at the same time that privatization of health care and cuts in social services eliminated state protection of the urban poor (*Envío*, 1994: 7). Since 1990, there has been a gradual erosion of small industries and an expansion of the informal sector, particularly as the state sector has been cut back.

Urban Cooperatives in the Transition from Revolutionary to Neoliberal Nicaragua

As small industries have been reconfigured as microenterprises (defined as working units of up to five individuals), numerous women workers have been affected; some have benefited from new employment opportunities, but many others have had adverse consequences. The Nicaraguan case may be considered alongside other formerly socialist countries to examine whether women are set back disproportionately to men as work is transformed to meet the requirements of the neoliberal capitalist development model (Einhorn, 1993).

Various interviews and conversations in Managua during the years following the 1990 elections suggest some ways that new policy directions, motivated by an ideological shift to the right, have attempted to close many of the openings that were won under Sandinista leadership. For example, a meeting with Fatima Reyes, author of the Ministry of Finance's Occupational Conversion program, disclosed the view that cuts in public sector employment would allow many female employees to return home to care for their families (Reyes, interview, July 18, 1991). Indeed, a disproportionate number of women, and Sandinistas in general, were among those to adopt the plan, often establishing small businesses out of their homes that were destined to fail. Yet, when the special obstacles confronting women in small industries and commerce were addressed with ministry officials, few were interested in discussing the effects that current policy was having on these women. Heavier burdens at home, resulting from cuts in such areas as child care, health care, and education, were apparently invisible to the officials, just as the impact of a free-market-oriented national economy was apparently invisible as a force driving women's small enterprises out of business.

The rapid decline of women's economic base can be illustrated through a study of four urban cooperatives that were formed over the last decade in various parts of Managua. These four working groups were seamstresses, welders, bakers, and artisans—traditional as well as nontraditional occupations for women (Babb, 1992, 1996). Two of the cooperatives, the bakers and the artisans, include men as well as women as members. All of the cooperatives have had to struggle to survive in the post-1990 period. Two of them, the seamstresses and the bakers, came together in the period soon after the Sandinistas rose to power and encouraged collectivization of small industries. They organized service co-operatives, which meant that members worked at home but had a central location for selling their product, holding regular meetings, and other activities. However, these two co-ops have been forced to put their office spaces up for sale in the last few years since they have been unable to keep up payments. Declining sales of bread and locally produced clothing have resulted both from Nicaraguans' inability to afford even these basic goods and from changing economic conditions which favor imported goods and larger industries. Individuals and families continue to produce without the support of the co-ops, but the bakers report that bread production is down as much as 50 percent, and clothing production in the cooperative has ground nearly to a halt.

The cooperative of women welders, formed in 1991 after a dozen housewives completed a ten-month training program, suffered a number of setbacks and now has ceased to function. Working together out of a workshop in a women's center in Managua, these women saw their membership drop steadily as a result of a number of problems that included interpersonal difficulties, resistance of husbands to their wives' working, and a lack of steady work. Although they had a space in which to work, they could not be sure that it would remain available to them, making the absence of a secure work environment an issue for them as well. By early 1993, the women had disbanded, some of them seeking work elsewhere and others once again at home with their families. One of the two former co-coordinators of the cooperative, the only single woman in the group, had recently been featured in a newspaper story. As a result she had received offers to join a couple of male welders in their work. She was ready to join them, but a few months later she reported that things did not work out, and she was out of work. Interestingly, the other co-coordinator had taken the opportunity to go with a group of USAID-funded Nicaraguans for technical training in the United States; what lies ahead for this select group remains to be seen.

The cooperative of artisans included several women and men making silver and coral jewelry along with two women making decorative wall hangings and other items with bark from the tuno tree. The cooperative members, who joined together in 1987, pride themselves on the high quality of their work, but they experienced a severe drop in sales as the economy worsened and as fewer international visitors were on hand to buy from them. In 1992 the bark workers left the cooperative for family reasons, another woman left because her husband opposed her working, and still another left because she felt that her children needed more attention at home. The women's low level of business may well have contributed to their decisions, although this was not expressed directly.

Despite this cooperative's setbacks, it may in a certain sense be regarded as successful. After a long wait, members were able to secure a loan and a grant from a nongovernmental organization (NGO) to construct a spacious new workshop, which was completed in 1992. The cooperative was also singled out as one of ten to receive extra support from CONAPI, the trade union organization of small- and medium-sized industries. Now the artisans are seeking new markets and trying out new creative techniques, but it is still unclear whether they will succeed in the long run. Their viability depends in part on the degree to which they turn from a Sandinista-identified work organization to a "microenterprise" orientation of competing in the open market, though that approach offers no guarantee of success.

Formed in 1983 under the Sandinistas, CONAPI remains the major organization representing the interests of workers in small industries (of the four cooperatives studied, only the welders had not joined). Still identified with the FSLN, CONAPI is now somewhat more diverse politically. The organization's assistance to selected cooperatives was an effort to demonstrate to USAID the promise of small industries in the country and to attract more external support. CONAPI has nonetheless experienced a loss of political strength in Nicaragua as the number of member cooperatives has fallen dramatically.

The structural adjustment measures that have been imposed since 1990 in Nicaragua are part of an IMF formula similar to that followed in other Latin American countries since the 1980s, but the impact may be substantially greater. The neoliberal plan has been set in place more quickly in Nicaragua, with harsher consequences for the majority of the population who cannot compete with large industries or with newly imported goods flooding the market. Moreover, the subsidized production provided under the Sandinista government was eliminated so quickly that even smaller industries with the potential to be competitive do not survive long. Even so, the Nicaraguans' past revolutionary experience has given them the ability to organize opposition and to win some limited concessions from the government.

For many of those whose businesses have failed or whose jobs in the public sector have been eliminated, the only option is to seek work in the informal sector of small-scale manufacturing, commerce, and services. In one popular barrio in Managua a mix of low-income merchants, artisans, and service workers, as well as a number of professionals, live and work. Many are informally employed women, working out of their homes and earning a marginal income. A good number, including some who adopted the Occupational Conversion plan, have invested in a freezer and set up a front room store to sell soft drinks, ice, and often an array of other products. Unfortunately, there is such an abundance of these small stores that few do very much business. Many women expressed the great difficulty in providing food for their families and in meeting other expenses.

From Cooperatives to Microenterprises in
Post-Sandinista Nicaragua

In this bleak economic context, the UNO government made several initiatives to promote the development of microenterprises—or at least gave the impression of promoting them. Defined as productive units of up to five individuals working together, microenterprises, in relatively modest but growing numbers, were given loans to begin operating. Among these, women workers were prominent. The new Office of Small Industries and Microenterprises within the Ministry of the Economy was established to oversee the development of these enterprises, providing loans and technical assistance. Several NGOs also offered support to microenterprises on a limited basis. The directors of these offices and organizations revealed the high failure rate of the microenterprises, many of which have been unable to repay loans and have gone out of business. However, this did not prevent the government from carrying out broad publicity campaigns or from holding highly visible fairs for the sale of items produced by microentrepreneurs. Thus, while the UNO government sought to dismantle the urban cooperatives that signal the persistance of Sandinista work organization, it was intent on replacing them with microenterprises that symbolize the success of the free market model.

Contradictory objectives were expressed by María Hurtado de Vigil, the director of the Ministry's Office of Small Industries and Microenterprises. While she stated that the government sought to support those small enterprises that were most likely to succeed, she acknowledged that even those promising industries stood little chance of success in a context of shifting policy that favored the entry of imported goods and increasing competition. Stressing the benefits of liberalization of the economy, she said she had not considered the implications for women microentrepreneurs deemed "likely to fail" (Hurtado de Vigil, interview, May 8, 1991).

Between 1991 and 1993, several interviews were conducted with Stefan Platteau, the head of the National Program to Support

Microenterprise (Programa Nacional de Apoyo a la Microempresa, or
PAMIC), also created by the Ministry of the Economy. A European econo-
mist based in Nicaragua, he shared a view held by many others, including
some Sandinistas, that the revolutionary government had "spoiled" workers by offering handouts and support without offering the training that
would make them self-sustaining. Thus, he was intent upon finding highly
motivated individuals to train in microenterprises in order to make his
program a success. In 1992, a year after his job was created, he was still
optimistic that individuals with management abilities and determination
could succeed with credit and training (Platteau, interview, February 24,
1992). By mid-1993 he revealed much more cynicism about the prospects for the five thousand microentrepreneurs his office had assisted. He
noted a problematic "work culture" in Nicaragua, in which people feel
that it doesn't pay to work, that he traced to the last decade and the
Sandinistas. He says that he now tells people that if they want loans and
want to succeed, there will be "blood, sweat, and tears"—a remark he
repeated several times for emphasis. While his cynicism extends to doubt-
ing that the growth of microenterprises would turn around the economy,
he thinks that much is at stake in demonstrating the good results of his
program (Platteau, interview, July 23, 1993).

An interview with Antonio Chávez, a leading official in CONAPI,
presented a different perspective. When asked about the impact of recent
economic measures on small industries, Chávez reported that the sector
had been particularly hard hit and that women, who made up 54 percent
of their membership, were the most affected. The largest number of women
workers are in the garment and food industries, which have experienced
great losses as import tariffs have been lowered on goods entering Nicaragua. He acknowledged that the decline in the sector began under the
Sandinistas, but he argued that the current "shock treatment" is far worse
(Chávez, interview, May 8, 1991). CONAPI reported that some seven
thousand small- and medium-sized industries and services closed in 1992,
leaving just three thousand shops registered with the Ministry of the
Economy (*Barricada Internacional*, 1993).

In an economy in which the majority of urban and rural workers are
located in small industries and microenterprises, it is useful for the Nicaraguan government to give the impression of concern and support for
workers in this sector (Leguizamon, 1990). The new administrative apparatus and discourse around microenterprises seems designed to offer hope
to the most vulnerable economic sector, at the same time that neoliberal
policies further undermine the chance of success of the sector. The difference between the Sandinista-organized cooperatives and the UNO-
promoted microenterprises is largely political—the former based on the

principle of state-led development and the latter based on the model of free market competition—yet both types of work organization are suffering under present conditions.

Alternatives for Social Mobilization

In the absence of a viable economic program supported by those critical of neoliberalism, and with the FSLN party split into two factions since late 1994, what are the alternatives for economic and political change? To address this question it is useful to turn attention to new forms of social mobilization in evidence since 1990. While this essay has focused on the harsh economic measures and the changing organization of work since the UNO government was elected, the 1990s have also seen growing political participation at the grassroots level on a range of issues. Breaking from party lines, autonomous social movements, or sometimes loosely organized networks, have taken up concerns as wide-ranging as the environment, health, women's rights, and, not surprisingly, the economic crisis. There is a significant connection between the changing political economy, with the new emphasis on privatization and export-led industrialization, and the expansion of political activism around issues of human rights and gender politics, at a time when the government has swung sharply to the right (Babb, 1997). Critics of the former Sandinista government argue that this movement is the result of a post-electoral democratization process, and partisans of the FSLN call it a continuation of the last decade of social mobilization. In fact, it is not simply one or the other. Rather, the emergence of more independent social movements may be the result of a questioning of top-down Sandinista party politics, a strong opposition to UNO government policy, a continued mobilization under a government that tolerates a degree of political dissent, and a desire to raise issues that had been overlooked or silenced by established political parties both before and after the 1990 elections.

Many of those who have been affected most harshly by recent policies are beginning to negotiate the terms of their wider participation in society through forms of collective action (Escobar, 1992: 83). In Nicaragua, the relationship is evident between such apparently disparate developments as the economic crisis, UNO government infighting and political dislocations on the left, and ideology veering to the right on the one hand and the rise of autonomous social movements on the other. These related though somewhat contradictory developments can be understood through the historical conjuncture of events following the 1990 elections. First, the Sandinistas' loss brought not only an abrupt political transition but also a more reflective period for the FSLN. Forced to acknowledge past errors of a top-down leadership, the party opened the way for more independent organizing to occur. Second, it may be precisely in the context of the most difficult times that Nicaraguans are seeking not only new lives but new meanings by which to apprehend their lives. Putting forward issues of gender, race, and class, as well as substantive matters such as health and environment, as key elements in a new political agenda is a way that marginalized groups are resisting the conservative ideology of the UNO government and finding openings for collective expressions of identity. There are indications that these recent "cultural" movements are breathing new life into ongoing struggles for economic and social justice.

Conclusion

The changes in Nicaragua's economy and in the organization of work since 1990 have been in some ways transformative and in other ways illusory. The unexpected juxtapositions remain, with elements of both state-directed and market-driven development—though the latter is rapidly gaining force. In 1979 the Nicaraguan revolution brought substantial changes to a small, underdeveloped nation, but rather than following any particular model of socialist development, the Sandinistas allowed for a mixed economy and heterodox policies and practices. When the Contra war demanded increased defense spending and an austerity economy, measures were introduced that bore resemblance to structural adjustment mandated by the IMF elsewhere in Latin America. However, the FSLN remained committed to delivering basic needs and services to the population—an orientation that was sharply reversed after the UNO coalition came to power.

The neoliberal project ushered in by the UNO government called for a reorganization of work as the state sector was cut back, industry was privatized, and national production was challenged by conditions favoring imports. Even so, Nicaraguans were vocal in their criticisms of the harsh consequences of the new free market orientation and they won some important concessions, including assistance to small-scale producers. The present government's support for microenterprise development, at the same time that urban cooperatives and small industries in general are seriously undermined by neoliberal policy, reveals a determined effort to contain the opposition of a large population in urban Nicaragua. However, judging from the continued failure of so many small production units and the downturn of the economy overall, it will take far more to quell the opposition.

If the Nicaraguan election in 1990 marked the loss of another "historic model" of socialist-oriented development, it also presented us with the opportunity to follow the response of the left and of emergent popular movements to the challenge of neoliberalism in one small Central American nation. In recent years, Nicaragua has undergone a worsening economic crisis and a fitful political transition, but it has also experienced the productive tension of a society demanding democratic and pluralist approaches to national development. Social revolutions of the future will be, without a doubt, different from revolutions of the past, and we can learn as much from current struggles as we can from historical ones. As the old debates over state-sector versus private-sector development and over loyalty to a political party line subside, today's social movements in Nicaragua and elsewhere may prefigure, in all their uncertainties, alternatives for the future.

References

Babb, Florence E. "From Co-Ops to Kitchens." *Cultural Survival* 16, no. 4 (Winter 1992): 41–43.

———. "Discourses of Development in Post-1990 Nicaragua." Paper presented at the International Congress of the Latin American Studies Association, Atlanta, 1994.

———. "Unmaking the Revolution: From Cooperatives to Microenterprises in Urban Nicaragua." *Anthropology of Work Review* 16, nos. 3–4 (Fall–Winter 1995): 2–8.

———. "After the Revolution: Neoliberal Policy, Informal Economy, and Gender in Nicaragua." *Latin American Perspectives* 23, no. 1 (Winter 1996): 27–48.

———. "Negotiating Spaces: Gender, Economy, and Cultural Politics in Post-Sandinista Nicaragua." *Identities: Global Studies in Culture and Power* 4, no. 1 (May 1997): 45–69.

Chávez, Antonio. Interview with author, Managua, Nicaragua, May 8, 1991.

Einhorn, Barbara. *Cinderella Goes to the Market: Citizenship, Gender, and Women's Movements in East Central Europe.* London: Verso, 1993.

Enríquez, Laura J. *Harvesting Change: Labor and Agrarian Reform in Nicaragua, 1979–90.* Chapel Hill: University of North Carolina Press, 1991.

Escobar, Arturo. "Culture, Economics, and Politics in Latin American Social Movements Theory and Research." In *The Making of Social Movements in Latin America: Identity, Strategy, and Democracy*, edited by Arturo Escobar and Sonia E. Alvarez, 62–85. Boulder: Westview Press, 1992.

Fagen, Richard R., Carmen Diana Deere, and José Luis Coraggio, eds. *Transition and Development: Problems of Third World Socialism.* New York: Monthly Review Press, 1986.

Gibson, Bill. "A Structural Overview of the Nicaraguan Economy." In *The Political Economy of Revolutionary Nicaragua*, edited by Rose J. Spalding, 15–41. London: Allen and Unwin, 1987.

"Happy New Year from the IMF." *Envío* 12, no. 150 (January 1994): 3–9.

Hurtado de Vigil, María. Interview with author, Managua, Nicaragua, May 8, 1991.

Leguizamon, Francisco A. "The Small Business Sector in Central America: A Diagnosis." Working paper No. 46. Washington, DC: Commission for the Study of International Migration and Cooperative Economic Development, 1990.

Platteau, Stefan. Interviews with author, Managua, Nicaragua, February 24, 1992, and July 23, 1993.

"Recession Decimates Small Businesses." *Barricada Internacional* 13, no. 357 (January 1993): 7.

Reyes, Fatima. Interview with author, Managua, Nicaragua, July 18, 1991.

Ricciardi, Joseph. "Economic Policy." In *Revolution and Counterrevolution in Nicaragua*, edited by Thomas W. Walker, 247–73. Boulder: Westview Press, 1991.

Rosen, Fred, and Deidre McFadyen, eds. *Free Trade and Economic Restructuring in Latin America.* New York: Monthly Review Press, 1995.

"Separation Time." *Barricada Internacional* 15, no. 381 (January 1995): 4–5.

Spalding, Rose J. *Capitalists and Revolution in Nicaragua: Opposition and Accommodation, 1979–1993.* Chapel Hill: University of North Carolina Press, 1994.

———, ed. *The Political Economy of Revolutionary Nicaragua.* London: Allen and Unwin, 1987.

Spoor, Max. "Issues of State and Market: From Interventionism to Deregulation of Food Markets in Nicaragua." *World Development* 22, no. 4 (1994): 567–78.

Walker, Thomas W. *Nicaragua: The Land of Sandino.* Boulder: Westview Press, 1986.

Weisskopf, Thomas E. "Toward a Socialism for the Future, in the Wake of the Demise of the Socialism of the Past." *Review of Radical Political Economics* 24, no. 3/4 (1992): 1–28.

Zamora, Rubén. Foreword to *Free Trade and Economic Restructuring in Latin America*, edited by Fred Rosen and Deidre McFadyen, 7–13. New York: Monthly Review Press, 1995.

III

Restructuring Society and Nature

7

Neoliberalism and Public Education: The Relevance of the Bolivian Teachers' Strike of 1995*

Lesley Gill

The sound was unmistakable—pah! pah! pah! It rose above the din of traffic and punctuated the quotidian noises of mid-morning social life in El Alto. White smoke curled upward, wafting around buildings in the distance and dissipating in the city's thin air. "Be careful if you go outside," warned my friend and landlady, Felicidad, as we stood in the courtyard of her home. "It's the police and the teachers again."

Several days earlier, in late March 1995, thousands of striking public school teachers from the surrounding countryside arrived in El Alto, a 14,000-foot-high satellite city on the periphery of La Paz, Bolivia's capital. They had marched for days across the Bolivian high plateau to join their urban colleagues in protest against an education-reform law, but soldiers and police preempted their attempt to hold a demonstration by spraying them with rubber bullets and tear gas. In the days that followed, small bands of angry teachers, frustrated by continued police repression, staged "lightning blockades" in which they barricaded roads and interrupted traffic until police moved in to disperse them. The dismantling of one such blockade with tear gas was what Felicidad and I had heard.

Bolivia was not the only place where public education came under fire in the early months of 1995. Governor George Pataki of New York

*This paper is part of a broader project that examines the relationship between popular movements, labor unions, and nongovernmental organizations. Research was conducted in El Alto and La Paz for eight months between June 1994 and July 1995 and funded by American University, the American Council of Learned Societies, and the Aspen Institute. I would like to thank Guillermina Soria and Berta Chuquimia for their assistance.

pushed through deep cuts in his state's education budget, prompting protests by students and faculty in New York City. Nicaraguan teachers staged a forty-two-day strike to secure wage increases, and their counterparts in Haiti and Colombia mounted similar protests. These were just the latest in a rising number of demonstrations that have expressed the discontentment of public school teachers and public-sector employees.

The worldwide shift to neoliberal policies, which seek to resolve social and economic problems through an unquestioned belief in the "magic of the market," has jeopardized teachers' job security and forced state agencies to reduce the number of personnel. Declining wages and social services have simultaneously eroded the survival possibilities of peasants and poor urban dwellers, who have also resisted the assault on their living standard in a variety of settings (for example, Edelman, 1991; Walton, 1989; Nash, 1992). Yet, with few exceptions, Latin American public school teachers have not occupied a central place in the social science literature (Foweraker, 1993; Cook, 1990). Advocates of a major paradigm for explaining collective action—the so-called new social movements theory—have ignored or dismissed the "old" struggles for economic equality waged by unions and class-based organizations, which, they believe, have been largely superseded by a plethora of social movements whose goals center on forging new identities and advancing particular gender, ethnic, and cultural claims (Escóbar and Alvarez, 1992; Jelin, 1990; cf. Edelman, n.d.). In Bolivia, however, public school teachers are at the forefront of labor and popular struggles that challenge currently dominant neoliberal social and economic policies.[1]

This essay explores an eight-week national teachers' strike against a government-backed education reform law and the tensions from which it emerged. It focuses on the cities of La Paz and El Alto, where resistance to the reform is strongest. At stake for the teachers is job security and the right to continue practicing their profession amidst an eroding public education system. The government is concerned about whose vision of education will prevail at a time when international pressure has made "reform" virtually mandatory. The ferment has put enormous pressure on teachers. They must contend with a concerted effort by the state to undermine their job security, and they must confront parents for whom they are ambivalent figures. Parents frequently believe that teachers do not care about children and improving the quality of education but simply are looking out for their own selfish interests. However, parents understand that teachers—like most parents—earn paltry salaries that are inadequate for supporting a family. The experiences of Bolivian teachers are important, because they resemble those of public school teachers elsewhere.

Public Education in El Alto

Following the 1952 Bolivian national revolution, the National Revolutionary Movement (Movimiento Nacionalista Revolucionario, or MNR) supported the development of a public education system that sought to incorporate thousands of Quechua- and Aymara-speaking peasants. Free public education, its leaders believed, was not only a way to consolidate power and respond to the demands of newly enfranchised indigenous peoples but also an instrument for forging a national identity and overcoming deep ethnic and regional differences. At the same time, a number of state-sponsored teacher training schools emerged to prepare women and men for positions in the new schools. The state guaranteed jobs to graduates in a system that expanded during the 1950s. But, after a prolonged economic crisis that began in the late 1970s and a series of fiscal austerity measures adopted in 1985, public education, which was always underfunded, began to crumble. The state no longer guaranteed jobs to graduates of teacher training institutes, and the municipalization of the country in the 1990s placed much of the burden of public education on cash-strapped local governments at a time when public spending to improve urban living conditions was restricted by the International Monetary Fund. Critics claimed that these state policies would essentially privatize education in El Alto.

Bolivia is one of the poorest countries in Latin America, and today 35 percent of its six million inhabitants are functionally illiterate. In El Alto—a sprawling slum of 405,500 people—71 percent of the men and 77 percent of the women fifteen years of age or older have never completed elementary school (INE, 1990). The reasons for this situation are numerous.

El Alto is a city of poor immigrants that began to develop in the years following the 1953 agrarian reform, when the fragmentation of peasant land holdings and declining agricultural yields prompted peasants to seek jobs in La Paz. Over the last fifteen years, drought, economic crisis and the brutal effects of neoliberal reforms—wage freezes, mine and factory closures, social service cutbacks, and rising un- and underemployment—have only made life in the city more difficult. The majority of the immigrants to El Alto are peasants who have emigrated from rural areas in the hope of finding jobs and educational opportunities for their children. Others are former tin miners who lost their jobs in the mid-1980s, after the government closed state-operated mines. Still other immigrants are ex-residents of La Paz, where rising rents forced them to move to El Alto in search of cheaper accommodations. Most of the immigrants have incorporated themselves into El Alto's burgeoning informal economy of insecure, low-wage jobs, such as street vending and part-time construction work (see the Buechlers, Chapter 5, this volume).

Social services in the city have not kept pace with the burgeoning population. Rapidly expanding immigrant neighborhoods lack schools, and students from these areas must travel to other districts, where underfunded schools, inadequate and outdated instructional materials, and overcrowded classrooms of fifty to seventy students make learning next to impossible. To make matters worse, school instruction is taught in Spanish, yet Aymara and, to a lesser extent, Quechua, are the first languages of many children, who speak Spanish imperfectly, if at all. The exigencies of life in an impoverished city also contribute to high rates of school desertion. The demands of the agricultural cycle oblige children to leave school and assist rural kinfolk or parents who continue to hold small plots in the countryside. Children are also obliged to work in the city to provide an income to their cash-strapped households. Boys work as shoeshiners and assistants on the minibuses that troll the streets of the city for passengers. Girls become domestic servants, sell on the street, or remain at home to carry out household tasks and look after small children in the absence of parents.

Under these circumstances, El Alto's 18,196 public school teachers are hard pressed to deliver a quality education. They are also the products of the same deficient system and impoverished environment in which they work, and their salaries, which range from U.S.$98 to U.S.$170 a month, make satisfying the economic necessities of their own households a constant struggle. Transportation to and from work can easily cost U.S.$10 a month, and after deducting expenses for food, rent, clothing and electricity, it is not hard to understand the economic difficulties that teachers face. During a discussion of the problems of Bolivian education and the learning problems of malnourished children, Rubén Zambrano, a young teacher with a beginning salary, pointed out that teachers are also poorly nourished. "It's also a question of food," he said. "If we are not well fed, it's hard [to think about] the lessons. One falls asleep."

Because of the low salaries, teaching is widely viewed as a second-rate profession; it is not the career of choice for those with the means and the opportunities to study law, medicine, engineering and other more lucrative professions. Not surprisingly, 54 percent (2,224) of El Alto teachers are women, although in the countryside, where women rarely study beyond the third grade, teaching is dominated by men. Nearly a quarter (24.4 percent) of all El Alto teachers do not have a teaching institute degree and are congregated at the bottom of the pay scale, where they are classified as "interim teachers" (*maestros interinos*) (Unidad de Apoyo y

Seguimiento a la Reforma Educativa, or UNAS, 1994). Because of low salaries, women are either married to men who earn comparable wages, or, in the case of single parents, live with relatives who help defray some of their expenses. It is also common for teachers—men and women—to hold down two teaching jobs or engage in other activities, such as petty commerce, to support themselves.[2] But attrition due to "burn-out" is routine; almost half of El Alto's teachers have held their jobs for nine years or less (UNAS, 1994).

Clearly, the public education system is in dire need of reform, and El Alto residents, other Bolivians, and many teachers have long recognized this fact. In order to understand the controversy surrounding educational reform, however, and especially the 1994 Education Reform Law, public education and the reform legislation must be placed within the broader context of global economic restructuring.

Reform and Resistance

The impetus to reform Bolivia's educational system came during the 1992 National Congress of Education, when the National Council of Education (Consejo Nacional de Educación, or CONED) was formed to draw up a series of recommendations for a far-reaching education reform program. CONED produced a document backed by a broad consensus of labor and popular organizations that became known as the Ley Marco de la Reforma Educativa (Basic Principles for Educational Reform). Although a number of its suggestions—such as bilingual education, updated teaching methodologies, and a greater sensitivity to gender—appeared in the Education Reform Law of 1994, the law itself lacked the popular support of the Ley Marco. It was hurriedly passed by the Bolivian Congress, which took a dim view of the social groups aligned behind the Ley Marco, and which was under pressure from the World Bank to approve the law. Indeed, the Education Reform Law, passed on July 7, 1994, bore the heavy imprint of the Technical Support Group of the Education Reform (Equipo Técnico de Apoyo a la Reforma Educativa, or ETARE), a World Bank-sponsored, technical advisory group that submitted its own recommendations to the government for transforming public education (Codina, 1994).

The World Bank is financing many of the changes mandated by the new law, especially at the primary level. It has increased spending on primary school education in Bolivia and elsewhere as a way to increase the future productivity of Third World labor forces, make them more attractive to business and promote economic growth through investment in "human capital" (World Bank, 1993). To this end, the Bolivian Education Reform Law is designed to deepen the free market policies crafted by

President Gonzalo "Goni" Sanchez de Lozada. It emphasizes primary schooling and technical training at the secondary level. And, although not directly stated, the law seeks to reduce the state bureaucracy by eliminating teachers, whose salaries and benefits account for 95 percent of the state's education budget, and to generate greater productivity from the remaining teaching staff, by requiring higher professional standards. It also contains a series of statutes that demean the teaching profession and undermine the job security of public school teachers.

Teacher training school graduates, once classified as professionals, are recategorized as "superior technicians" (*técnicos superiores*), and hiring, job retention, and promotion under the new law are determined by the results of a competency examination, to be taken within five years time. Teachers are, in principle, not opposed to higher professional standards, and those interviewed for this study want to further their professional development by taking university courses, yet the state is not serious in assisting them to meet new goals. Thus, teachers argue, the exams will gradually thin their ranks because they will be unable to perform well on them.

Noel Aguirre is a thirty-three-year-old elementary school teacher who has taught in an El Alto primary school for eleven years. To supplement his salary and support his three children, Aguirre also works afternoons in a private school, where his wife teaches. He fully supports the idea of an educational reform but cannot afford the time off to take the courses that he needs to pass the competency exam. Moreover, his exhausting schedule leaves him little time to study. Aguirre's day begins at 8:30 A.M. and ends between 5 and 6 P.M. His classes typically contain fifty to seventy-five children, who completely drain him by the end of the day. "I leave school totally exhausted," he explains. "I don't have energy for anything. And my wife feels the same way. So she's tired; I'm tired; and both of us have little interest in the children. The kids make noise, and we get mad because we have absolutely no more energy. After a little dinner and some coffee we fall into bed so we can get up the next day and start the same routine all over again." In addition, Aguirre lives in a new settlement on the outer perimeter of El Alto, and traveling to the university in central La Paz for evening classes would take an hour to an hour and a half in each direction. "Give me time," he states emphatically, "but the government will not do this for us."

Teachers' suspicions of government intentions are only deepened by the law's contribution to undermining their union. The law makes it more difficult for the union to raise money by eliminating a 1 percent payroll deduction that is used to support union activities. Teacher Alex Morales—

the director of education and culture for El Alto's Regional Workers' Central—believes that the government wants to break the union, which is a constant thorn in its side. "[The government's behavior] is not gratuitous," he says. "The fewer unions that [the government] has before it, the easier it will be to implement neoliberal policy. A union without financial support cannot survive, because nothing is free." El Alto teacher Antonio Sanchez concurs. "The government wants to disappear the union."[3] Teachers also resent changes in the control of schools that take autonomy away from the teaching body by encouraging local entities to assume an active role in monitoring teachers and spending. Victor Prado, executive secretary of the Urban Teachers' Confederation, summarized the changes as ". . . an administrative reform and not [a reform] of education in general" (Painter, 1995: 4).

Opposition to the reform began to build nationwide immediately after its passage in July 1994, and a twenty-four-hour strike on February 10, 1995, only ten days after the initiation of the school year, was a harbinger of deeper strife. Many Bolivians saw this conflict as the opening gambit in what, they thought, would be a series of protests, strikes and negotiations between teachers and the state that had come to be almost routine at the start of every year. But 1995 was not like past years. In addition to the usual demands for wage increases, teachers insisted that the government repeal the Education Reform Law and thereby challenged a key element of the government's neoliberal doctrine.

Teachers' resolve to resist the law mounted throughout February and March. After two additional twenty-four-hour strikes in February, the union, on March 13, declared an indefinite national strike to force the government to repeal the reform and attend to their wage demands. They were supported by the Bolivian Workers' Central (Central Obrera Boliviana, or COB)—a national confederation of unions—which, on March 22, announced an indefinite general strike, after negotiations with the government deadlocked over a series of issues, including the education reform, minimum wage increases, and coca cultivation in the Chapare region. Although support for the general strike was weak, teachers in La Paz and El Alto, as well as those in the surrounding countryside, were generally supportive of it.

In the following weeks, the government used various tactics to pressure teachers back to work, including threatening to hire replacement workers and refusing to pay wages. The Education Ministry disseminated misinformation about the strength of the strike, exaggerating the extent to which teachers were working and ignoring the call to strike. Whenever they had a chance, government functionaries tried to isolate and discredit union leaders by branding them "Trotskyist extremists" and "dictatorial." When none of these tactics worked, the government reverted to overt repression.

On March 22, when rural teachers converged on El Alto, they were met with police and military troops. Soldiers wielding batons and shooting tear gas and rubber bullets broke up the march and arrested leaders. A week later, eighty thousand residents of El Alto, responding to a call by the COB, marched through the city, demanding that the government attend to their demands for wage increases, respect for peasant coca growers, and a repeal of the Education Reform Law. Unwilling to negotiate but threatened by the teachers' challenge and ongoing conflicts with peasant coca growers, the government, on April 18, declared a state of siege. Police rounded up over three hundred peasant and labor leaders and shipped them off to isolated prisons in the lowland jungles and frontier regions. A curfew was imposed, any meetings of more than three people were prohibited, and civil rights were suspended.

Coordinating the strike in the days that followed proved difficult. Union meetings were outlawed and all the major leaders were either in prison or in hiding. Rank-and-file teachers were also uncertain about how far the government would carry its campaign against them, and many were feeling the financial crunch of a strike that had already lasted five weeks. On the morning after the imposition of the state of siege, however, teachers began meeting clandestinely in their schools with local union delegates to assess the situation and plot a strategy for the days ahead. One such meeting occurred in the Colegio San Salvador.

Forging Solidarity in the Colegio San Salvador[4]

The Colegio San Salvador is a primary school in La Paz's northern zone, an area that, until recently, housed light manufacturing industries and an urban working class. Much of the industry is gone now and residents must make their living in the ubiquitous informal sector. Some 540 children attend the school, which is only two blocks from the headquarters of an elite army battalion, and they are taught by a twenty-nine-member teaching staff that, with only three exceptions, is all women.

Eleven of these women teachers gathered, nervously, in the school's courtyard on the morning of April 19. Earlier that morning their school representative was to have attended a city-wide meeting of union delegates to vote on continuing the strike, but the state of siege and the police occupation of the union hall precluded any type of major assembly. Although the San Salvador staff had met regularly in the school since the beginning of the strike, this meeting was clearly different. Individuals cast uneasy glances every time a new arrival knocked at the door, fearing that the police would break in and arrest them. One woman counseled others to tell the police, if they should appear, that the teachers were simply waiting for students to arrive. Indeed, on imposing the state of siege the night before, the government had ordered the teachers back to work and threatened to fire them and hire replacement workers if they did not obey.

Because of the uncertainty created by the state of siege, some teachers did not risk coming to school that day, but others, according to several women present, were simply treating the strike "like a vacation." These teachers, who supplemented their paltry wages with petty commerce, were using the freedom from teaching that the strike provided to dedicate themselves to their commercial activities. Those present, however, did not have other jobs and were borrowing money and relying on the support of spouses and relatives to see themselves through the strike. They wanted to discuss the implications of the state of siege, allay each others' fears, and, more than anything else, decide whether or not to continue the strike in light of the latest government actions.

The meeting was directed by Berta Choque, a single mother, who, in recent days, had been raising money to feed her child by selling a powdered milk allotment that the state provides to needy mothers. Choque was also the school's de facto union delegate. She had been the official representative for eight years but resigned after the birth of her child. The staff subsequently delegated the union responsibility to Etna Romero, an unlikely candidate because, as one teacher complained, "she is too influenced by the officialist views of her husband." Romero also had a reputation for acting against group decisions in the past. Yet, by imposing the job on her, teachers had hoped to develop Romero's sense of responsibility and involvement and limit her disruptive behavior. The success of this tactic, however, was not evident on April 19. Romero did not attend the meeting, and Berta Choque assumed her old responsibilities, which she had never entirely abandoned.

The first person to speak was Maria del Carmen Méndez, a forty-year-old woman with twenty-two years of teaching experience. Like other teachers in her position, Méndez resented being forced to take a competency examination after years on the job, but she expressed doubts about continuing the strike. "We have to analyze how far we are willing to go," she said. "After all, we depend on our work and don't want to go to such extremes as to get fired en masse and replaced by high school graduates." Other women expressed similar reservations, but to these people, Inés Velasco, a fifty-year-old widow, counseled caution and a wait-and-see attitude. Given the peripheral location of the Colegio San Salvador, she did not think that its teachers would be the first fired if, in fact, the government carried through with its threat. She urged those present to continue evaluating the situation one day at a time and not to be intimidated. After more discussion, the women agreed to continue the strike but resolved to meet again in three days' time to reassess their position. Choque and Vilma Peralta, the school's director, stressed the importance of frequent meetings, in spite of the state of siege, so teachers will not feel isolated and become susceptible to government propaganda.

Later that week, on Friday, April 21, the teachers met again. This time a majority was present, and anxieties ran high. Although the government had not fired anyone, the Ministry of Education continued to make threats. It announced that pay vouchers would be distributed the following Monday only to those teachers who showed up for work and that salaries would be discounted for every day of the strike. At the same time, radio stations sympathetic to the strikers broadcast statements from union leaders in jail or hiding that urged teachers to maintain the strike. The Colegio San Salvador teachers once again found themselves at a crossroad, where they had to make a decision that could potentially affect their jobs and their futures. And again, opinions were divided over the best course of action.

One young woman dressed in blue jeans indicated that other schools were slowly returning to work and that the Colegio San Salvador should do the same. Nanci, the school secretary and a widow from El Alto, declared that she would show up at 8:30 A.M. Monday so that nobody could fire her, and a woman seated next to her quickly asserted that she would do the same. Etna Romero, present for the first time since the state of siege, also felt that teachers should return to work.

The more radical teachers again counseled patience and caution. As she had done before, Inés Velasco advised people to come on Monday to evaluate the situation and make a decision based on developments in the rest of the city. By being present, she argued, they would be able to defend their jobs, but that did not mean that they had to teach, which, she felt, should not happen until the entire rank and file voted to end the strike and jailed leaders were released. Berta Choque and Vilma Peralta supported this position. In a subtle rebuke to those threatening to act on their own, Choque suggested that everyone arrive together on Monday at 8:30 A.M., so as to maintain unity. Solidarity, she stressed, was crucial. Why, she asked, should they return to work if the government discounted their paychecks? Given the length of the strike to date, they still would be left with virtually nothing. She further argued that nobody would be fired on the first day of a supposed return to work; only after a majority of schools had gone back, she claimed, would this really happen. Choque concluded by urging people to take with a grain of salt government claims about schools ending the strike. The Colegio San Salvador, she pointed out, was part of a list of schools broadcast on television that had supposedly reinitiated classes.

As teachers argued back and forth, several of the women present remained silent. One of them, Elia Ormachea, was deeply conflicted about the strike and her participation in it. As the mother of three children, Ormachea was having difficulty keeping food on the table. She was already in debt, and supplies that she had stockpiled after the last strike were running out. Ormachea was also a devout Seventh Day Adventist and acting against her religious beliefs by participating in a strike. "We [the Adventists] are supposed to support God and the authorities," she said in an earlier conversation, "therefore when I participate in a demonstration, I can't shout insults because we respect the authorities. More than anything, I go to avoid the fine that the union levies against those who do not participate." Why, then, would she risk imprisonment by attending an illegal meeting? "I have to support my compañeros," she said. "I obey whatever they decide so as not to divide us. It's a little conflictive for me." Given these contradictions in her own position, Ormachea did not venture any opinions, one way or the other, during the meeting, and other women, less torn by their religious beliefs, but insecure about expressing themselves in the debate, also remained on the sidelines.

The teachers once again decided to continue the strike, persuaded, in large measure, by the arguments of Choque and Velasco. They also resolved to continue meeting periodically. But their next meeting never occurred. As the teachers assembled a week later, an anonymous phone caller tipped them off about an imminent police raid. Alarmed by the call, people quickly dispersed, except Choque and director Peralta, who eventually discovered that the call was a hoax, perpetrated by an irate parent angered by the teachers' continued refusal to end the strike.

Parents and Teachers

Parents in the poor and working class neighborhoods of El Alto and La Paz are deeply committed to the education of their children. Education, they believe, is a road out of poverty and a way to insure a more secure future. Therefore, parents frequently make great sacrifices for education. Those who can afford the expense send their children to a growing number of private schools, where, they say, the quality of education is often no better, and sometimes worse, than the public schools. However, classes are never disrupted by the constant strikes that plague the public system since teachers are not unionized and are subjected to rigid administrative discipline. The vast majority of parents cannot furnish their children with the luxury of a private school education. They must make do with the public system, where labor unrest disrupts the educational process and, according to many parents, teachers are poorly prepared to exercise their profession. Given their views on education, parents' feelings about the strike understandably are mixed.

Those parents who back the teachers appreciate that they earn low salaries, and many fear that the Education Reform Law is an attempt to abolish public education. These parents may have also suffered from tear gas entering their homes during the frequent clashes between police and striking teachers in their neighborhoods. For these reasons, they support the teachers demands and are highly critical of the reform and the government's heavy-handed tactics. Women like Francisca Mendoza, whose six children attend public school and whose eldest son teaches in a public school, support the strikers because her son's wages are key to the survival of her household. "He has to strike because his wages are not enough," she explains. Taxi-driver Fermín Ortega, whose two children attend public school, also backs the strike. "The government isn't interested in solving anything," he says. "[Everything it does] is with bullets and gas."

Other parents, however, deeply resent teachers and feel that their children are the primary victims of the strike. Like all parents, they want their children educated by well-trained professionals, but they are not satisfied with teachers' professional behavior or their qualifications. The irregular attendance record of teachers is a constant complaint voiced by them. Teachers, they say, typically extend school vacations by failing to appear on the days preceding and following official holidays. Weekends also generate high attrition on Monday mornings, and when teachers do show up, they are invariably late. This, say angry parents, is unprofessional conduct that should be sanctioned by the state.

The teaching profession is also an avenue of upward mobility, despite the proletarian salaries, especially for individuals in rural areas and urban immigrant slums. It confers a higher social status than that of day laborer or peasant and enables individuals to distance themselves from their peasant and Indian backgrounds. Many parents and students charge that teachers who have obtained this limited social mobility discriminate against their own people by denigrating the Aymara language and becoming abusive and authoritarian in the classroom. To them, teachers appear less as the exploited victims of an unjust state policy than as domineering social climbers.

The strike, for these parents, was not about improving education for their children; it reflected the intransigency and self-serving attitudes of teachers and their union. The elderly grandmother of five students at the Colegio San Salvador was disturbed by the teachers' refusal to return to work. "My grandchildren are tired of playing," she fumed. "They want to go back to school." This woman, who sold sweets in front of the school, was also distressed by the strike because business at her small stand had dropped off dramatically with the suspension of classes. Another angry mother complained that "a year never passes with normal classes. There are always strikes and that is why public education is viewed so poorly. The teachers never agree with anything that the government says. They're really not so badly paid given the number of hours that they work, and they get two long vacations a year. Any other public employee has to work all day long." She further criticized the low professional qualifications of public school teachers. "They call themselves professionals," she said, "but many have not gone to the normal school."

Parents' divided opinions about the strike were reflected in the Federation of Parents of El Alto, an organization that represents a majority of the parents of public school children. The Federation, which is dominated by members of an opposition political party—Conscience of the Fatherland (Conciencia de la Patria, or CONDEPA)—and belongs to the COB, supported the teachers insofar as their demands for higher wages were concerned, but it refused to call for the repeal of the education reform legislation. The Federation backed the Education Reform Law because it believed that the law would compel teachers to improve themselves. It was also sympathetic to the notion that parents should have more control over the education of their children. As one Federation leader explained, "We must realize that there are teachers who are not even high school graduates. These people have encrusted themselves onto the current struggle as a way of blocking changes to the system. They are never going to agree with the reform, because they are the ones who will never pass the test. . . . They entered the profession through political favoritism, . . . or family connections." Desperate parents in several local-level affiliations organized funds to pay teachers to work during the strike, but because of union vigilance, they were generally not successful in getting them back to work.

The government's intransigence and repression finally prevailed. The COB called off the nationwide general strike on April 30, when three leaders, operating clandestinely and without consulting the rank-and-file, signed an agreement with the government. Without the COB's support, the teachers had little choice but to follow suit. They could not hold out indefinitely without a strike fund, and the eight-week strike had already exacted a high price from teachers and their families. It was a crushing defeat: not only did the Education Reform Law remain intact but teachers were not even sure that their lost wages would be paid. Teachers' union leaders—the most radical in the Bolivian labor movement—were irate and accused COB leaders of selling out the movement. Rank-and-file teachers also felt disillusioned that their long weeks of sacrifice had brought nothing.

Conclusion

The debate about public education is likely to continue whether or not the current education reform law is repealed. Shorter work stoppages continue in the wake of the strike; opposition to the Education Reform Law remains strong; and government officials and labor leaders are discussing possible revisions of the law, albeit not its total repeal. Despite its failure to completely reverse the reform, the teachers' strike galvanized a level of popular support in El Alto and the poor neighborhoods of La Paz that has not been seen in the recent past. Former executive secretary of the COB and peasant leader Genáro Flores found reason for hope in the popular response. "[The strike] was not a total defeat. In the past, it was the miners who fought for the poor and the working class. Now it is the teachers, and the population supported them and understood that it is not just a wage problem. The strike was a way for people to reorganize themselves and become [more] conscious of the problems with education in Bolivia. The reform came very quickly without anyone really understanding what it was about, because it's a project of the International Monetary Fund and the World Bank" (Flores, interview, May 1995).

Contrary to one sector of public opinion in La Paz, teachers did not oppose the law because they were against reforming education in Bolivia. Rather, they were struggling to protect the few shreds of job security that remain after more than a decade of neoliberal reforms in Bolivia and to preserve their dignity as teachers.

The strike and teachers' conceptions of themselves demonstrate that class remains a central organizing dimension in the conflicts over public education. Contary to the views of new social movement theorists, class is not just one of a multiplicity of "identities," nor can it be consigned to the dustbin of history by linking it to the "old" labor movement, which other kinds of social movements have ostensibly surpassed. Although new social movement theorists have shown that a narrow, class-based perspective is insufficient for understanding the complexities of collective action, they have unwisely jettisoned the concept altogether. But, as Genáro Flores indicates, class-based struggles and organizations in Bolivia have an enduring history, and they are key to understanding how people conceptualize themselves and their ongoing relationships to others. "Class," according to Argentine sociologist Carlos Vilas, "doesn't replace . . . other identities, nor does it necessarily take precedence over them. Rather, it organizes them" (Vilas, 1993: 39).

The Bolivian teachers' strike not only promoted greater consciousness of the class warfare that the International Monetary Fund, the World Bank, and the Bolivian government are waging against teachers and poor urban dwellers and peasants, but it also intensified the debate about racism and teacher accountability in the public school system. Building solidarity in the future will depend upon the ability of teachers, parents, and students to engage in discussions about educational quality, professional responsibility, and cultural integrity as well as the broader issues of political and economic inequality that shape public education. Skeptics need to be convinced that teachers are genuinely concerned about educating children, who also bear the brunt of the public education system's numerous inadequacies, and that they are, indeed, the champions of a public education system that is currently threatened by the reformist zeal of neoliberal planners in state agencies and distant international organizations.

Notes

1. The peasant coca growers of the Chapare region are also defending their right to grow coca in the face of increasing U.S. pressure to eradicate coca fields and eliminate a major source of primary material for the international cocaine traffic. Their protests multiplied in 1995 after the United States intensified pressure on the Bolivian government to eradicate coca fields and were also a major factor in the government's decision to impose a state of siege (see Painter, Chapter 2, this volume).

2. Ricardo Humerez Machicado has even suggested that because teachers are forced to have alternative sources of income to survive, their strikes are more successful in achieving stated goals, especially in the absence of a union strike fund. Teachers, he argues, rely on these alternatives during a strike and are thus able to hold out longer than workers dependent on only one source of income. However, Humerez Machicado is critical of a system that forces teachers to have other means of support, because they are essentially subsidizing public education with their low wages (Humerez Machicado, 1995: 2).

3. The use of "disappear" as an active verb came into use in Latin America during the era of military dictatorships in the 1970s and 1980s. "To disappear" refers to the way that people were kidnapped and murdered by military and paramilitary death squads, who subsequently denied any knowledge of the victims' whereabouts.

4. The names of the school and the teachers have been changed.

References

Codina, Gabriel. "Los rostros de la reforma educativa." *Cuarto Intermedio*, no. 33 (November 1994): 26–45.

Cook, Maria Lorena. "Organizing Opposition in the Teachers' Movement in Oaxaca." In *Popular Movements and Political Change in Mexico*, edited by Joe Foweraker and Ann L. Craig, 199–212. Boulder, CO: Lynne Rienner, 1990.

Edelman, Marc. "Shifting Legitimacies and Economic Change: The State and Contemporary Costa Rican Peasant Movements." *Peasant Studies* 18 (1991): 221–49.

———. "Defying the Invisible Hand: Peasant Politics and the Free Market in Costa Rica." Unpublished manuscript, n.d.

Escóbar, Arturo, and Sonia Alvarez. *The Making of Social Movements in Latin America*. Boulder: Westview Press, 1992.

Flores, Genáro. Interview with author, La Paz, Bolivia, May 1995.

Foweraker, Joe. *Popular Mobilization in Mexico: The Teachers' Movement, 1977–1987*. New York: Cambridge University Press, 1993.

Humerez Machicado, Ricardo. "Por que tienen éxito las huelgas del magisterio." *Presencia* (June 13, 1995): 2.

Instituto Nacional de Estadistica (INE). *Censo nacional de población y vivienda*. La Paz, Bolivia: INE, 1990.

Jelin, Elizabeth. *Women and Social Change in Latin America*. London: Zed, 1990.

Nash, June. "Interpreting Social Movements: Bolivian Resistance to Economic Conditions Imposed by the International Monetary Fund." *American Ethnologist* 19, no. 2 (May 1992): 275–93.

Painter, Michael. "Maestros cuestionan espíritu de Ley de Reforma Educativa." *Presencia* (March 29, 1995): 4.

Unidad de Apoyo y Seguimiento a la Reforma Educativa (UNAS). *Registro de docentes y personal administrativo*. La Paz, Bolivia: UNAS, 1994.

Vilas, Carlos. "The Hour of Civil Society." *NACLA Report on the Americas* 27, no. 2 (1993): 38–42.

Walton, John. "Debt, Protest, and the State in Latin America." In *Power and Popular Protest: Latin American Social Movements*, edited by Susan Eckstein, 299–328. Berkeley: University of California Press, 1989.

World Bank. *Annual Report*. Washington, DC: World Bank, 1993.

8

Vital Signs: The Dynamics of Folk Medicine in Northwestern Argentina

Constance Classen and David Howes*

Northwestern Argentina borders on Chile to the west and Bolivia to the north. The region was once part of the Inca empire and participates in a general pan-Andean culture with local variations. The language spoken is Spanish, inflected by words and modalities from Quechua (with pockets of Quechua-speakers present in the province of Santiago del Estero). The region is primarily agricultural, producing sugar cane and citrus fruits among other crops.

In the Northwest, traditional or folk medicine combines indigenous healing practices with colonial Spanish medicine and other more recent influences. While the ethnomedicine of the region is a syncretism of traditions rather than a purely "indigenous" body of knowledge and practice, the people who make use of it treat it as an integral whole and a valued part of their cultural heritage.

Within the increasingly heterogenous medical marketplace of global society, the place of ethnomedicine, and the relationship between "traditional" medicine and "modern" biomedicine, constitute important areas of research. It has been noted that the postmodern condition of the late twentieth century is characterized by, among other things, a mélange of styles and trends from various cultures, producing sometimes conflicting influences of modernity and postmodernity on Latin America (Canglini,

*Among the many people who helped us during our stays in Argentina, we would like to express our special thanks to Emilia Núñez de Fritsch, Francisco Maza, Simona Moya de Maza, Luís Acosta, Cristina Contreras, Elsa Núñez de Battich, the Quiroga family, and the Sturla family. The field research on which this essay is based was made possible by a grant from the Social Sciences and Humanities Research Council of Canada. An earlier version of parts of this essay was published in *The International Journal of Aromatherapy* 5, no. 4 (1993/94): 19–23.

1995). While the processes of modernization have displaced traditional medicine in Northwestern Argentina, this essay explores the possibility that the ostensibly pluralist ethos of postmodernity has permitted space for the growth and development of ethnomedical practices and beliefs.

The Vocation of *Curandero*

In Argentina, ethnomedical practitioners are commonly known as *curanderos* and may be either men or women. They customarily learn their trade as apprentices to other *curanderos*, often a parent or grandparent, although many healers will state that they were born with the gift or that their ability to heal came to them through some transformative experience, such as being struck by lightning. A *curandero* will often have passed middle age before he or she begins practicing, as an indication of the responsibility which healing is understood to entail. The better-known *curanderos* can draw patients from great distances and may receive substantial monetary rewards for their assistance. However, most *curanderos* do not live off their medical practice, but rather dispense their aid as a favor to their neighbors in return for small gifts.

Attaining information from *curanderos* about their techniques of healing can be difficult since they are often secretive about their practices. This secrecy is due in part to a desire to prevent competition and in part to an association of secrecy with healing power. Furthermore, official attempts to suppress folk medicine have made *curanderos* reticent to reveal information about their practice. Once they overcame their initial suspicions, most of the *curanderos* interviewed were quite willing to discuss their methods of healing, although they were never pressed to reveal practices that they wished to keep secret.

The desire for secrecy increased proportionally with the renown of a *curandero*'s practice. In such cases it is probable that the high demand for their services, together with the occasional media interview, had taught the *curanderos* to regard their medical knowledge both as a personal possession and a potentially valuable commodity. The less-known or more remote *curanderos*, however, were apt to treat their knowledge as part of a common fund of folk wisdom, with the exception of certain "words of power," which were believed to require secrecy in order to be effective.

The *curanderos* interviewed for this essay lived primarily in the small mountain towns of the Northwest, although a selection of *curanderos* and their patients in the cities of the region were also surveyed. The information given to us by the various *curanderos*, whether male or female, and by their patients largely agreed, indicating a broadly shared understand-

ing of illness and its treatments. While many *curanderos* are general practitioners in that they treat a wide range of ailments, they may also spe-
cialize in one form of treatment. One common example of a folk-healing
specialist is the bonesetter, who both sets broken bones and treats such
ailments as arthritis or backache through massage. An annual visit to such
a bonesetter for a "work over" is said to keep one's skeleton in good
working order. Other *curanderos* may treat only toothaches or the "evil
eye."[1]

Since the illnesses diagnosed and treated by *curanderos* are consis-
tent with popular or folk models of health and disease, they are not always compatible with biomedical models. The folk model of disease often
includes fluid boundaries among physiological, spiritual, and social ailments. Indeed, virtually any sensation of unwellness comes under the
domain of the *curandero*, and not simply physiological disorders. Common folk illnesses such as *mal ojo* (the evil eye), *susto* (fright), and *mal
aire* (bad air) are considered to affect a person both in body and spirit.
Problems apparently social or economic in origin, such as unemployment,
may also be included within the general model of illness and treated by
the *curandero*. Treatment typically includes prayers, vitalizing teas, and
protective amulets designed to fortify the individual in his or her areas of
weakness and integrate the person into a network of positive energy.

Folk models of the organization and functions of the human body in
Northwestern Argentina are likewise often incompatible with the structural and functional paradigms of the body posited by biomedicine. A
good example of this incompatibility is the *paletilla*, which is held by
ethnomedicine to be a small bone suspended from the point of the ster-
num. This bone is said to occasionally become loose and sink or fall,
causing grave illness. Biomedicine does not recognize the existence of
such a migrant bone, and, in fact, the *paletilla* has become a literal "bone
of contention" between practitioners of the two forms of medicine in the
region. That physicians do not recognize the role of the *paletilla* in illness is taken by *curanderos* to signal the limits of biomedical knowledge.
Conversely, that *curanderos* deem the *paletilla* capable of causing disease is taken by physicians as evidence of the fanciful and unfounded
nature of ethnomedicine.

These differences in opinion over the basic organization of the body
between the community of *curanderos* and the community of physicians
are indicative of the extent to which the body is a cultural object, subject
to widely different constructions. However, it must be recognized that
body models are not static—as is a diagram in a medical textbook—in
either ethnomedicine or biomedicine but are continually adapted and re-
interpreted according to new concerns and developments.

Healing through the Senses

What holds true for the body also holds true for the senses, the media through which we experience our bodies and the world outside. While possessed of a basic physiological form, the senses are endowed with meaning and employed according to cultural dictates. This "cultural construction" of the senses means that societies can differ significantly in the ways in which they perceive and make sense of the world (Howes, 1991; Classen, 1993b).

In the case of the ethnomedicine of Northwestern Argentina, the different senses play distinct roles in both the diagnosis and treatment of illness. Diverse methods of diagnosis are used by *curanderos* in the Northwest. The patient's narrative of symptoms is usually an important factor in the arrival at a diagnosis. It is supplemented by the information gathered by the *curandero* from a number of other sensory diagnostic techniques.

Certain healers, for example, diagnose primarily by looking at and smelling a sample of a patient's urine. The *curandero* notes whether the urine is cloudy or clear, light or dark, and may observe the pattern cast by a ray of light passing through the urine. Other healers diagnose by reading the pulse, or by examining the form of the hand, the shape of the fingers and knuckles, and the temperature of the skin.

Divinatory aids may also be employed to determine the cause of the illness. A handful of coca leaves, for example, may be thrown on a table to provide a "reading." The shapes of the individual leaves as well as the position in which they fall are said to offer information about the patient. A *curandero* may also define a patient's illness by watching the flickering of a candle flame for supposedly telltale signs relating to the patient's condition. Alternatively the patient's body may be rubbed with wool that is then thrown into the fire. The resulting colors, forms, and cracklings are interpreted by the *curandero* (Palma, 1973: 77–82). The mode or modes of diagnosis employed by a *curandero* depend on his or her personal preference and training and the suspected illness of the patient.

As with the methods of diagnosis, the treatments employed by the *curanderos* of the Northwest have a strong sensory foundation. The *curandero* is attentive to colors, forms, sounds, smells, and tactile sensations according to the particular methods employed. In treatment the patient absorbs a similar range of sensory stimuli, from an aromatic tea to a massage with herbal ointments.

In the case of a serious illness, an attempt will often be made to treat the patient through all of her or his senses. Such is the case with *susto—*

fright sickness—a common ailment in the region, as in other parts of Latin America. *Susto* is said to occur when a person suffers a strong fright, which has the effect of separating the soul from the body. In the countryside, coming close to being struck by lightning is cited as a typical event that will result in *susto*. In the cities, almost being hit by a car may produce *susto*. In the case of children, the most frequent sufferers of *susto*, simply wandering alone outside after dusk is thought to be enough to result in a "soul loss."

A person affected by *susto* will feel weak and nervous, may spend long periods crying, and may also have bouts of vomiting. The *curandero* usually visits the place where the fright occurred, if nearby, and attempts to lure the soul back to its body by calling out the name of the patient. The *curandero* will also drag a piece of the patient's clothing on the ground to leave a trail for the soul to follow home. During this ceremony it is important that there be complete silence, for even the bark of a dog is said to be enough to scare the already frightened soul away again.[2]

In the meantime, the patient will have been treated with a range of therapies. The sufferer from *susto* is kept warm in bed and given hot, aromatic herbal tea to drink. Incense composed of a variety of substances, such as rosemary, rue, sugar, and dust, is burned. This incense has multiple purposes, including those of soothing the patient, attracting the wandering soul, and keeping away evil spirits. The patient's body is carefully massaged according to specific techniques in order to assuage the physical consequences of *susto*. Prayers to the Pachamama, "Mother Earth," and to a number of saints invoke divine aid on behalf of the patient. Finally, a bright red charm, often in the form of a bracelet, may be used to strengthen the patient's resistance to evil forces. This multisensory therapy creates a pleasant aesthetic environment in order to encourage healing. At the same time it integrates the patient into the healing process through all of her or his senses.

Aromatic Cures

Andean healers have traditionally had access to a wide variety of plants for their cures due to the nature of the Andean environment, which supports very different plant life at different altitudes, and the varying amounts of precipitation that fall from region to region (Lira, 1985; Villafuerte, 1984). Aromatic plants are administered to patients by *curanderos* in a variety of ways, the most common method being in the form of a tea. For example, *muña muña*, a strong, musky-smelling shrub, is made into tea to alleviate stomachaches. *Muña muña* is also said to be an aphrodisiac—its

Quechua name, in fact, means "love." Such teas are believed to work upon the patient both through being swallowed and through their aromatic vapors.

Aromatic plants may also be burned to produce an incense, called *sahumerio*. Such incense, in addition to being inhaled, is thought to penetrate the whole body of the patient. Sometimes incense will consist of only one substance. For example, rosemary incense is said to be good for head colds. More often, however, an incense will be composed of several ingredients. For instance, an incense consisting of rue, anise, black wool, and eucalyptus was said to have cured a patient suffering from a postpartum illness.

While odors are thought able to cure diseases, they are also believed to be able to cause them.[3] The general name for air-borne illnesses is *mal aire* (bad air). *Mal aire* is a vapor or emanation thought to be present in places containing stale air, such as caves, and where there is putrefaction, such as swamps or cemeteries. Certain trees are also believed to give off a *mal aire*, which infects those who rest in their shade.

The primary symptoms of *mal aire* are a stiffness in the body or a rash. *Mal aire* is often treated with incense, such as tobacco smoke, or by the application of an aromatic ointment. The foul emanation of *mal aire* is countered by strong-smelling herbs in the belief that the "good air" administered by the *curandero* will drive out the harmful "bad air." Through this economy of odors, the *curandero* is able to augment the patient's olfactory vitality.

The importance assigned to odors in the medicine of this region can be seen as evidence both of a "non-modern" understanding of odors as sources of disease and well-being and of an Andean preoccupation with olfactory sensations. The Quechua language, for example, contains a wide range of verbs describing subtle variations in olfactory experience. Such verbs include terms meaning "to smell a good odor," "to smell a bad odor," "to smell the traces of an odor," "to make someone smell an odor," "to let oneself be smelled," and "to smell something as a group." The prominence given to smell is due to its close association with the breath and therefore with the life force (Classen, 1993a: 165–66).

The sensory dimensions of the ethnomedicine practiced in Northwestern Argentina are similar in many ways to those found in colonial Spanish medicine and among certain folk healers in contemporary Europe (Howes, 1995). Before the advent of clinical biomedicine in the late eighteenth century, European physicians and folk healers alike made use of such sensory therapies as incense, herbal teas, and aromatic baths. Diagnosis would likewise usually be undertaken through various sensory channels. Galen, the primary medical authority for premodern physicians, recommended that a physician use all his senses to examine a patient: hearing, to listen to the patient's narrative and to attend to the gurgling of the intestines or the trembling of the voice; smell, to assess the odors emanating from the patient's body and excretions; touch, to take the pulse and temperature; sight, to examine the patient's appearance and living conditions; and taste, to sample the patient's sweat and thereby ascertain the balance of the humors in the patient's body (each of the four humors being associated, and sometimes identified, with a corresponding flavor) (Nutton, 1993).

By contrast, in modern biomedicine, diagnosis and treatment are largely desensualized. The thermometer substitutes for a hand on the forehead as a means of ascertaining body temperature. Charts, graphs, x-rays, and chemical analyses provide graphic information hitherto ascertained, if much less exactly, directly through the senses. Treatment consists of pills to be swallowed—without being tasted if the patient can avoid it— or surgery, during which the patient is anaesthetized. Rather than being an important agent in the healing process, the senses are usually bypassed as much as possible in modern medicine. Thus, the involvement of the senses constitutes a fundamental distinction between ethnomedicine and biomedicine.

Folk Medicine and Modernization

It has often been assumed that biomedicine would supplant traditional medical systems throughout the world since this medical revolution was generally thought to be beneficial. While ethnomedicine might be appreciated as a form of folklore, biomedicine was believed both to offer the best system of health care in the world and to play an essential role in Third World development. However, at the end of the twentieth century it is evident that the universalization of modern medicine is by no means assured. One apparent reason for this is that modern medicine is too capital-intensive for many Third World peoples to afford, requiring massive investment in hospitals, technologies, and the training of physicians (Bastien, 1992: 12). Another less expected reason is that biomedicine, in its spread across the world, has proved unable to displace ethnomedicine. Two distinct tendencies have contributed to the continuing survival and reinvention of ethnomedical practices in areas where biomedicine has been made available. The first is the adherence of local peoples to their own medical systems. The second is the growing interest shown by users of modern medicine in folk therapies.

In Northwestern Argentina the availability of modern health care services has not resulted in the elimination of traditional practices of healing. In fact, as in many other regions of Latin America, the inhabitants
are likely to resort to both ethnomedical and biomedical practitioners at
different times, rather than exclusively patronizing one system or the other.
Furthermore, the movement of rural populations into urban areas over
the past decades has increased the number of folk healers available to
urban dwellers—normally the consumers of biomedicine—just as the establishment of biomedical clinics in rural areas has made biomedicine
more accessible for country dwellers—normally the consumers of
ethnomedicine. Thus, the current health care scene in Northwestern Argentina is marked by strong medical pluralism.

Although most people interviewed recognized various advantages to
modern medical treatment, and even its necessity on certain occasions,
there was nonetheless a widespread distrust of biomedicine. A prevalent
concern was that biomedical care was too expensive and that physicians
sometimes prescribed unnecessary treatment simply to increase their fees.
As well, many persons associated modern medicine with invasive procedures, and in particular, surgery, of which they were afraid. Even medica-
tions administered by physicians were often distrusted out of a fear of
dangerous side effects. In contrast, herbs "never do anyone any harm."
The general idea seemed to be that the "natural" cures of the *curandero*
worked in harmony with the body, while the "artificial" cures of the physician assaulted the body.

Patients tended to feel more at ease being treated by herbs well known
to them than by mysterious foreign substances procured at a pharmacy
(although a "mysterious" substance may sometimes be considered to have
superior healing power). Related to this feeling of greater ease is the fact
that *curanderos* work within a setting familiar and comfortable to their
patients—that of the home—while physicians work in an alien and alien-
ating environment—the hospital or the doctor's office. Similarly, especially for patients with rural backgrounds, the diagnoses and treatments
suggested by the *curandero* are usually grounded in local cultural beliefs,
while those put forward by the physician pertain to an unfamiliar and
often incomprehensible worldview.

Ethnomedicine incorporates a spiritual dimension to healing which
modern medicine lacks. Modern physicians do not pray for their patients,
as *curanderos* do, because that is in no way part of their job. However,
curanderos not only invoke divine aid on behalf of their patients, but
they also offer remedies for spiritual, as well as emotional and social,
problems of their clientele. Ironically, modern medicine is not thought fit
by many people of the region to cure the very ills that are perceived lo-

cally as being caused by modernization, such as stress, unemployment, and the disintegration of the family.

The different sensory therapies offered by *curanderos* would appear to constitute another major element in the appeal of folk medicine. These therapies provide patients with forms of treatment they find sensually satisfying that are not used in modern medicine. While taking a pill containing the extract of a certain medicinal herb may have the same curative effect as ingesting an infusion of that herb, swallowing a pill cannot compare to drinking an aromatic tea, in experiential terms. The domain of the *curandero* is characterized by a rich sensuality, while that of the physician is de-sensualized and aesthetically sterile.

Traditional urban users of biomedicine have their own reasons for turning to ethnomedical practitioners. Biomedicine is widely perceived as having failed in its goal to provide a comprehensive system of health care. Despite many decades of medical research, cures are still lacking for many illnesses, from shingles to cancer. In fact, the habitual user of the resources of modern medicine has had more occasion than anyone else to become acquainted and frustrated with biomedicine's failures and drawbacks. This accumulated disappointment and frustration has created a large base of people willing to explore alternative means of therapeutic intervention, if not to entirely give up on biomedicine.

In an era of expanded consumer choice, people want to be able to "shop" for health care, just as they shop for other consumer products. In this regard it is important to note that traditional ethnomedicine provides only one of a variety of alternative therapies available in the urban centers of Northwestern Argentina. These alternative therapies include homeopathy, faith healing, and a range of Eastern and New Age-inspired practices.

In the first half of the twentieth century, modernization was associated with a monolithic social, scientific, and technological model drawn from the First World. The attempt to impose this model on Northwestern Argentina led to, among other things, the marginalization of ethnomedicine in the region. However, at the end of the century, due in part to the forces of consumer capitalism and a general disillusionment with monolithic ideologies (or "metanarratives"), being "modern," or rather "postmodern," appears to mean being able to select the elements of one's life-style from a range of choices that includes elements marked "traditional." This development may contribute to the survival of ethnomedicine by presenting it as one more consumer option in a pluralized medical marketplace. Indeed, given the current interest in alternative healing, ethnomedicine has become a more "modern" medicine than biomedicine, which now seems to belong to a prior era of faith in science and technology.

The Dynamics of Folk Medicine

The fact that ethnomedicine is surviving in Northwestern Argentina does not mean that this medicine is not undergoing changes. Only a very few communities remain so remote from the medical trends of modernity as to be relatively unaffected by them. Traditional *curanderos* gather information about new trends not only through direct encounters with physicians or alternative practitioners but also through radio programs, newspaper articles, and patients who have tried various therapies. As a result, when one speaks with a *curandero* today—particularly with an urban *curandero*—one occasionally finds traditional medical lore combined with notions drawn from germ theory, yoga, or the shamanic books of Carlos Castaneda.

Changes in living and working situations are also contributing to the alteration of ethnomedicine in the Northwest. The increased pace of modern life makes it difficult for potential healers to devote the time deemed necessary to acquire medical knowledge and for patients to submit to full-length treatments. As a result, both ethnomedical knowledge and ethnomedical therapies appear to have been simplified over the last decades in order to make them suitable for healers and patients on the go. A healing rite that once involved days of treatment as well as community participation might now consist of a quick consultation and a protective amulet for the (perhaps out-of-town) patient to take home.

Nevertheless, it is important not to underestimate the continued resistance to folk healing, particularly among some professionals. The medical profession in Argentina is far from ready to accord an official status to ethnomedicine. Physicians in rural communities sometimes attempt to prohibit local *curanderos* from practicing by denouncing them to the police. Many physicians claim that people put their own or their children's lives at risk by seeking treatment from a *curandero* when the situation calls for urgent biomedical assistance. *Curanderos*, therefore, have to negotiate a place for themselves in the current medical scene. One *curandera*, Doña Marcela, spoke of how she had arrived at an uneasy truce with her community's physician: they had agreed to disagree as to the correct diagnosis and treatment of different ailments, with the proviso that the *curandera* send those patients with serious problems on to the physician.

The opposition to *curanderos* is not only based on their unofficial status as medical practitioners. Various physicians, academics, and administrators express the concern that turning to *curanderos* for solutions to health problems contributes to the neglect of neccesary changes—such as ensuring the provision of potable water—that could radically improve people's living conditions and their well-being. Also, turning to *curanderos* for personal solutions to difficulties such as unemployment can be seen as distracting attention from the "real" sources of such social problems, namely, the marginalization of Northwestern Argentina within the national economy and of the working class within the Northwest. However, while it is true that individuals, believing themselves unable to change political or economic structures, will sometimes choose a consultation with a *curandero* over social action, the two approaches are not mutually exclusive. The most active of labor leaders in Northwestern Argentina might well consult with a *curandero* concerning personal economic difficulties. Similarly, the establishment of basic sanitary measures in rural households and villages is not necessarily incompatible with the continued practice of ethnomedicine. Even physicians and health care workers are known to occasionally seek treatment and advice from their ethnomedical colleagues for problems beyond their own compass.

A factor that may support the survival of ethnomedicine in Northwestern Argentina and elsewhere, or may lead to its further transformation, is the growing interest of First World peoples in Third World practices of folk healing. In the era of the global consumer, one can imagine a stream of dissatisfied and unhealthy Europeans and North Americans, anxious to get in touch with "ancient traditions of knowledge," lining up to be treated by Argentine *curanderos* as they currently do with renowned folk healers in China, the Philippines, and Peru (Joralemon, 1990; Howell, 1995). One foreseeable consequence of the current First World interest in ethnomedicine is that local beliefs and practices would become inserted or "packaged" within foreign discourses of "shamanic healing" and "Native American spirituality." Indeed, with New Age discourses becoming global phenomena, many folk healers may, on their own account, rethink their practices in light of current therapeutic and spiritual trends.[4]

These developments may be seen as leading to the disintegration of ethnomedicine in Northwestern Argentina. At the same time, however, they point to the continued vitality and relevance of ethnomedicine. It is significant that city dwellers with complete access to biomedicine are nonetheless interested in ethnomedicine, for this demonstrates that the *curandero* has a viable role as an alternative therapist in the modern urban environment. The fact that *curanderos* are able to adapt their practice to urban settings and modern life-styles ensures that, while specific elements of ethnomedicine may be transformed, the practice will be able to persist under changing social conditions into the next century. From the point of view of the historian or cultural purist, the new ethnomedicine that results from this persistence will have lost its former authenticity, just as indigenous medicine lost authenticity when it became integrated with Spanish medicine in the colonial period (see, for example, Pérez de Nucci, 1986: 30). From the perspective of the people who make use of ethnomedicine, however, such medicine must respond to the dynamics of contemporary culture in order to remain authentic and relevant to their lived experience.

Notes

1. The evil eye (*mal ojo*), in its simplest form, refers to the notion that the envious glance of another can have a debilitating effect on one's health or fortune.

2. For further descriptions of the symptoms and treatment of *susto* and other "folk" illnessses in Northwestern Argentina, see Rosenberg (1939) and Pérez de Nucci (1988).

3. A historical and cross-cultural examination of the role of odors in medicine is presented in Classen, Howes, and Synnott (1994).

4. Yet, at the same time as the phenomenon of globalization contributes to the valorization of certain local traditions by placing them on a world stage, it also contributes to their homogenization and cultural dislocation by framing them within a universal consumer discourse (Howes, 1996).

References

Bastien, Joseph. *Drum and Stethoscope: Integrating Ethnomedicine and Biomedicine in Bolivia.* Salt Lake City: University of Utah Press, 1992.

Canglini, Néstor García. *Culturas híbridas: Estrategias para entrar y salir de la modernidad.* Buenos Aires: Editorial Sudamericana, 1995.

Classen, Constance. *Inca Cosmology and the Human Body.* Salt Lake City: University of Utah Press, 1993a.

————. *Worlds of Sense: Exploring the Senses in History and Across Cultures.* London: Routledge, 1993b.

Classen, Constance, David Howes, and Anthony Synnott. *Aroma: The Cultural History of Smell.* London: Routledge, 1994.

Howell, Signe. "Whose Knowledge and Whose Power? A New Perspective on Cultural Diffusion." In *Counterworks: Managing the Diversity of Knowledge*, edited by Richard Fardon, 65–79. London: Routledge, 1995.

Howes, David, ed. "The Senses in Medicine." *Culture, Medicine, and Psychiatry* 19 (1995): 125–33.

————. *The Varieties of Sensory Experience: A Sourcebook in the Anthropology of the Senses.* Toronto: University of Toronto Press, 1991.

————. *Cross-Cultural Consumption: Global Markets, Local Realities.* London: Routledge, 1996.

Joralemon, Donald. "The Selling of the Shaman and the Problem of Informant Legitimacy." *Journal of Anthropological Research* 46 (1990): 105–17.

Lira, Jorge. *Medicina andina: Farmacopea y rituales*. Cuzco: Centro de Estudios Rurales Andinos "Bartolomé de Las Casas", 1985.

Nutton, Vivian. "Galen at the Bedside: The Methods of a Medical Detective." In *Medicine and the Five Senses*, edited by W. F. Bynum and Roy Porter, 7–16. New York: Cambridge University Press, 1993.

Palma, Nestor Homero. *Estudio antropológico de la medicina popular de la puna Argentina*. Buenos Aires: Ediciones Cabargon, 1973.

Pérez de Nucci, Armando. "Medicina popular en el valle Calchaquí." In *VI Jornadas del Valle Calchaqui*, vol. 6, 29–34. San Miguel de Tucumán, Argentina: Universidad Nacional de Tucumán, 1986.

———. *La Medicina tradicional del Noroeste argentino*. Buenos Aires: Ediciones del Sol, 1988.

Rosenberg, Tobias. *Curiosos aspectos de la terapeútica Calchaquí*. San Miguel de Tucumán, Argentina: General Impresora, 1939.

Villafuerte, Carlos. *Diccionario de árboles, arbustos y yuyos en el folklore argentino*. Buenos Aires: Editorial Plus Ultra, 1984.

9

Eco-Imperialism? Environmental Policy versus Everyday Practice in Mexico

Marilyn Gates

> Who is to say that a hungry man should not make his milpa [corn field], cut a tree, shoot a deer? . . . To prevent this, first you must provide him with alternative ways of making a living.
> —Forest manager, Campeche, January 1990

Article 27 of the 1917 Mexican constitution established that all lands and waters are part of the national patrimony, subject to control by the state for the public good. The state also claimed the right "to regulate use of exploitable natural resources in order to make an equitable distribution of the public wealth and to care for its conservation" (Zaragoza and Macías, 1980: 52, author's translation). Nevertheless, articulation of effective environmental legislation has been slow as a result of the adopted economic development models and the belated recognition of the extent of the ecological degradation that they incurred.

By the mid-1980s, however, the environmental crisis was widely acknowledged. Media attention focused on spectacular disasters such as birth defects in the vicinity of border *maquiladoras* (export manufacturing plants), massive oil spills, factory and pipeline explosions, clandestine dumping of toxic wastes, and the asphyxiated capital, Mexico City, arguably the world's most polluted metropolis. These horror stories overshadow the more mundane aspects of the country's environmental crisis such as bad water, tainted food, open sewers, urban congestion, and mountains of garbage that millions of Mexicans have to cope with routinely in their daily lives. In their struggle to make a living, Mexicans are faced with both the ongoing depletion of natural resources—widespread destruction of ecosystems, poisoned or eroded soils, contaminated lakes and rivers, desertification, and rapidly vanishing forests—and with increasing constraints resulting from attempts by the government and by environmentalists to arrest this degradation.

Paradoxically, Mexico's environmental crisis has come to a head at a time of recent impressive achievements with respect to environmental legislation, mitigation, and conservation initiatives. However, the gap between environmental policy and practice remains vast. An incompatibility with cultural mores, social structural conditions, fiscal austerity, and other contradictions in the political economic context militate against enforcement of and compliance with regulations and enduring changes in attitudes to natural resource exploitation.

Achieving solutions to this problem is complicated by the conceptual distance between Western environmentalism and the diverse attitudes of Mexicans about their lived environment. While some Mexicans express a need to live in harmony with their natural surroundings, many do not recognize the concept of environmental degradation, or have become inured to its daily manifestations. If problems are admitted, often they are considered to be the responsibility of the government, rather than of the individual, a legacy of the highly interventionist role of the Mexican state in economic and social life over much of this century. Although public awareness of the environmental costs of modernization is increasing, fifteen years of economic crisis associated with neoliberal restructuring have ensured that relatively few people have the resources to attempt to improve environmental practices.

Some fundamental ethical issues emerge. Do "outsiders" have the right to tell people to change their economic ways, clean up their lifestyles, or leave their homes in order to protect the environment? What is the likelihood of effective modification in environmental behavior if the implications of resource degradation are not universally recognized? Proponents of neoliberalism argue that free trade brings increased prosperity and that it is easier for rich nations to be environmentally responsible, but until this proposition is proved by example, why should anyone else believe it? If the First World—with its belated and often superficial environmental consciousness, extensive financial resources, and technological sophistication—has achieved only limited success in containing ecosystemic damage resulting from its commitment to industry-based growth, how can Third World countries prevent the accelerating depletion of global resources? In this context, does pressure by the United States and Canada for environmental adjuncts to the North American Free Trade Agreement (NAFTA) constitute eco-imperialism—an exercise wherein Northern interests are being imposed under the guise of "greenness"? In the same vein, do the efforts by the Mexican government to articulate an environmental policy that is compatible both with the NAFTA and the goals of the environmental movement constitute a form of internal eco-colonialism, where the interests of dominant domestic elites are being imposed on a diverse population?[1]

The Roots of the Environmental Crisis

The structural roots of Mexico's current environmental crisis lie in the post-World War II import-substitution industrialization model (ISI). Until the late 1950s, a rough balance between agricultural and industrial development was maintained, contributing to the "Mexican miracle" of unprecedented growth and diversification. However, there was a net transfer of value from agriculture to industry through the production of cheap food for the new urban areas.

By the late 1960s, critical economic bottlenecks began to emerge as the industry-first priority exacerbated preexisting problems such as skewed income distribution, increasing regional disparities, rural-urban migration, and inefficient, overprotected industries (Street, 1981). Agricultural growth rates declined and market forces reshaped production as staples increasingly were replaced by export, industrial, and animal feed crops. From 1970 on, Mexico was forced to import large quantities of basic foods as a consequence of technological modernization, the fruit of the internationalization of the economy (Barkin and Suárez, 1982).

The consolidation of the shift toward an export-led economy in the 1970s and 1980s reinforced development imbalances and accelerated ecological decline. The "petrolization" of the economy in the late 1970s contributed to the 1982 debt crisis and the transition to free market policies.[2] Mexico joined the General Agreement on Tariffs and Trade (GATT) in 1986, and the NAFTA with the United States and Canada was implemented in 1994. Ongoing austerity measures, including social spending cuts and wage and price controls, together with the December 1994 peso crisis, cumulatively had a severe impact on many sectors of the population. The continuing decline in living standards, together with frustration over the apparent failure of political reform, fostered an unprecedented level of popular protest, including a growing emphasis on environmental issues. At the same time, the structural adjustment required by the neoliberal transition reduced the resources available for the protection of the environment. This has occurred at a time when the environment is most under stress because of the imperative to become economically competitive. Modernization has been achieved at high economic, social, and environmental costs. Yet, public pressure to encourage economic diversification, foster civil empowerment, and promote resource renewability appears to be on the rise (Barkin, 1990; Barry, 1995; Goldrich and Carruthers, 1992; Simonian, 1995).

The Evolution of Environmental Policy

The articulation of formal environmental policy in Mexico was prompted by the widespread international concern over the impact of industrialization on the environment that emerged from United Nations initiatives in the late 1960s and early 1970s (López Portillo y Ramos, 1982). In 1971 the first comprehensive environmental legislation was enacted in Mexico. It established principles for decreasing contamination of air, water, and soil, together with the corresponding penalties for contravening these principles. Unfortunately, the law did not stipulate the norms and standards necessary for implementation and lacked effective regulatory authority. Consequently, throughout the 1970s environmental enforcement was negligible (Mumme, 1992).

A more focused environmental law was proclaimed in 1982, prompted by growing public concerns about rising levels of smog in Mexico City, domestic nuclear power development, and the impact of oil exploitation. In 1982 incoming president Miguel de la Madrid established Mexico's first cabinet-level environmental agency, the Secretaría de Desarrollo Urbano y Ecología (Ministry of Urban Development and Ecology, or SEDUE). In addition, the president encouraged the formation of environmental organizations through an extended national campaign to promote public awareness of the impact of human actions on the natural surroundings. However, the onset of the debt crisis and ensuing fiscal restraints reduced SEDUE's budget. The ministry was criticized for its failure to confront Mexico City's air pollution, its response to the 1985 earthquake and other environmental disasters, as well as for generalized corruption and patronage (Mumme, 1992, 1994). The de la Madrid government's commitment to environmental protection remained largely symbolic until the end of its term when an environmental law with more juridical teeth and greater regulatory capacity was enacted.

The 1988 Ley General de Equilibrio Ecológico y Protección al Ambiente (General Law of Ecological Equilibrium and Environmental Protection) differs from its predecessors in its integral ecological approach to the goal of environmental "preservation, restoration and improvement" (Mexico, Secretaría de Gobernación, 1988: 33). The law underscores the connections between rapid economic modernization, population growth, and environmental deterioration, and the fallacy of assuming that industrialization and urbanization automatically improve quality of life. However, the law's preamble maintains that the solution to Mexico's environmental problems is not to abandon the pursuit of development, given the country's pressing needs for food, employment, and housing security. Rather, the answer lies in continuing development from the perspective of a more environmentally aware economic growth following the neoliberal path to prosperity "without interrupting or interfering excessively in production processes" (Mexico, Secretaría de Gobernación, 1988: 15, author's translation). In other words, the law opts for economic development on a sustainable basis, rejecting the thesis implicit in prior legislation that Mexico should develop first and worry about the environment later. On paper, at least, environmental concerns had attained the same level as economic considerations, but in practice the growth imperative continued to be paramount in the haste to embrace free market policies (Simonian, 1995).

The next president, Carlos Salinas de Gortari (1988–1994), emphasized a range of environmental protection issues early in his term of office. However, after 1990, Salinas's environmental policy focused on concerns about the NAFTA raised by environmental groups and other interests in the United States and Canada and by domestic critics. In May 1992, SEDUE was replaced by the Secretaría de Desarrollo Social (Ministry of Social Development, or SEDESOL) in an attempt to improve policy implementation. Factory inspection rates, fines and other penalties, and closures of some of the worst sources of industrial pollution increased, while public relations exercises directed at the appearance of environmental sensitivity proliferated (Mumme, 1994).

Other significant actions by the Salinas regime to improve Mexico's environmental image at home and abroad included the elaboration of the Integrated Border Environmental Plan in collaboration with U.S. agencies, measures to protect endangered species and biodiversity, and the creation of a variety of national parks, wildlife preserves, heritage sites, and biosphere reserves. This conservationist thrust was due in part to energetic action by Mexican environmentalists, on occasion in collaboration with international organizations such as the World Wildlife Fund and Conservation International (Simonian, 1995). However, at the same time, land reform legislation was revised and new national forestry and water laws proclaimed in order to open up previously protected sectors to private investment. While the neoliberal claim is that such measures will improve management efficiency and economic competitiveness, critics argue the likelihood of accelerating resource depletion under diminished state stewardship (Barry, 1995; Barkin, 1994; *El Financiero Internacional*, January 25, 1993).

Overall, these initiatives constitute an impressive conservation and protection package, at least on paper. They are part of an ongoing

preemptive reform strategy aimed at both incorporating the rapidly growing environmental movement and smoothing the path of structural adjustment (Mumme, 1992). This strategy seems to have been successful in
reassuring the international financial community that Mexico is "modern" enough to respect environmental concerns in the process of opening
the country to free trade. The government's role in encouraging the formation of environmental interest groups in the early 1980s—via campaigns to promote public awareness of the negative impact of human
actions on their natural surroundings—initially facilitated the political
manipulation of such organizations to legitimize the administration's actions (Barkin, 1990; Barry, 1992; Mumme, 1992; Mumme, Bath, and
Assetto, 1988). This strategy may have backfired, however, because a
number of these groups have broken with their original sponsors and act
instead as independent lobbyists for environmental policies, often in direct conflict with government interests (Barkin, 1990; Mumme, 1992).

Environmental Attitudes in Mexico

The Mexican environmental movement is largely urban based and mainly
has involved the intelligentsia and middle classes in the larger metropolitan areas. The environmental interests of these groups are similar to those
of their counterparts internationally. Neither these concerns nor those of
the government, however, reflect the range of attitudes to the environment within the population overall—a consequence of the extreme regional and local diversity of the "many Mexicos" (Simpson, 1941) which
have been forged by an interplay of geographical, cultural, and historical
factors.

The term *el medio ambiente* (environment; literally, ambient surroundings) is almost a neologism in Mexico. It was used only rarely fifteen
years ago outside of scientific and technical circles and still has not gained
currency beyond the major urban areas. Similarly, universal terms for
"pollution" or "environmental degradation" do not exist. More common
are circumlocutions such as *asaltos a la naturaleza* (assaults on nature).
For most Mexicans, "nature" is the usual reference for the physical realm
that envelops human lives. It is something that can be *profanada* (de-
filed) or *inficionada* (infected).

Mexican environmental attitudes relate in part to the character of the
Spanish conquest of the New World. The Spanish came to Latin America
not only to mine gold and silver, extract valuable timber, and to plant
cash crops, but also to be "planters" of cities (Wolf and Hansen, 1972).
This compulsion derived, in large measure, from the tradition of urbanity

in the Mediterranean realm, where even peasant farmers tended to dwell in small towns and villages, focused on the symbols of civic life such as the central plaza and the surrounding edifices of religious, administrative, and mercantile power. In these nucleated settlements lived farmers who "go out to cultivate the earth, but who do not love it" (Pitt-Rivers, 1961: 47), as urban life was esteemed and the rural denigrated. This observation may look like an ethnocentric overgeneralization to the contemporary anthropological gaze. Nevertheless, it underscores the sharp demarcation between urban and rural which was reinforced in the New World by the contrast between the new cities and the surrounding sparsely settled hinterland, sometimes polarized as civilization and barbarism. This hinterland was not wilderness to be tamed in the name of progress, however, as in the case of the settlement of the North American frontier. Rather, nature was to be exploited, but not dominated, respected in its own right, but kept at a distance.

In Mexico, environmental attitudes have been further syncretized through *mestizaje*—racial and cultural mixing with Amerindian populations for whom unity with nature was a dominant theme. For example, contemporary Maya sacred cosmology has a strong pragmatic and personal dimension linked to the imperative of agricultural production in an uncertain natural order. This cosmology is laced with Spanish Catholic symbols and concepts but is structured through complementary dualities rather than Western dichotomies (Faust, 1988). Thus, the spiritual and tangible aspects of everyday life are interwoven rather than mediated. Humans, as a part of nature, must interpret and appease the rains, the wind, and the land itself if a successful corn harvest is to be obtained. Agricultural practices in themselves are important religious rituals with immediate practical meaning (Gates, 1993).

This blending and parallelism of cosmologies has resulted often in an apparent lack of congruence between environmental attitudes and behavior. For example, the Maya live in an intimate relationship with nature in their agricultural lives, but mostly are congregated in small towns, villages, and hamlets rather than dispersed in the fields; the urbanity of pre-Columbian ceremonial life was reinforced by Spanish colonial management and the federal agricultural policy of this century. Other paradoxes abound. Large landowners extol the virtues of the rural ambience but rarely live on their estates, relying on resident managers. Urban families love to spend the day at a remote beach or in a country restaurant, but make sure to be home before dark. The intelligentsia crusade for biosphere reserves but show little enthusiasm for wildlife at close quarters. In other words, frequently the idea of nature seems to be preferable to the reality.

These contradictions also affect the design and implementation of official development strategies for natural resources as well as public responses to these measures. The urban legacy of the colonial era favors the pursuit of "clean professions," such as law and teaching. However, other professions, like agronomy and engineering, can be followed via an "arm's length" approach, which emphasizes plans designed in the office. Government rural development agencies in particular have been dominated by an engineering mentality, wherein tangible projects like the construction of dams and drains are favored over holistic ecosystemic approaches to resource management. Often, this is part of a *proyectismo* (project fever) syndrome, characterized by a preoccupation with physical infrastructure and expressed in a compulsion to proliferate costly developments that serve primarily as a monument to the developers (Gates and Gates, 1976). In this context, opportunities for personal enrichment are abundant. Although the bureaucracy has been streamlined, and a high-profile anticorruption drive has been initiated as part of the neoliberal reforms, the institutional structure still represents a considerable impediment to the enforcement of environmental regulations. This problem is compounded both by widespread public ignorance of the legislation and limited recognition of the problems it is intended to solve.

A final paradox is that the heritage of urbanity as well as the interventionist role of the modern Mexican state has reinforced a clear distinction between the public and private realms. This seems to promote abdication of individual responsibility for the commons, such that people tend to rely on the government to protect the environment if necessary, without having much confidence in its ability to do so. However, the slow but steady growth in public environmental consciousness, widespread disaffection over the ongoing economic crisis, and the gradual disintegration of the political system that held sway for much of this century is fostering a groundswell of popular social movements, often with at least an indirect ecological slant. At this juncture, there may be a window of opportunity for local community action to bridge individual and state responsibility for the commonwealth.

Environmental Problems, Perceptions, and Practices in Campeche

The state of Campeche is located in the tropical lowlands of southeastern Mexico on the Gulf side of the Yucatán Peninsula. A classic example of the "development of underdevelopment" (Frank, 1967), Campeche has been dependent since the Conquest on the export of natural resources in a series of boom-and-bust cycles. The colonial extraction of dyewood and tropical hardwoods was replaced at the end of the nineteenth century by chicle (for chewing gum) and henequen (for twine and cordage), which were in turn supplanted by shrimp (after 1960) and petroleum (after 1976). Agriculture was neglected until 1970, when a barrage of government-sponsored rural development projects was launched with the goal of modernizing peasant production on ejidos, the unique corporate land tenure category generated by the 1910–1917 Revolution. The result was the institutionalization of an *industria de siniestros* (industry of disasters) in which crop failure, corruption, and chronic indebtedness became the norm. With little dynamism outside the sector producing the current global boom commodity (petroleum), Campeche was particularly hard-hit by the 1982 debt crisis and the subsequent austerity and restructuring (Gates, 1993).

Today, outside of the major export enclaves, the bulk of the population makes a living much as it has since the Spanish conquest. In the towns and cities, Campechanos engage in primary-product processing and small manufacturing industries, petty retail and distribution businesses, provision of services, employment in the bureaucracy, and casual labor, particularly in construction. In the countryside, the sparse population relies on subsistence agriculture, cottage handicrafts, small-scale exploitation of forest products, and extensive cattle rearing. The majority of the Maya inhabitants, clustered mainly in the center and north of the state, make a precarious living from cultivation of milpa, employing tools and techniques probably little different from those of their pre-Columbian ancestors. Fishing and boat-building involve both urban and rural dwellers. In-migration from more densely populated areas of Mexico and the onset of the debt crisis also prompted an expansion of the informal and underground economies. This is evidenced by the growing numbers of itinerant vendors, unregistered businesses, drug dealers, purveyors of contraband, and traffickers in human lives such as the *polleros* (chicken-wranglers) who smuggle Central Americans into the country through the forests of southern Campeche and Quintana Roo.

The above sketch may seem to present a picture of relatively small-scale and unobtrusive alteration of the physical landscape. However, five hundred years of dependence on one or two exports at any given time have taken their environmental toll and recent economic development strategies have been particularly destructive. Twenty-five years ago almost two-thirds of the state of Campeche was forested (FIRA, 1972). At least half a million hectares have been cleared in the interim for frontier colonization, mechanized agriculture, or pasture, often in that sequence, with cattle as the end phase in the cycle of destruction now typical of the tropical forests of Central and South America. At the same time, the absence of effective and enforceable forest management practices has allowed much wastage of common species and decimated the precious tropical hardwoods. Sales of ejidal timber have taken place without permits, often with official collusion. Meanwhile, fragile soils have been stripped by the use of heavy machinery in clearing and cultivation, and massive applications of agrochemicals have turned the earth into an exhausted wasteland. Clear-cutting has caused changes in the microclimate, the extent of which is still unknown. Further environmental degradation has resulted from the oil boom in southern Campeche, where pollution has affected fruit and vegetable crops and has contributed to the decline of fisheries in the Gulf of Campeche. Meanwhile, the population of Campeche's two major cities, Campeche and Ciudad del Carmen, has swelled in recent years as a result of both in-migration and rural-urban drift within the state, producing an explosion of *colonias* (shantytowns) and *barrios populares* (people's suburbs) along with the attendant environmental problems of urban poverty.

Today, Campeche is far from possessing the resource potential it claimed only a few decades ago. The delicate natural equilibria of diverse and complex tropical ecosystems have been disturbed, in some cases irreversibly. Do Campechanos agree with this assessment? If so, what do they identify as environmental problems and how do they think these can be solved? These topics were addressed through in-depth, open-ended interviews on the Mexican agricultural, debt, and environmental crises conducted from 1989 to 1990.[3]

One half of the urbanites and a little over one quarter of the rural peasants interviewed acknowledged the existence of environmental degradation (see table). However, two-thirds of the informants in both categories felt that this was more of a concern in Mexico City than in Campeche's cities, with only nine urban and eight rural informants identifying degradation in the Campeche countryside. By and large environmental degradation was seen as a metropolitan phenomenon—somebody else's problem. As one ejidatario put it, "There is no contamination here in Campeche. That's a condition they have in Mexico [City]. It's their problem. Here, everything is clean and quiet."

The thirty-three urban dwellers who acknowledged degradation of the environment in Campeche cities listed a range of local concerns (see table). The main problem identified in the city of Campeche was air and water pollution from industrial emissions, in particular from the storage depot of Petróleos Méxicanos (PEMEX, the state oil monopoly) and the diesel-run thermal electric plant of the Comisión Federal de Electricidad (the Federal Electricity Commission, or CFE). Air pollution from automobiles, trucks, and buses also is seen to be increasing as a consequence of the rapid population growth and the deteriorating quality of vehicles on the road due to the cumulative effects of post-1982 austerity.

Perceptions of Environmental Problems, Campeche, 1989–1990

	Number of Responses		
	Urban	*Rural*	*Total*
Acknowledged Environmental Degradation, General	50	32	82
In Mexico City	48	23	71
In Campeche cities	33	20	53
In rural Campeche	9	8	17
Environmental Problems Identified			
Industrial emissions	28	4	32
PEMEX	15	4	19
Thermal electric plant	13		13
City of Campeche public market	25	3	28
Sewage	22	2	24
Campeche municipal dump and garbage services	17		17
Nondegradable consumer goods	5	10	15
Deforestation	9	5	14
Agricultural practices	4	9	13
Colonization	4	9	13
Illegal resource exploitation	9	3	12
Colonias and public health	11		11
Flora, fauna, and endangered species	8	2	10
Air pollution—vehicular	8	1	9
Maritime and fisheries contamination	8		8
Potable water	7	1	8
Fisheries practices	7		7
Noise	5	2	7
Slaughterhouses	3	3	6
Street peddlers	5		5
Bad odors	3	2	5
Railroad waste	4		4
Highway construction	3		3
Environmental Actors and Actions Identified			
SEDUE and other state agencies	13	3	16
Enforcement of environmental laws	7	4	11
Public health	10	1	11
Biosphere reserves and other protected areas	5	3	8
Environmentalists	6		6
Archaeological and heritage sites	5		5
Urban parks and beautification	5		5
Environmental education	4		4
Recycling	3		3
Reforestation	1	2	3

Source: Field interviews (see note 3)
Total informants: 215 (100 urban, 115 rural).

Other major environmental problems identified in the city of Campeche included the public market, sewage, and garbage disposal. The market is an older facility. In this humid tropical climate, meat and fish spoil quickly as few butchers have refrigeration and local fishermen neither clean fish prior to sale nor use ice. Complaints about food contamination in the public market have increased since the first supermarket in the city opened ten years ago offering more hygienic conditions. Poor sanitation facilities particularly in the new migrant *colonias,* as well as sewers that are open or incapable of handling effluent in heavy rains are regarded as health hazards by many. The municipal dump also is criticized widely. Although it claims to be a "sanitary landfill," garbage normally is burned, enveloping neighboring suburbs in noxious fumes. Meanwhile, domestic garbage-disposal service is erratic, while in public areas waste barrels are scarce and usually overflowing. Instead, people are accustomed to dumping their trash along roadsides on the outskirts of the city. Indeed, many do not identify public waste as trash. As one unskilled laborer put it, "What garbage? There isn't any garbage here. All these things will have a use, sooner or later. If not, you pitch it in the gully."

With respect to degradation of the rural environment, less than 10 percent of the urban informants identified specific problems such as deforestation, illegal resource exploitation, agricultural practices, and colonization. Slash-and-burn cultivation practiced both by the Maya and in-migrants to Campeche's frontier from other regions of Mexico received much of the blame for deforestation, especially through forest fires, which are regarded by government agencies as especially destructive. Eight individuals also expressed concern about the effects of frontier settlement on wildlife, although traditionally the major threat has been from urban hunters.

Solutions to these problems mainly were believed to be the responsibility of government agencies. However, it was doubted that environmental laws and regulations would be enforced because of corruption, lack of resources, and widespread poverty. Environmental protection initiatives such as the creation of the 723,185-hectare Calakmul Biosphere Reserve in southern Campeche by presidential decree in 1989 were felt to be unlikely to succeed for these reasons. Furthermore, the reserve is surrounded on three sides by an active settlement frontier with a "Wild West" reputation. In this context, the designation of a protected core, where exploitative economic activities that may disturb ecosystems are prohibited, and of a surrounding buffer zone where low-impact land use is permitted subject to strict rules, is regarded by many as futile. As a Campeche civil servant noted in January 1992, "the reserve is in the middle of the frontier, far from anywhere. Down there, it's truly the law of the jungle. And hungry men are desperate. Who would be stupid enough to deny their right to make a living? All the regulations in the world won't stop them."

Actions proposed by environmental groups such as community work parties for street clean-up, reforestation drives, and ecotourism promotions were mentioned only by six informants, and were regarded with skepticism or irritation as the ideas of *ecolocos* (crazy ecologists): "Can you imagine planting trees in Campeche? Here, there are too many [expletive] trees. If you don't attack the vegetation constantly, it eats everything. And this ecotourism? Who would want to spend their vacation in the forest with the animals? Not natives [Mexicans], that's for sure. We like our nature on the Disney Channel. *¡Ecolocos!*" (Professional, Campeche, November 1989).

Environmentalists were also accused of trying to impose Mexico City ways on the provinces in order to show their "modernity" or to appease American economic interests, while being out of touch with local realities: "Our manager is from Mexico [City] and is always proposing crazy ideas to impress the *gringos*, like to put cans in a special barrel for recycling. There isn't any recycling here, or rather, yes, we have recycling—the little boys who spend their days collecting cans support their whole families from this. And the garbage collectors or the scavengers have the rights to our cans. The chief doesn't understand that garbage is big business here. You don't want to interfere" (Processing plant employee, Campeche, January 1992).

Garbage picking in Campeche is not a major semiunderground industry run by powerful caciques sponsored by the ruling party, the Partido Revolucionario Institucional (Institutional Revolutionary Party, or PRI), as it is in Mexico City where some seventeen thousand people work in the dumps (Guillermoprieto, 1995). However, it is highly organized in a web of patron-client relations, wherein both municipal employees and sanctioned scavengers pick through the garbage at every stage of its collection so that nothing goes to waste. In this context of poverty and inequality, Western notions of tidy recycling bins seem alien indeed.

The rural dwellers interviewed identified fewer specific problems with environmental degradation. Mainly, informants discussed the differences between urban and rural life in general terms, characterizing the former as crowded, noisy, dirty, and more prone to crime and vice, while the latter was seen as clean, tranquil, and safe—a good place to raise a family. However, a major problem identified was the increase in nondegradable consumer goods, packaging, and residuum (see table). Over the past two decades, many rural households have become reliant on the cash income of at least one occasional wage laborer, with an accompanying rise in the purchase of consumer goods despite austerity. Accustomed to consuming virtually everything they produce or acquire, Campeche peasants only recently have had to deal with postconsumption detritus such as plastic bottles, cans, dead batteries, and broken television sets. The quantities of such litter surrounding rural villages may seem insignificant to urbanites, but to the Maya, who believe in living in harmony with nature in every daily activity, such monuments to waste are both an eyesore and a reminder of the assaults on traditional life. "In the beginning, the containers were a dividend. You consumed the product and got to use the bottles, the jars, for your honey or your preserves to keep or to sell. Now, it's too much. You see everywhere the useless waste products of the expenditure of work and money. It's an affront to nature, to the old ways" (*Ejidatarío*, Tinun, March 1990).

As with the urban informants, discussion of environmental protection issues centered on deforestation, agricultural practices, and colonization. Urban dwellers echoed the attacks on traditional agriculture made by government agencies, while the campesinos naturally defended their own customs. However, agricultural practices and problems in the peasant sector are far from homogeneous. The Maya are particularly concerned about declining maize yields under the milpa system, particularly in areas where increasing population pressure and the incursion of government development projects has shortened the fallow period. With reference to forest destruction, the Maya make an emphatic distinction between their conservationist approach to slash-and-burn agriculture and the exploitative mentality of the out-of-state migrants to the southern frontier: "Agriculture has to follow nature's rhythm, nature's signs or the land will be offended and not give. If the campesino does not show respect according to the customs, if he disturbs the balances beyond his needs, the *aluxes* (pixie-like sacred beings of the milpa) get angry. This is special to the world of the Maya. It's like our permission to cultivate here. Down there, they [the migrants] consume everything so that there is nothing left, not a stick. They have no respect for the natural order, nor for those who come after" (*Ejidatario*, Ucum, February 1992).

A migrant confirms this difference in agricultural philosophy: "When we arrived, it was all forest here. But we have felled all the trees and it looks nice, right?—clean and open for our maize. And when that is exhausted, we will put in more cattle and put maize over there where the land is new. Here, they [the Maya] don't know how to combat the vegetation that promotes diseases" (*Ejidatario*, Silvituc, March 1990).

Both the migrants and the Maya do share the conviction that the bulk of the damage to the rural environment in Campeche has been done by the government in the course of the "industry of disasters," wherein a succession of agricultural modernization projects for peasants has resulted in outright failures in agricultural production or small increases achieved at high investment and opportunity cost. In particular, attempts to turn Campeche's tropical lowlands into a granary via the direct transfer of agricultural technologies from temperate zones have done incalculable harm ecologically: "After 10 years of rice, they left a desert, not even good for maize. When they saw that agriculture was finished here, they abandoned us with no help, no prospects. Goodbye, boys! There is no life left here now. When they cleared, they burned the valuable timber and fried the wildlife. . . . Everything the government touches turns to dust" (*Ejidatario*, Yohaltún, March 1990).

Against this backdrop, there is little confidence in the government's ability to take effective action on environmental protection. Rather, those campesinos who identify deterioration of the rural environment suggest that an important step toward a solution would be for the government to withdraw completely from intervention in peasant agriculture and the natural resource sector. The designation of the Calakmul Biosphere Reserve was seen, by the three campesinos who had heard of it, as proof of the increasingly anti-peasant policies of the government, contrary to the agrarian populist rhetoric of the Revolution: "Now they put even the birds ahead of the campesinos. It is more important for them to have a good way of life than for Mexican citizens. They don't care if we eat or not, if we live or die. It's the ultimate injustice of a failed revolution" (*Ejidatario*, Ucum, February 1992).

The attitudes of Campechanos to the environment vary considerably between and within the categories of urban dwellers and rural inhabitants. On the whole, those urbanites who recognize environmental degradation in Campeche seem to regard such problems as relatively minor or remote from their own immediate lives, ranking them well below the economic and political perturbations that have racked Mexico in recent years. Many rural people, on the other hand, seem to have a more acute and holistic sense of the threshold of ecological damage that has been reached and the implications for their way of life in the future. This is particularly the case for the Campeche Maya, who have long demonstrated an intimate understanding of the environment and of ecosystemic interrelationships.

Developing Sustainability

Perhaps more significant than the specific issues and actions identified in this study is that the majority of the participants did not acknowledge environmental degradation at all, at least not in "Western" terms. In this context, it seems both unrealistic and unethical to expect environmental behavior to conform to current "international" (that is, First World) standards of acceptable practices for sustainable development.

Sustainable development has become a core concept in environmentalism and a buzz phrase within the political and economic mainstream. However, there is little consensus as to what it involves other than a concern for resource renewability via ". . . development that meets the needs of the present without compromising the ability of future generations to meet their own needs" (World Commission on Environment and Development, 1987: 89). Nor is there agreement as to how sustainable development can be achieved, nor by whom.

For large corporations, sustainable development is likely to mean sustainable profit through expedient strategies for apparent or minimal compliance with environmental standards and to assuage public concerns. For bureaucrats, sustainable development often becomes a planning exercise, or just another roll of red tape. For neoliberal governments, it seems to be used as a rationale for cutting social welfare provisions or other subsidies for those on the margins while claiming a concern for continuing economic growth in a less environmentally destructive manner (Nozick, 1992). For environmentalists and alternative development theorists, the only common ground appears to be the imperative of grass-roots participation in resolving locally as well as globally defined problems through the promotion of self-reliance, community initiative, and political empowerment. For these groups, sustainable development cannot be imposed unilaterally and hierarchically if it is to have any chance of enduring success. People need to define their own problems and identify their own solutions in congruence with their life-ways and aspirations.

The dimensions of Mexico's environmental crisis attest to the failure to date to implement sensitive growth management practices, in large part as a result of the essentially preemptive nature of reforms (Mumme, 1992). Although conservation seems to be gaining ground on utilitarianism in Mexican environmental policy, in practice the neoliberal focus on privatization and foreign investment, together with the immense scale and scope of environmental problems and the chronic shortage of resources for combating them, makes implementation of the new ecological law a formidable task. However, at the local level, particularly in the rural areas, there is a long record of successful ecological adaptations, especially when unimpeded by external interventions in the name of modernization.

These local histories form the basis for another approach to sustainable development calling for a radically different economy, producing much lower rates of growth, to ensure future ecological stability by fully recognizing the processes and limits of the biosphere (Rees, 1990). This approach, with an additional emphasis on the importance of cultural as well as biological diversity, the right to democracy, and the satisfaction of basic human needs, has been embraced in Mexico by a number of rural communities, citizens' groups, ecological organizations, and segments of the intelligentsia (Barry, 1995). In this view, sustainable development becomes more than "green" rhetoric or a mask for "business as usual." Instead, it constitutes a direct challenge to neoliberalism, an alternative to development.

A key opportunity to promote this kind of sustainability may arise, paradoxically, from the current crisis in the Mexican countryside (Barkin, 1990, 1994; Goldrich and Carruthers, 1992). To date, development policies have degraded the resource base, promoted inefficient land use, created massive unemployment and underemployment, and promoted ongoing out-migration. These crisis conditions could provide a starting point for sustainable development via small-scale, diversified production to meet basic needs and stimulate local economies in combination with employment of the surplus workforce in environmental reconstruction (Barkin, 1990, 1994; Goldrich and Carruthers, 1992). This intermediate strategy could act as a bridge between the government's commitment to confront environmental problems and spontaneous, bottom-up initiatives, through an emphasis on the process of developing sustainability rather than the elusive concept itself (Carley and Christie, 1993; M'Gonigle and Parfitt, 1994). Such an approach is likely to involve new forms of policy and practice, with priorities given to community initiative, building knowledge about ecosystems, and holistic planning and management, emphasizing mediation of environmental, economic, and social goals at local and regional levels.

This type of pragmatic approach might be particularly appropriate in regions such as Campeche, with its history of resource extraction in boom-and-bust cycles and the continuing depredation of its natural riches today. It could be argued that Campeche is on the path to sustainable development by default, as small-scale, diversified production for a local market is already in place as a concomitant of the dependence on exports. Furthermore, the widespread mistrust of state initiatives seems conducive to civil empowerment, which may be an inadvertent concomitant of the neoliberal thrust. The new dimension would be the employment of the surplus work force in environmental reconstruction and regeneration. For example, SEDESOL has been experimenting with planting rapid-growth melina in regions near the Calakmul Biosphere Reserve for the international pulp market, with the active involvement of local ejidatarios. This type of regeneration model appeals to the Maya because, in essence, it is what they already do—tending the forest—but in the guise of resource enhancement instead of slash-and-burn agriculture, which is widely perceived as destructive. It is attractive even to the migrant colonists, despite their short-term, exploitative vision of the frontier, for the opportunities for paid labor in the plantations.

Sustainable development as an ecological way of life cannot be planned or legislated, only facilitated, and to do this, diverse attitudes to the environment must first be identified. This scenario may not be unrealistic, whether or not free trade promotes significant economic growth and increased employment in Mexico, especially if the hemispheric trading partners see a common interest in breaking the linkages between economic restructuring, environmental degradation, poverty, and social unrest. The January 1994 Chiapas uprising may have provided some incentive in this direction. The December 1994 peso crisis and subsequent increased austerity underscore the imperative of promoting local environmental solutions rather than relying on government actions in a time of extraordinary economic, political, and social adjustment.

Notes

1. Pablo González Casanova maintains that colonialism does not only apply to relationships between nations: "It also pertains to relationships within a nation, insofar as a nation is ethnically heterogeneous and certain ethnic groups become the dominant groups and classes and others become the dominated. Despite the long years of revolution, reform, industrialization, and development, inheritances from the past—marginality, plural society, and internal colonialism—persist today in Mexico in new forms" (González Casanova, 1970: 72). The outbreak of an armed rebellion of indigenous peasants in Chiapas on the day that the NAFTA took effect (January 1, 1994) is testimony to both the enduring relevance of González Casanova's statement and the eroding public tolerance for Mexico's pursuit of modernization at the expense of the marginalized.

2. "Petrolization" of an economy refers to over-dependence on oil exports with concomitant growth in capital and luxury imports, increased foreign indebtedness as a result of the attractiveness of oil wealth to foreign bankers, inflation, and a skewed income distribution (Grayson, 1981).

3. Interviews were conducted with 115 male campesinos in seven ejidos in diverse regions of the state. In addition, 100 urbanites in the city of Campeche, including development agents, politicians, businessmen, housewives, and workers, were interviewed about broader aspects of the crises and the implications of economic restructuring (Gates, 1993). These were supplemented by interviews with 50 campesinos in two ejidos and 43 urban dwellers in the city of Campeche in 1992, with a specific focus on environmental issues.

References

Barkin, David. *Distorted Development: Mexico in the World Economy.* Boulder, CO: Westview Press, 1990.

————. "The Specter of Rural Development." *NACLA Report on the Americas* 28, no.1 (July/August 1994): 29–34.

Barkin, David, and Blanca Suárez. *El fin de la autosuficiencia alimentaria.* Mexico City: Centro de Ecodesarrollo and Nueva Imagen, 1982.

Barry, Tom. *Zapata's Revenge: Free Trade and the Farm Crisis in Mexico.* Boston: South End Press, 1995.

————. *Mexico: A Country Guide.* Albuquerque, NM: Resource Center Press, 1992.

Carley, Michael, and Ian Christie. *Managing Sustainable Development.* Minneapolis: University of Minnesota Press, 1993.

Crump, Andy. *Dictionary of Environment and Development: People, Places, Ideas, Organizations.* Cambridge, MA: MIT Press, 1993.

El Financiero Internacional, January 25, 1993.

Faust, Betty. "Cosmology and Changing Technologies of the Campeche Maya." Ph.D. thesis, Syracuse University, 1988.

Fondo Instituido en Relación a la Agricultura (FIRA). *Estudio agropecuario del estado de Campeche y algunos consideraciones para su desarrollo.* Campeche: FIRA, 1972.

Frank, Andre Gunder. *Capitalism and Underdevelopment in Latin America: Historical Studies of Chile and Brazil.* New York: Monthly Review Press, 1967.

Gates, Marilyn. *In Default: Peasants, the Debt Crisis, and the Agricultural Challenge in Mexico.* Boulder, CO: Westview Press, 1993.

Gates, Marilyn, and Gary R. Gates. "Proyectismo: The Ethics of Organized Change." *Antipode* 8, no. 3 (1976): 72–82.

Goldrich, Daniel, and David V. Carruthers. "Sustainable Development in Mexico? The International Politics of Opportunity." *Latin American Perspectives* 19, no. 72 (Winter 1992): 97–122.

González Casanova, Pablo. *Democracy in Mexico.* Mexico City: Siglo Veintiuno, 1970.

Grayson, George. "Oil and Politics in Mexico." *Current History* 80, no. 469 (November 1981): 379–83, 393.

Guillermoprieto, Alma. *The Heart That Bleeds: Latin America Now.* New York: Vintage Books, 1995.

López Portillo y Ramos, Manuel, comp. *El medio ambiente en México: Temas, problemas, alternativas.* Mexico City: Fondo de Cultura Económica, 1982.

Mexico, Secretaría de Gobernación. *Ley General de Equilibrio Ecológico y la Protección al Ambiente.* Mexico City: Secretaría de Gobernación, 1988.

M'Gonigle, Michael, and Ben Parfitt. *Forestopia: A Practical Guide to the New Forest Economy.* Madeira Park, B.C., Canada: Harbour Publishing, 1994.

Mumme, Stephen P. "System Maintenance and Environmental Reform in Mexico: Salinas's Preemptive Strategy." *Latin American Perspectives* 19, no. 1 (Winter 1992): 123–43.

————. "Mexican Environmental Reform and NAFTA." *North American Outlook* 4, no. 3 (March 1994): 87–101.

Mumme, Stephen P., C. Richard Bath, and Valerie Assetto. "Political Development and Environmental Policy in Mexico." *Latin American Research Review* 23, no. 1 (1988): 7–34.

Nozick, Marcia. *No Place Like Home: Building Sustainable Communities*. Ottawa: Canadian Council on Social Development, 1992.

Pitt-Rivers, J. *The People of the Sierra*. Chicago: University of Chicago Press, 1961.

Rees, William. "The Ecology of Sustainable Development." *The Ecologist* 20, no. 1 (1990): 18–23.

Simonian, Lane. *Defending the Land of the Jaguar: A History of Conservation in Mexico*. Austin: University of Texas Press, 1995.

Simpson, Lesley Byrd. *Many Mexicos*. Berkeley: University of California Press, 1941.

Street, James H. "Mexico's Economic Development Plan." *Current History* 80, no. 469 (November 1981): 373–78.

Wolf, Eric R., and Edward C. Hansen. *The Human Condition in Latin America*. New York: Oxford University Press, 1972.

World Commission on Environment and Development (Brundtland Commission). *Our Common Future*. New York: Oxford University Press, 1987.

Zaragoza, José Luis, and Ruth Macías. *El desarrollo agrario y su marco jurídico*. Mexico City: Centro Nacional de Investigaciones Agrarias, 1980.

10

Neoliberal Recipes, Environmental Cooks: The Transformation of Amazonian Agency

Gustavo Lins Ribeiro and Paul E. Little

The metaphor of the "shrinking of the world" captures some of the profound tendencies unfolding within the world system. The development of the transportation, communication, and information industries, the globalization of financial markets, and the diffusion of segments of productive processes to different areas of the world have provided for an unprecedented increase in the circulation of capital, information, and people. This is an era of flexible accumulation, of postfordist capitalism, in which profound transformations in the logic of capitalism produce differing impacts on nation-states, multilayered agencies, private corporations, and other political and economic actors (Harvey, 1989). The relative weakening of the nation-state with the unleashing of transnational forces and actors is one example of these transformations. The emergence of global, fragmented space produces new relationships between different localities and between these localities and the world system.[1] New communication media, such as the Internet, make possible, under the aegis of computer and electronic capitalism, the existence of a virtual-imagined transnational community (Ribeiro, 1995).

Global governability becomes a matter of explicit concern when environmental problems, financial "earthquakes," world trade, terrorism, drug trafficking, and international migration are measured against an increasingly integrated world. In this context, transnational corporations flourish and promote visions of a world without frontiers; multilateral agencies such as the World Bank, the International Monetary Fund, the United Nations, and others have their regulatory power increased; new supranational entities (for example, the European Union, the North American Free Trade Agreement, Mercado Común del Sur) reshape economic and political relationships in different areas. Nongovernmental organizations (NGOs), in the midst of a crisis of power and legitimacy among traditional political and economic actors (including political parties, government agencies, and unions), appear to be representative of a new civil society or a different kind of political subject.

The growth of neoliberalism as an ideology of the world elite needs to be understood within the context of the unification of world markets, the transnationalization of the capitalist political economy, and the end of the bipolar, Cold War world, fostering a triumphant view of capitalism as the sole option for humankind. Neoliberal discourse pontificates upon the need for a major restructuring of national economies in order to adapt to the new international division of labor. By the early 1990s the neoliberal "recipe" came to be widely known in Latin American circles as the "Washington Consensus," a series of policies that called for monetary stabilization (that is, the end of rampant inflation) and structural adjustments (that is, the end of a strong, interventionist state). Albeit implemented through states vigilant of their neoliberal missions, the free market has so far meant the privatization of public companies and services, the "junking" of the welfare state, and the opening of formerly protected national markets to transnational capitalism, the latter requiring stability and predictability to operate on a global scale. The control of inflation has been achieved, at least by Latin American standards, again through the actions of strong state policies.

However, the policies rooted in the Washington Consensus do not have the same implications for all countries in Latin America. They encounter political, economic, and social systems that are a result of previous developmental cycles and insertions within the world system and which maintain differentiated relationships among each other. Within Brazil, neoliberal perspectives and pressures have been felt since the 1980s. They experienced a strong surge during Fernando Collor de Mello's administration in the early 1990s, and have continued to exert a strong influence. Although neoliberal policies are increasingly hegemonic, the tensions between neoliberal positions and defenders of Brazil's national market within Brazilian political and economic elite cannot be overlooked. These tensions were expressed in the national elections of 1989 and 1994, when the opposition Workers' Party received an impressive number of votes (almost winning the 1989 election). They can also be perceived in the relatively slow pace of the Brazilian privatization program and, during Fernando Henrique Cardoso's first year as president, in the somewhat contradictory opening to the global economy, in which powerful industrial lobbies, such as the automobile sector, have managed to interfere with the speed and intensity of import flows.[2]

This chapter explores the complexity of globalization and neoliberalism by focusing on the Brazilian environmental sector. This examination shows that powerful forces of homogeneity, such as neoliberal formulae, are not created in constraint-free environments, nor do they have uniform effects and outcomes. For example, Brazil's environmental sector presents an apparent anomaly in a context of overall neoliberal pressures: state responsibilities, expenditures, and administrative structures have expanded amidst stringent structural adjustment policies in other sectors. A power struggle within a major Brazilian federal environmental program will illustrate the complexity of this political field. At the same time, the interfaces between global and local forces generate new social actors that change power relationships. The importance of Amazonia within the environmentalist discourse provides for new types of agency, which are used to empower, to varying degrees, political subjects within the environmental sector, particularly among local populations.[3] This point is illustrated through the power struggles over the environmental destiny of the Amazonian region of Brazil.

When coping with globalization and transnational phenomena such as environmentalism, anthropologists must consider different textual and analytic strategies. This approach, on the one hand, tends to blur the frontiers between anthropology and other disciplines such as sociology, political science, and geography. But, on the other, it reinstates the richness of anthropological approaches, which can present the variety of voices that—spanning from local, regional, national, international, and transnational levels—are always involved in certain dramas. In the end, plurality and sensitivity to the perspectives of "others" different from those representative of the hegemonic, expansive Western powers will remain as anthropology's mark of distinction.

Contemporary Environmentalism in Global Context

The international rise of the environmental movement during the 1980s is an important feature of the changing nature of the contemporary political economy. The destructive power, locally and globally, of industrial development placed environmental issues on the agenda of peoples throughout the world. The lack of correspondence between the boundaries of ecological and political systems, exemplified by such problems as acid rain, global warming, nuclear fallout, the depletion of the ozone layer, and the destruction of biodiversity, calls for political and economic arrangements that are not contained by the existing nation-state structure. In an era of transnational flexible capitalism marked by the growth of "cleaner" industries and the service sector (for example, electronics,

computers, communications, entertainment, tourism), the diffusion of a
new metanarrative on nature and society has gained added impetus.[4]

The crisis of alternative ideologies and utopias rooted in the nineteenth century, clearly portrayed by the decline of Marxism, Leninism,
and "really existing socialism," opened up a space of uncertainty that
powerfully rearranged metanarratives about humankind's destiny. The
focus on human/nature relationships, the main axis of environmentalism's
master discourse, acted as an efficient substitute for the previously dominant emphasis on human/human relationships, typical of alternative
formulations, and favored the emergence of wider alliances. As a consequence, the political spectrum of the international environmental movement shows a variability of positions and labels that includes ecofeminists,
ecosocialists, ecoanarchists, and ecofascists, among others.

The environmental movement established diverse relationships with
government and multilateral agency officials, politicians, the media, scientists, and the academic community that led to its entrance into the mainstream of developmental policy and planning. This process gained
momentum with "sustainable development," a notion popularized amongst
public policymakers by the United Nations-sponsored Brundtland Commission report of 1987. The Rio-92 United Nations Conference on Environment and Development represented the climax of this trend when more
than 100 heads of state pledged their commitment to a style of development that would not endanger the needs of future generations (Little, 1995).
The Earth Summit, a mega rite of passage through which the world
transnational elite anticipated and celebrated the coming of a new age,
was properly held in Brazil, a country that had been for many years in the
center of hotly debated global environmental problems such as the burning of tropical rainforests and the loss of biodiversity (Ribeiro, 1994a).

The Brazilian Environmental Sector

Brazil's environmental sector can be characterized as a political and economic field composed of at least five segments of differentiated actors
that maintain unequal and contradictory relationships over time (Ribeiro,
1994b). These segments, which often overlap, include the state, multilateral and bilateral financing agencies, national and international NGOs,
local populations, and market-oriented actors.

The history of Brazil's environmental federal institutions can be seen
as formally starting with the creation, in the early seventies, of the Environment Secretariat, established under the influence of the 1972 U.N.
conference in Stockholm on the environment. This small agency would

play regulatory roles of minor incidence in the state administrative structure and in the developmentalist and expansionist policies of that decade. The growing influence of environmentalism in the eighties within Brazil, together with the heightening of worldwide criticism of the burning of the Amazon jungle channeled through foreign governments, multilateral agencies, and international NGOs, prompted the federal government to launch an ambitious program in 1989. The "Our Nature Program" restructured environmental state apparatuses and policies, constituted a Ministry of the Environment, and formed a new federal agency—the Brazilian Institute for the Environment and Renewable Resources (Instituto Brasileiro de Recursos Naturais Renovaveis e do Meis, or IBAMA) in order to fuse four previously existing entities. Environmentalism was becoming an important political force capable of forming heterodox, transnational alliances with powerful economic and political ramifications.

A second major segment of Brazil's environmental sector is composed of multilateral and bilateral financing agencies and other international organizations. These institutions are largely responsible for the diffusion of environmental models and variables in development planning at the global level. While recognizing the importance of the United Nations, the Inter-American Development Bank, official foreign aid agencies, the European Union, and semi-formalized political and economic groupings such as the Group of Seven (G-7), this chapter will concentrate on the key role of the World Bank due to its financial and economic power as a development agency in Latin America and the rest of the world.[5]

Because the World Bank has a wide range of goals, from education to infrastructure projects and energy development, it is the single most important foreign agency to exert direct influence on Brazilian environmental issues. The introduction of environmental conditionalities in project appraisals fuels contradictions between credit-hungry countries and world centers of political and economic power. While the Bank is a notorious instrument of the Washington Consensus, it also allows for local population and NGO participation in the development process.

The relationship between multilateral lending agencies like the World Bank and NGOs is characterized by the mutual use of one another for their own specific goals. International lending agencies often seek to channel funds through NGOs because they feel that these offer greater guarantees that the monies lent will be spent on direct programming and not be lost in government bureaucracies. In this arrangement, NGOs not only provide for a mechanism to bypass government bureaucracy, but also serve (often unwittingly) to promote neoliberal policies designed to weaken the power of the state by finding viable substitutes to it. For their part, NGOs gain both economic clout and political bargaining power by entering into a direct relationship with multilateral lending agencies and can use these to gain concessions from the state.

The increased importance of civil society within the international arena is a direct result of the worldwide strengthening of local organizations and social movements rather than the ceding of political space by dominant social actors.[6] Nongovernmental organizations, the third segment of the environmental sector, represent a key vehicle for articulating civil society interests. Brazilian NGOs comprise a field of political actors that is highly structured through interactions and partnerships with international political forces, such as multilateral agencies, international NGOs, foundations, and other organizations. In the 1980s they experienced a rapid growth in number and importance as advocates of different social and political issues. While some of the largest NGOs started out performing advisory and technical assistance roles to social movements, others began by directly addressing environmental issues. Brazilian NGOs, characteristically staffed by highly educated members of the middle class, now strive for increased professionalism in their work in order to survive in an unstable milieu and have gained varying degrees of autonomy.

By the mid 1990s, the new dynamics of the world system had rearranged the relative powers and conceptions of the major players within the international cooperation field (Durão, 1995). Brazilian NGOs, highly dependent on international funding, began facing harsh budgetary cutbacks, provoking a maturation crisis in which competition for resources often meant the fusion or the disappearance of many NGOs. National policies of structural adjustment worsened the situation. In 1994 a new set of economic policies known as the Plano Real installed a new currency in Brazil, overvalued vis-à-vis the U.S. dollar, and stopped runaway inflation. NGOs started to suffer with the loss of surplus profits generated by the maintenance of foreign currency accounts and the ability to manipulate exchange rates. In spite of these adjustments, NGOs experienced a growth in their relative political power and entered into a relationship of tension with the Brazilian government over issues of public policy and political representation.

The fourth major segment of Brazil's environmental sector, the local populations, includes many diverse groups. One set of local groups refers to urban populations that are subject to forced resettlement or that are struggling for housing, basic sanitation, health care, and pollution control. However, rural groups are most often associated with the environmental sector in Brazil. Indigenous peoples, rubber tappers, fishing communities, and maroon societies (former runaway slave communities) have their own political dynamics based on cultural norms that seldom match those of central governments.[7] Each of these populations has particular relationships to territories and ecosystems that place them directly within the environmental sector due to the rights they claim over natural resources and the cultural knowledge systems they possess.

These groups often find themselves in subordinated positions in their encounter with multiple outside forces, a situation that has fostered the appearance of numerous resistance movements and grass-roots leaders. The rubber tappers movement that emerged in the Amazonian state of Acre illustrates this process. Throughout the 1970s local rubber tappers organized *empates* (stand-offs) in which they prevented the felling of the native forest by large ranching interests as part of the defense of their homelands. Chico Mendes emerged out of this struggle as a dynamic leader who was instrumental in organizing the rubber tappers into the National Rubber Tappers' Council (Conselho Nacional dos Seringueiros, or CNS), founded in 1985. The CNS established the rubber tappers as a political force that pressured the government into creating Extractive Reserves, a new environmental policy instrument that formalized the territorial rights of extractivist populations.

Our fifth and last segment is composed of market-oriented actors that range from large, capital-intensive industries that are adopting cleaner and less destructive technologies to small-scale sustainable agricultural cooperatives trying to create a niche within the burgeoning national and international "green" market. Aracruz Celulose, one of the largest paper companies in the world, is an example of a major Brazilian corporation that is being "modernized" by the discourse of sustainable development through the introduction of new techniques of forestry management and pollution control. However, the growing market for Amazonian forest products such as Brazil nuts, vegetable oils, fruits, and natural rubber has generated a large number of commercial initiatives (sometimes subsidized by NGOs, the state, and multilateral agencies) that exploit their "environmental-friendliness" to increase sales. Rainforest Crunch ice cream, body oils derived from nuts hand-picked by Indians, and Amazonian nut bars and cereals are but a few of the examples of this new trend that seeks to fulfill the fantasies of consumers in shopping malls and supermarkets throughout the world. This segment also includes private capital and entrepreneurs who are required by law to commission environmental impact assessments prior to the implementation of development projects. These assessments created an entirely new field of consulting and engineering firms that often benefits from environmentally earmarked credit.

Actors within the five segments of the environmental sector must function in a larger economic and political power field. However, they have their own political agenda that they promote through a complex web of political relationships marked by temporary alliances and conflicts.

Within each segment of social actors there are internal struggles over representation, control of financing, and political status that directly influence the way external relationships are conducted.

A Power Struggle within the Brazilian Environmental Sector

In the years leading up to the Earth Summit, the Group of 77 formed a common negotiating strategy based upon the realization that "the North's stated environmental concerns might be used to extract economic concessions" as part of the much broader category of "development aid" (McCoy and McCully, 1993: 81).[8] This strategy was supported by international NGOs and generated a political negotiating climate favorable to the financing of new environmental programs and policies within the development aid network. The industrialized donor countries preferred to channel their funds through the World Bank, an agency over which they hold majority control. In 1991, for instance, the Global Environmental Facility (GEF) was established by the World Bank with a clear eye toward becoming the funding body for new financing to come out of the Earth Summit. In spite of sustained objection of most NGOs and the Group of 77 at the Earth Summit, GEF was selected as the mechanism through which sustainable development aid would be administered, thus making it one of the "de facto 'winners' in the debates held during the Rio Conference" (Little, 1995: 271).

The World Bank was also the principal lending agency for the Brazilian National Program for the Environment (Programa Nacional do Meio Ambiente, or PNMA) set up in August of 1990 as "the first large-scale environmental program in Brazil to be co-financed by an international lending agency" (Ros Filho, 1994: 89). The relationships between multinational financing agencies and the Brazilian government have been plagued with problems rooted in the incompatibility between two different bureaucratic and financial systems that tends to spawn even more bureaucracy and financial inefficiency. For example, the problems encountered during the first three years of the PNMA program included chronic failures to meet deadlines, depreciation of monies lent due to inflation, internal transfer problems within the federal and state levels of government, lack of an adequate administrative structure capable of dealing with the program in an integrated way, and a shortage of trained personnel needed for the effective implementation of the program. While the multilateral lending agencies and the Brazilian government often blamed each other for these problems, the end result was that after three years—the projected period for total implementation—most of the money had not been spent.

In 1993, when the failure of the PNMA program to spend its allotted money was evident, a three-year extension was granted and the Projects of Decentralized Execution program (Projetos de Execuçao Descentralizada, or PED) was created as a mechanism for breaking the bureaucratic impasse that had prevented the government from financing local projects. In this new federal program, Brazilian municipalities, NGOs, social movements, and local organizations were to participate directly in the elaboration and implementation of environmental projects.[9] During 1994, statewide meetings throughout the country were sponsored by the national PED office in Brasília to explain to local groups the program's new decentralized guidelines and procedures. Preproject proposals submitted by local groups were screened at a state and national level and predominantly came from NGOs and grass-roots organizations.

In May 1995, while these groups were in the process of elaborating their definitive projects to be submitted to Brasília for final approval and financing, the national director of the PED program announced that only municipal governments would be eligible for funding, thereby effectively eliminating civil society representatives from the entire process of decentralization. Since under Brazilian law private organizations could not receive government funds to buy permanent equipment or build infrastructure, NGOs and grass-roots organizations were not legally qualified to implement these projects.

The law, however, does not prohibit private organizations from receiving and using public monies and the director's restricted interpretation went against the grain of the partnerships made over the previous year between local organizations and municipalities that were allowed to buy equipment and build infrastructure with public funds. Yet, because PED was a new program without clearly established norms, it became open for the play of power concerning whose interpretation would prevail. An organized response was next to impossible, given that local groups were scattered throughout the country and time was running out for the presentation of the final projects. Thus, due to widespread governmental incompetence, one federal government official was able to use his position of power to preempt previously negotiated agreements and impose an interpretation that maintained total government control over a program ostensibly designed to involve civil society.

The Environmentalist Appropriation of Amazonia

Within the worldwide environmental movement, Amazonia came to occupy a privileged space during the 1980s and 1990s. The specific ways in which world environmentalism has discursively and practically appropriated Amazonia are important for understanding the projects, programs, and policies that have been implemented in its name. First, environmental groups, particularly those of Western Europe and the United States, see Amazonia as the world's largest remaining tropical rainforest, which must be saved for posterity from predatory forces. A second dimension of this appropriation is Amazonia as home to numerous traditional peoples who are considered allies in the struggle to stop deforestation. A third dimension involves a discourse that highlights the region's world-record levels of biodiversity.

The environmentalist appropriation, although certainly founded upon empirical facts, hides from view and even distorts other realities of Amazonia. In writing about the economic importance of Amazonia to the world, Lúcio Flávio Pinto affirms that "in spite of all the discussion about sustainable development and a biological diversity bank, in concrete terms today . . . Amazonia is a mining, metallurgy, and siderurgy area" (1994: 114). Another neglected fact is that over 60 percent of the Brazilian Amazonian population is urban and lives in such cities as Belém, Manaus, Santarém, Macapá, and Porto Velho. The residents have a host of concerns centered around improved housing, expanded sanitation services, employment, better schools, and paved streets, issues which are not directly related to deforestation. In fact, the world environmental movement has few specific proposals to deal with gold miners, agricultural colonists, ranchers, loggers, businessmen, and the host of other peoples that make up the majority of the over ten million people who currently live in the region. These people are spurred by powerful market forces which provide incentives for invasions of new areas for farming, ranching, and the extraction of economically valuable resources such as gold and mahogany.

A Power Struggle over Amazonia

A "mini-boom" of initiatives for the entire Amazonian region occurred in the late 1980s and early 1990s, particularly in Brazil, which contains over 60 percent of the total area of this biome (ecological community). The initiatives were designed to reduce deforestation rates, establish new conservation areas, protect existing biodiversity, and promote indigenous peoples' rights to land. The Pilot Program for the Protection of the Brazilian Tropical Forest is the largest new Amazonian environmental undertaking and grew out of discussions held at the annual G-7 meeting in Houston in July 1990, during which the leaders of the industrialized nations expressed their concerns over the destruction of the world's tropical forests. Upon the initiative of Helmut Kohl, the German chancellor, the

G-7 leaders formally agreed to finance an environmental program that was to serve as a replicable model (hence the name "Pilot" Program) for international protection (Fatheuer, 1994). After a series of negotiations lasting nearly two years, the G-7 countries agreed to allocate U.S.$250 million for the Pilot Program to be dispersed over a three-year period among four separate subprograms, while using the World Bank as the main financial administrative agency.

In June 1992, in conjunction with the Earth Summit, the Pilot Program was officially created within Brazil and a coordinating committee was established to oversee the program, consisting of representatives from six federal ministries, two executive secretariats, and three NGO representatives. In addition, an International Advisory Group comprised of twelve eminent scientists and environmental leaders was established to provide technical guidance for the program. Another key actor that emerged during this period was the Amazonian Working Group (Grupo de Trabalho Amazônico, or GTA), a network comprised of environmental NGOs, indigenist groups, anthropological institutions, and grass-roots organizations. The GTA grew rapidly in size through the incorporation of over three hundred different groups and organizations and became the major representative of civil society in the Pilot Program.

A power struggle developed within a German-funded project of the Pilot Program over the demarcation of a number of Indian lands. This is a highly polemical issue within Brazil that pits powerful mining, logging, and ranching interests, who are eager to gain access to resources located in indigenous territories, against indigenous peoples and their allies, who see the formal demarcation of Indian lands by the government as a crucial step toward guaranteeing indigenous rights and protecting the Amazon rainforest.

In 1994 a unilateral decision by the Minister of Justice (who in Brazil has authority over the government-run National Indian Foundation [Fundacão Nacional do Indio, or FUNAI]) excluded this project from the Pilot Program, claiming that it was not a current priority and that the federal government was capable of financing the demarcation of indigenous lands without the aid of foreign governments.[10] By refusing to accept this secure funding source, the minister was virtually suspending the demarcation effort. His decision provoked the immediate outcry of indigenous organizations, indigenist and environmental NGOs, and FUNAI within the very Ministry of Justice. In seeking to reverse this situation, these groups appealed to and gained the support of distinct segments of the environmental sector.

The International Advisory Group, set up to provide expert counsel to the Pilot Program, was meeting in Brasília at the time and expressed its adamant opposition, claiming that the project was essential to the adequate fulfillment of the program's overall goals. Meanwhile, the German government also opposed the decision and, as a major funder of the G-7-sponsored Pilot Program, wielded considerable clout within its overall decision-making structure. After several tense negotiating meetings, the Minister of Justice reversed his decision and the project began to be implemented.

Local Agency and Global Forces in Amazonia

Environmentalism, more than any other movement, has stressed in its programs the value of local/global relationships for political action. "Think locally, act globally" is now a slogan that synthesizes the mind frame necessary to allow actors to intervene in the scenario of relationships typical of a globalized world. At the same time, this slogan alludes to many levels of contradictions that can hardly be understood by all social actors. The transit from local to global levels requires a major investment of energy and resources not always available to local social movements or institutions. This is one of the reasons why political networks capable of articulating different levels of action, something highly valued by NGOs, are becoming increasingly effective.

The relationships between local populations and outsiders are mediated by brokers. Brokerage operates within a field of its own—stimulated by external agents with variable degrees of membership in the community such as churches, political parties, unions, and NGOs—which can become highly institutionalized. An idiom of "participation" develops to regulate the power imbalances common to local/outsider encounters. Though participation has now become a mandatory demand of social movements, local leadership, and development agencies, its control by institutions external to the communities almost always leads to clientelism or a distorted form of development pedagogy. Furthermore, the risk of co-optation of grass-roots leaders is ever-present.

Another issue of contention is the variegated meanings that "local" may have for social actors since, in many senses, life always unfolds in given local scenarios. Thus, social actors always have a sense of what is local. The main issue is how different actors within each segment of the environmental sector conceptualize the local, place it within a hierarchy of values, and use it as a means to cope with the multitude of other interlocutors. For example, in the PNMA and Pilot Program cases, the social actors used their strategic positions and power to manage conflicts and form coalitions in order to promote their ends and gain control of financial resources that were destined for local populations. In the former case, the timely imposition of a unilateral decision by a government official regarding who was to represent the local (NGOs, social movements, or municipalities) was upheld within a field of poorly defined policy guidelines and fragmented partnerships and thus reinforced state power. In the latter case, the ad hoc alliance of diverse international and national actors standing in for indigenous peoples' interests was able to reverse a decision made by a minister and forced the immediate implementation of the project. In both cases, the local social actors who were the supposed beneficiaries of these programs were underrepresented and, in effect, tokens in the hands of institutional actors and brokers in wider struggles over resources.

The forging of the Forest People's Alliance presents a different situation. Powerful environmental NGOs at a global level needed a unified front of Amazonian populations, particularly indigenous groups and rubber tappers—the privileged actors of the environmentalist appropriation of Amazonia—to provide the local foundation for the launching of international campaigns. Though the Forest Peoples' Alliance was created in 1989 at the behest of environmental groups, it has never truly functioned as a dynamic entity capable of representing the common interests of indigenous peoples and rubber tappers. Historical tensions accruing from conflict over lands between these groups made their joint collaboration problematic. Here we see how a local population was homogenized for global purposes, only to have its underlying heterogeneity reemerge in the course of further events.

Still other examples show how active participation by local populations in environmental struggles can be effective in promoting their interests. A historic meeting held in the Amazonian town of Altamira in 1989 gathered international and Brazilian NGOs, members of the world press, federal government officials, high-level management of a state-owned electric company, and Kayapó Indians to discuss the construction of the Kararaô Hydroelectric Dam that would flood extensive areas of the rainforest in Kayapó territory. A dramatic confrontation between the Indians and government officials unfolded in front of world cameras at the meeting. In a well-orchestrated local/global action, simultaneous protests against the building of the dam were held in European and U.S. cities. These initiatives culminated in the halting of the hydroelectric project.

The case of the rubber tappers exemplifies how local groups appropriated the environmental ideology for their own needs and goals. The rubber tappers' movement, which grew out of a tradition of labor organizing, only entered into a strong working relationship with environmentalists during the 1980s, under the leadership of Chico Mendes. The "environ-mentalization" of a long-standing agrarian problem gave rise to the con-cept of extractive reserves, an environmental and territorial policy that consolidated rubber tappers' interests. After Mendes's tragic assassina-tion in December 1988, rifts emerged between the labor and environmen-tal sides of this coalition over, among other issues, who should receive and administer new environmentally earmarked funds.

The idealized appropriation of Indians by environmental and indigen-ist groups has often discursively transformed them into a type of "hyperreal Indian," a category useful to the goals of outside groups but one that rarely takes into account the day-to-day needs and conflicts of indigenous peoples (Ramos, 1995). The Yanomami Indians have suffered from appropriations that characterize them as a "fierce people" and the last and largest surviv-ing "primitive tribe" in Amazonia. However, new leaders, such as Davi Kopenawa, have managed to appropriate the environmental discourse, fuse it with Yanomami cosmology in a criticism of the destruction of their habitat by gold miners, and open up new alliances and channels that strengthened their claims within Brazilian national society and interna-tional forums (Albert, 1995).

The agency of local Amazonian groups has been transformed by the environmentalization of social conflicts and Amazonian peoples. The cases just mentioned exemplify how the environmental discourse is a two-way street that cannot be viewed as simply an external imposition since it may foster internal reappropriations that differentially empower local groups. The presence of grassroots leaders capable not only of understanding glo-bal forces, but of translating them into forms comprehensible to their peoples and channeling collective action based on new visions, repre-sents the foundation upon which local actors become agents in their own right. This new agency modifies local groups' specific relationships with the environmental sector and provides them with discursive and political weapons useful to their struggles. In order to create a just and equitable power dynamic within the environmental sector that is coherent with its programmatic principles, it is clear that local populations must be con-sidered as subjects and not as rhetorical partners.

Conclusion

To the degree that the environmentalist ideology gains force, allows for the expansion of state apparatuses, and is enriched by the active partici-pation of local groups, it counterbalances the harsh structural adjustment policies being implemented throughout Latin America that are almost exclusively designed to promote capital investments, deregulation, and economic growth. The consolidation of a new environmental sector in Brazil is tied to the broader process of globalization and has produced an entirely new realm of interactions at multiple levels between the five major segments previously analyzed. In the process several contradictions of neoliberalism have become apparent.

As this chapter has shown, certain state sectors expand in the midst of major fiscal and governmental cutbacks. Within the Brazilian government, a secretariat, a new Cabinet ministry, and regulatory agencies were created, and then enlarged, in order to accommodate new financing and programs dealing with the environment and, in particular, the Amazon rainforest. This growth is contradictory in another manner since it strengthens coalitions that oppose hegemonic forces of the state linked to traditional developmentalist initiatives. This entire process was fueled by financing which originated in large part from outside Brazil. While international NGOs provided some of these new funds, the bulk of them came from foreign governments or from multilateral lending agencies. In this way the expansion of the environmental sector is part and parcel of the globalization process that has grown in strength and scope during the past two decades. The analysis of Brazil's environmental sector underlines the need to place all worldwide processes—in this case, neoliberalism and globalization—within specific historical and ethnographic contexts.

Nongovernmental organizations also thrived during the past decade and were integrated into the institutional structures of the new environmental programs as representatives of the civil society and depositories of technical skills and knowledge. Nonetheless, their brokerage functions based in networking placed them in ambiguous positions whereby they can simultaneously represent local populations, challenge state policies, perform quasigovernmental activities, and receive direct financing and administrative powers from multilateral agencies to implement their programs.

In the case of Brazilian Amazonia, the local/global dynamic—founded on two-way appropriations of environmentalist ideologies—has given new visibility to local populations, promoting their interests in national and international forums. The transformation of local agency that resulted from these processes has recast the political forces of this region and created new opportunities for defending their interests against dominant economic interests promoted by sectors of the state and its allies. The strategic use of these situations offers hope that Amazonian peoples, along with others throughout Latin America, will not simply be subjected to crude economic calculations of the "bottom line," but will be able to emerge as a powerful set of social actors capable of shaping a more promising destiny within the constraints of a shrinking world.

Notes

1. In a context of globalizing forces, the physical distance between localities radically decreases and the mediation of the nation-states becomes less important.

2. Other factors that further complicate the Brazilian case vis-à-vis other Latin American nations are the weight of Brazil in the global economy; the size of its national market; a high institutionalization of the public sphere; a National Congress that, though dominated by conservative parties and coalitions, also contains significant forces of opposition; a high level of unionization of industrial workers and public servants; and the growing visibility and influence of movements such as the landless rural workers who struggle for agrarian reform.

3. In his discussion on agency and power, Anthony Giddens states that "to be an agent is to be able to deploy (chronically, in the flow of daily life) a range of causal powers, including that of influencing those deployed by others. Action depends upon the capability of the individual to 'make a difference' to a preexisting state of affairs or course of events. An agent ceases to be such if he or she loses the capability to 'make a difference,' that is, to exercise some sort of power" (1984: 14).

4. Metanarratives are master discourses that guide the political and ideological visions and goals of citizens. Categories such as progress, freedom, and democracy can be seen to be metanarratives that are anchored in the Enlightenment and that are an essential part of the Western imagination.

5. The G-7 is a political body that serves to voice the concerns of the North and includes Canada, France, Germany, Great Britain, Italy, Japan, and the United States.

6. The term "civil society" refers to politically active organizations not directly a part of the state apparatus, such as churches, labor unions, charities, NGOs, and social movements. Although these last two entities share a similar political space, social movements are led by grass-roots leaders and unofficially represent local populations in wider political arenas.

7. Within the Brazilian environmental sector, these peoples have come to be known as traditional peoples whose adaptive system does not depend upon extensive deforestation.

8. The G-77 is a political body made up of the world's poorest nations that serves to voice the concerns of the South and functions as an informal negotiating group within the United Nations.

9. Brazil is a federation based upon three distinct levels of government: federal, state, and municipal. Brazilian municipalities roughly correspond to the combined functions of county and city governments within the U.S. governmental structure.

10. In making this decision, he was tacitly enlisting the support of the nationalist element within the Brazilian armed forces that is critical of the creation of indigenous territories as a potential threat to national sovereignty and that views foreign financing of indigenous organizations as a violation of this sovereignty.

References

Albert, Bruce. "O ouro canibal e a queda do céu: Uma crítica xamânica da economia política da natureza." *Série Antropologia* (Brasília: Universidade de Brasília), no. 174 (1995): 1–29.

Durão, Jorge Eduardo Saavedra. "Perspectivas de parceria com a cooperaçao internacional." *Cadernos ABONG*, no. 9. São Paulo, 1995.

Fatheuer, Thomas W. *Novos caminhos para a Amazônia? O Programa Piloto do G-7: Amazônia no contexto internacional.* Rio de Janeiro: FASE/SACTES, 1994.

Giddens, Anthony. *The Constitution of Society: Outline of the Theory of Structuration.* Berkeley: University of California Press, 1984.

Harvey, David. *The Condition of Postmodernity: An Enquiry into the Origins of Cultural Change.* Oxford, England: Basil Blackwell, 1989.

Little, Paul E. "Ritual, Power and Ethnography at the Rio Earth Summit." *Critique of Anthropology* 15, no. 3 (September 1995): 265–88.

McCoy, Michael, and Patrick McCully. *The Road from Rio: An NGO Action Guide to Environment and Development.* Amsterdam: World Information Service on Energy, 1993.

Pinto, Lúcio Flávio. "A Amazônia entre estruturas desfavoráveis." In *A Amazônia e a crise da modernizaçao*, edited by M. A. D'Incao and I. M. da Silveira, 111–18. Belém: Museu Paraense Emílio Goeldi, 1994.

Ramos, Alcida Rita. "O Índio hiper-real." *Revista Brasileira de Ciências Sociais* 10, no. 28 (June 1995): 5–14.

Ribeiro, Gustavo Lins. "The Condition of Transnationality." *Série Antropologia*, no. 173 (1994a): 1–13.

———. "Uma introduçao para pensar o setor ambiental." In *Financiamentos para o meio ambiente*, edited by Luiz Carlos Ros Filho. Brasília: Instituto de Estudos Amazônicos e Ambientais, 1994b.

———. "Internet e a emergência da comunidade transnacional imaginada." *Revista Sociedade e Estado* 10, no. 1 (January–June 1995): 181–91.

Ros Filho, Luiz Carlos. *Financiamentos para o meio ambiente.* Brasília: Instituto de Estudos Amazônicos e Ambientais, 1994.

Conclusion: Anthropology in the Age of Neoliberalism

Lynne Phillips

Perhaps one of the most important conclusions that can be derived from these essays is that Latin America can no longer be viewed simply as the "other" America. The issue of production and consumption alone demonstrates that important commonalities intimately link the Americas together: Rainforest Crunch ice cream, Levi jeans, fresh fruit and vegetables, and even drugs and violence.[1] The current global changes mentioned in these pages affect North as much as South America. Perhaps one of the positive products of globalization is that it brings out these interconnections and forces us to see that, ultimately, the "other" is also us.

Anthropology is typically known for its study of the "other" and the "local." The essays in this volume attempt to move beyond the limitations of this focus by developing a global vision within which to understand the creation, differences, and similarities of localities. In developing this global vision, the authors share a common concern to transcend dichotomies (traditional/modern; them/us) and to reconnect with the lived experience of people. The chapters discuss people who are not real (in the sense that anthropologists construct them), but who are after all "really there."[2]

These essays show the range of ways in which anthropologists are attempting to make theoretical sense of current global changes. The relationship between culture and political economy has always been a problematic one for anthropology; an interest in one almost always has meant an underemphasis of the other.[3] Many of the authors here are concerned with showing the necessity of grappling with economic and political transformations without sacrificing people's understanding of the world. The tool kit from which they draw in order to consider both arenas is not always the same. Some, such as Babb and Ribeiro and Little, draw on the insights of Michel Foucault to look at the economy—and things economic—as discourse, dissecting economic terms for the cultural meanings and intent. Others, such as Beaucage and Painter, turn to history to see how economic labels and policies have changed over time. This

strategy helps to uncover the social and cultural foundations of those phenomena considered "natural."[4] Others, like Gill, attempt to rethink class,
to consider how class is made and how it organizes gender and ethnic
relations. Classen and Howes turn to postmodernism to celebrate the cultural vitality of medical "traditions" despite economic changes. Green,
Seligmann, and Gates consider the interstices of culture and economy
with the understanding that capitalism is not an abstract model but a process that today is taking a different form and, as such, is reshaping notions of time and space.[5]

Neoliberalism and the Social Sciences

These contributions lead us to question the place of the social sciences in
the current global economic situation and to consider how globalization
shapes the knowledge we produce and what implications this might have
for effecting social change. The question of how best to challenge
neoliberalism as social scientists is a thorny one. Given the hegemonic
component of neoliberalism, it is not surprising that much of how we
think theoretically is informed by neoliberal views of the world. Perhaps
social scientists do have a responsibility to participate, as citizens, in the
debates surrounding neoliberal policies, but it is argued here that their
critical edge as social scientists will ultimately depend on their engagement with the concerns of those people, whether in North, South, or Central America, who are maginalized or excluded by those policies.

The social sciences have two paradigms for critiquing neoliberalism.
One approach details the impact and implications of the neoliberal process. Focusing on poor economic performances under neoliberal policies,
on the social costs of neoliberalism, and on the extent to which the state
has been (contrary to neoliberal rhetoric) highly interventionist in implementing neoliberal policies, these empirically based studies have been
extremely important for documenting the gap between neoliberal rhetoric and neoliberal reality.

The underlying goal of this approach is that by providing concrete
proof that neoliberalism has a negative impact on people's lives, the power
of neoliberalism may be dismantled. But does this strategy, in itself, challenge the neoliberal worldview? Skepticism about its potential is based
on a number of observations. First, there are clear indications that the
proponents of neoliberalism have little interest in engaging with the details of arguments; nor do they feel compelled to provide empirical proof
(beyond Gross National Product increases) for their belief that neoliberalism is a positive contribution to people's lives. The current economic crisis has caused some to call neoliberalism the "law of the jungle" (Peck

and Tickell, 1994). As such, logical arguments and empirical studies can be easily dismissed in the name of crisis management. It is in this way that the proponents of neoliberalism can also argue that the social costs of policies are inevitable or that analysts should spend more time documenting "the long-term pain caused by the failure of many Latin American countries to embrace neoliberalism" (Lynch, 1994: 98). With no alternative development strategies being given equal consideration, it is easy for neoliberal supporters to rely on the basic claim that this is the best model we have for the future, irrespective of its documented "faults."

A related observation is that neoliberal assumptions about society are radically different from those generally supported by social scientists. The most important difference to note is that neoliberal advocates generally view the social as something that should be replaced rather than supported. As Margaret Thatcher declared in 1987, "There is no such thing as the social; there are only individuals and families" (cited in Taylor, 1991). The assumption here is that the market will take care of what was previously the responsibility of government and society. Hence, it is not difficult to see that criticizing neoliberalism for undercutting the fabric of society is rather beside the point from the neoliberal perspective.

This issue is all the more worrisome when we note that neoliberalism proposes itself to be gender, race, and class neutral. As feminist anthropologists have pointed out for other apparently neutral paradigms, neutrality often masks an implicit discrimination that pretends that all women and men live the same lives, with the same responsibilities and opportunities. It is critical social analysis that best clarifies that such equality does not exist, in either North or South America. Yet, by rejecting the significance of the social, and of the social sciences, neoliberalism can easily sidestep accusations of sexism, classism, or racism. Thus, while the documentation of the social and economic consequences of neoliberalism is necessary work, it is not likely to be sufficient for challenging neoliberalism in today's global context.

Is there an alternative strategy in the social sciences that might more effectively take on this task? It is worth considering whether postmodernism, an increasingly important perspective in the social sciences, offers a more effective critique of neoliberalism.[6] While it is recognized that postmodernism is not a unified, homogenous school of thought, it should be noted that some variants of neoliberalism and postmodernism share a striking number of similarities. Both delight in experimentations involving the collapse of time and space, emphasizing the metaphor of a shrinking world where anything is possible. These experimentations permit a play with reality that offers the illusion of a level playing field where everyone has the freedom to experience mobility and "dislocation."

"Fixities" (social categories such as community and class and gender) become "unhelpful grids" for analysis (Nederveen, 1995). Both neoliberalism and postmodernism also have a curious amnesia about the past, much of which becomes "junked history." Both "schools" share a methodological disinterest in empirical studies (Vieux, 1995), and accept the market as the foundation of social life, particularly emphasizing consumption as the means through which globalized individuals may satisfy their needs.

Stephen Vieux (1994) has argued that postmodernism is not up to the challenge of criticizing neoliberalism. By noting the above similarities, I simply want to point out that postmodernist approaches may help to protect neoliberalism in insidious ways, a matter that needs further investigation. Certainly the combined assumptions of postmodernism and neoliberalism do little to encourage the view that it is possible or even desirable to organize for alternative futures.

Meanwhile, neoliberalism continues to erode social and economic environments throughout the world that might provide alternatives to the current situation. Moreover, an emphasis on a politics of the aesthetic, a favorite strategy of some postmodernists, almost appears perverse in a world where the contrasts in wealth have become so stark. Vidal (1993) suggests that some Chileans may have taken on postmodernism as an aspect of the post-traumatic stress associated with the terror of living under a highly authoritarian regime: they want to ignore the reality of the economic and political violence, make peace with the enemy (the neoliberal military), and distance themselves from former alliances (movements in defense of human rights).

Yet, we live in a time when we very much need to link our theory to real life. A critical social science cannot afford to move away from empirical studies, not because they are essential to challenge neoliberal arguments but because they are essential to those for whom we do research: marginalized people who are otherwise denied important information about their lives (and the lives of others), but who must assume the costs of how social relations are currently being organized.[7] Critical social science requires an engagement that recognizes the connections between research and politics and that actively listens to representations of the world that vary from those being offered by this political project called neoliberalism.

The Value of Anthropology

What specific contributions might anthropology have for understanding this "third wave" of modernization in Latin America? As editor, I asked the contributors to this volume informally about the value of anthropology in their current work. Despite the various critiques that the discipline has sustained over the last decade, each of them emphasized the importance of an element they define as "anthropological" in their perspectives. Most find that the micro-level approach—the cornerstone of classic anthropology—is still essential for exposing the fallacies of bureaucratic modernization (Beaucage), examining the everyday lives of low-income people (Babb; Gill), and giving people a voice so that they can express their own lives (Buechlers). Furthermore, through anthropological fieldwork, that is, intensive qualitative research through participant observation, anthropologists are confronted with political complexities that challenge their own sense of what is important (Painter). Fieldwork, as Marilyn Gates puts it, helps to keep us honest.

Others point to concepts such as agency and local-global relations as anthropology's most valuable asset. Anthropology offers "a view of the nexus where structure and agency come together" (Seligmann) and is particularly apt for dealing with macro-level processes because the plurality of actors involved is always considered (Green; Lins Ribeiro and Little). It "obliges one to take up a position on the border—the border of one's own and another culture, the border of local lives and anthropological discourse—and to keep looking both ways" (Classen and Howes).

In this volume we have seen how anthropology, with its various theoretical perspectives and methodological strategies, can contribute alternative interpretations to the apparent naturalness of neoliberalism as a modernizing process for Latin America. We have also seen that the kinds of arguments we see daily in the press about the need for less state intervention and market flexibility often have a devastating impact on people's lives when they are made into policy. Given anthropology's methodological and theoretical strengths, it may well be the best-placed social science to understand the "awkward" relationship that Latin Americans currently have with neoliberalism. But anthropology is what anthropologists make it, and the future will depend on whether or not anthropologists are prepared to recognize the value of an engaged social science that remains attuned to people's lives.

Notes

1. For an interesting assessment of the connections regarding the consumption of hamburgers, see Mark Edelman's "From Costa Rican Pasture to North American Hamburger" (1987).

2. This comment is playing on an observation by Gertrude Stein (1940).

3. A remarkable Latin American ethnography that breaks through this age-old anthropological problem is Nancy Scheper-Hughes's *Death Without Weeping* (1992).

4. The work of Emily Martin (1994), an anthropologist, is a useful resource for understanding how something as apparently natural as biology is culturally constructed. Also see Evelyn Fox Keller (1995).

5. This approach builds on the work of David Harvey (1989), who argues that this emerging period of flexible accumulation is a new form of capitalism that goes some way toward explaining the current popularity of postmodernism.

6. It is noteworthy that intellectuals in Latin America are also engaging in the postmodern debate (see the special issue of *Boundary 2* [1993].

7. This argument draws on the insights of Sandra Harding (1996).

References

Edelman, Mark. "From Costa Rican Pasture to North American Hamburger." In *Food and Evolution*, edited by M. Harris and E. Ross, 541–61. Philadelphia: Temple University Press, 1987.

Fox Keller, Evelyn. *Refiguring Life: Metaphors of Twentieth Century Biology*. New York: Columbia University Press, 1995.

Harding, Sandra. "Science Is 'Good to Think With.' " *Social Text* 14, nos. 1 and 2 (Spring 1996): 15–26.

Harvey, David. *The Condition of Postmodernity: An Inquiry into the Origins of Social Change*. Oxford: Blackwell, 1989.

Lynch, Edward. "Ecuador under León Fébres Cordero: The Folly of Halfway Measures." In *Economic Development under Democratic Regimes*, edited by Lowell Gustafson, 83–89. New York: Praeger Press, 1994.

Martin, Emily. *Flexible Bodies*. Boston: Beacon, 1994.

Nederveen Pieterse, Jan. "Globalization as Hybridization." In *Global Modernities*, edited by M. Featherstone, S. Lasch, and R. Robertson, 45–68. London: Sage Publications, 1995.

Peck, Jamie, and Adam Tickell. "Jungle Law Breaks Out: Neoliberalism and Global-Local Disorder." *Area* 26, no. 4 (December 1994): 317–26.

Scheper-Hughes, Nancy. *Death Without Weeping: The Violence of Everyday Life*. Berkeley: University of California Press, 1992.

Stein, Gertrude. *Paris, France*. London: B. T. Batsford, 1940.

Taylor, Ian. "Introduction: The Concept of 'Social Cost' in Free Market Theory and the Social Effect of Free Market Policies." In *The Social Effects of Free Market Policies: An International Text*, edited by Ian Taylor, 1–26. New York: St. Martin's Press, 1991.

Vidal, Hernan. "Postmodernism, Postleftism, Neo-Avant-Gardism: The Case of Chile's *Revista de Critica Cultural*." *Boundary 2* 20, no. 3 (Fall 1993): 203–27.

Vieux, Steve. "In the Shadow of Neo-liberal Racism." *Race and Class* 36, no. 1 (July–September 1994): 23–32.

About the Contributors

FLORENCE BABB is an associate professor in the Departments of Anthropology and Women's Studies at the University of Iowa. She is currently working on a book on gender, economics, and cultural politics in post-Sandinista Nicaragua.

PIERRE BEAUCAGE teaches in the Department of Anthropology at the University of Montreal in Canada and has been involved in a long-term research project with the Nahua Indians of the Sierra Norte de Puebla. He is currently carrying out research on Mexico's Indian political movements.

HANS BUECHLER is professor of anthropology at Syracuse University. His most recent books on Bolivia, both coauthored with Judith-Maria Buechler, are *The World of Sofia Velasquez: The Autobiography of a Bolivian Market Vendor* (1996) and *Manufacturing Against the Odds: Small-Scale Producers in an Andean City* (1992).

JUDITH-MARIA BUECHLER is professor of anthropology at Hobart and William Smith Colleges. In addition to the coauthored books *The World of Sofia Velasquez* and *Manufacturing Against the Odds*, she has published several articles on rural and urban markets in Bolivia and with Hans Buechler has coauthored *The Bolivian Aymara* (1971).

SIMONE BUECHLER is currently earning a doctorate in urban planning at Columbia University. She has worked as a consultant on microcredit for the UN Development Fund for Women (UNIFEM) and Women's World Banking and has written on women and microcredit programs.

STEPHANIE BUECHLER is a doctoral student in sociology at the State University of New York, Binghamton, and plans to write her dissertation on economic strategies of women and children in rural Mexico. She has undertaken a study of women and credit in Bolivia and is the director of a film, *Dona Avelina, a Bolivian Artisan: Credit and Production*, for the International Coalition for Women and Credit and BancoSol.

CONSTANCE CLASSEN, a writer based in Montreal, Canada, is doing research in Andean studies and the history of the senses. Her books include *Inca Cosmology and the Human Body* (1993), *Worlds of Sense* (1993), and *Aroma: The Cultural History of Smell* (1994), the last coauthored with David Howes and Anthony Synnott.

MARILYN GATES is an associate professor in the Department of Sociology and Anthropology at Simon Fraser University, British Columbia. She is the author of *In Default: Peasants, the Debt Crisis, and the Agricultural Challenge in Mexico* (1993).

LESLEY GILL teaches anthropology at The American University in Washington, DC, and is currently involved in a project on compulsory military service in Bolivia.

LINDA GREEN is an assistant professor in the Departments of Anthropology and International and Public Affairs at Columbia University. Her latest book is *Fear as a Way of Life: Mayan Widows in Rural Guatemala* (1998).

DAVID HOWES is chair of the Department of Sociology and Anthropology at Concordia University in Quebec. He has edited a number of books, including *The Varieties of Sensory Experience* (1991) and *Cross-Cultural Consumption* (1996).

GUSTAVO LINS RIBEIRO is associate professor in the Department of Anthropology at the University of Brasília. He is the author of *Transnational Capitalism and Hydropolitics in Argentina* (1994) and is currently a visiting scholar at the Institute for Global Studies in Culture, Power, and History at Johns Hopkins University.

PAUL LITTLE completed his Ph.D. in anthropology at the University of Brasília in 1996 and is currently involved in research on territorial disputes in Amazonia.

MICHAEL PAINTER is a social science adviser to the Department of Wildlife and National Parks of the Government of Botswana and an adjunct research associate professor at the State University of New York at Binghamton. Prior to accepting his present position, he undertook extensive research on land degradation and the organization of coca leaf production in Bolivia.

LINDA SELIGMANN is an associate professor of anthropology at George Mason University and is also the director of the Center for the Study of the Americas. She is the author of *Between Reform and Revolution: Political Struggles in the Peruvian Andes* (1995).